A Moment In Time

Issues That Enhance Spiritual Multiplication

Mark Spencer

WestBow Press books may be ordered through booksellers or by contacting:

WestBow Press
A Division of Thomas Nelson
1663 Liberty Drive
Bloomington, IN 47403
www.westbowpress.com
1-(866) 928-1240

ISBN: 978-1-4497-4846-3 (hc)
ISBN: 978-1-4497-4847-0 (sc)
ISBN: 978-1-4497-4848-7 (e)
Library of Congress Control Number: 2012907313

Printed in the United States of America

WestBow Press rev. date: 4/15/2014

Table of Contents

For

Ann Malone

&

Donna Neill

Two of Phoenix's finest . . .

Foreword

Mention the word "theology" and most people think of dusty libraries and esoteric debates about how many angels can stand on the head of a pin. You might also think that theology is only a topic for evangelists, pastors or professors of theology. But it is unlikely that you would ever think of theology being connected with a "cop." Although Mark Spencer is a veteran policeman of over twenty-five years, he is also an intentional and effective evangelist, and a good theologian.

This book provides a summative survey of the mandate, method, and motivation for living the Christian life of discipleship and some great cop stories! This book will also provide significant insight and understanding of Free Grace Theology. It is grounded in the exegetical exposition of the biblical text. You may not agree with every interpretation but you will be informed concerning the various options and opinions of interpretation. The book provides an excellent discussion of the biblical text clarifying the distinction between the requirement for gaining eternal life and the rigorous decisions essential for living the Christian life.

Eternal life is exquisitely free and discipleship is extremely costly. In confusing the two there results not only a theological, but also a pastoral and personal catastrophe. Both Calvinism and Arminianism, although using different means, produce similar ends. For the Calvinist, "Christians" who do not grow enough are said to have never been alive. For the Arminian, the Christian who is alive but fails to thrive loses their eternal life. In either case these theological systems result in eternal death.

Free Grace Theology affirms that the Grace of God in justification is an unconditional free gift. The sole means of receiving the free gift of eternal life is faith in the Lord Jesus Christ, the Son of God, whose substitutionary death on the cross fully satisfied the requirement for our justification. Faith is a personal response, apart from our works, whereby we are persuaded that the finished work of Jesus Christ has delivered us from condemnation and guaranteed our eternal life.[1]

This is not cheap grace or "easy believism" and it does not result in being guilty to the charge of Antinomianism. Free Grace Theology demands the call to a consecrated life for the Christian. It simply is aware that not all believers will always behave like believers. Although one's eternal security is forever settled, eternal significance is not certain. Being declared righteous is the final and finished act of God. Being rewarded for a faithful Christian life of service to the Lord is an ongoing process contingent upon continued faithfulness.

Mark Spencer has provided a clear exposition of the text and concise distinction of the theology of grace in both justification by faith and sanctification by faithfulness. Although this will not be the last book on this subject, I believe it is a great place to start.

Fred Chay Ph.D.
President, Free Grace Alliance
Associate Professor of Theological Studies Phoenix Seminary

---

1 Free Grace Alliance Covenant

Acknowledgements

Someone took the time to teach me to walk and talk, to read and write, to dress and drive, to shave and shower. Someone took the time to tell me how to obtain eternal life. Someone took the time to instruct me how to be a parent and a husband. Someone took the time to train me how to make an arrest, how to write a report, how to testify in court, how to drive a police car, how to interview a suspect, how to produce a search warrant, how to shoot a gun, how to identify drugs, how to manage an informant, how to represent officers in the grievance process, how to negotiate contracts, and how to interact with the media – no one is born with these skills. These abilities are learned because someone took the time to teach. I didn't invent police work or the biblical principles expressed in this book. Scripture is a wonderful reminder of just how brilliant I'm ***not!***

> That which has been is that which will be, and that which has been done is that which will be done. So there is nothing new under the sun. Is there anything of which one might say, "See this, it is new"? Already it has existed for ages which were before us. (*Eccl. 1:9,10*)

I know what's presented in the following pages isn't new—just easily forgotten and overlooked. Even though the applications and perspectives behind the principles presented might be unique, certainly the principles themselves are not sourced in me. To represent myself as the genesis of this book's content would be utterly disingenuous. The only thing I mastered in life all by myself was sin. I'm grateful for the scholarship, input, and work of other men who came before me. Like me, these men were students under the tutelage of others before them. I'm compelled to thank God for allowing the influence and thoughts of these men to intersect with my mind and enhance my role in the Great

Commission. Even though the following acknowledgements may fall short of thoroughness, the grateful intent behind them is sincere.

Dr. Dave Anderson
Dr. Charlie Bing
Dr. Lewis Sperry Chafer
Dr. Fred Chay
Dr. Joseph Dillow
Dr. Zane Hodges
Dr. T. Kem Oberholtzer
Dr. Earl Radmacher
Dr. Charles Ryrie
Dr. Charles Swindoll
Dr. Don Sunukjian
Dr. Bob Wilkens
Dr. Bill Yarger

> The things which you have heard from me in the presence of many witnesses, entrust these to faithful men who will be able to teach others also. (*2 Tim. 2:2*)

On one hand there's Calvinism. On the other hand there's Arminianism. The free-grace position is a third theological system that is held by many believers. The ideas and principles presented in this book are reflective of this system. I would encourage the reader to utilize the included recommended reading section. The writings and studies of others committed to a free-grace theology are great resources in expanding one's understanding of a grace-based, cohesive, and biblically consistent Christian worldview.

Introduction

You never know how fast you can move until bullets are bouncing all around you. It's amazing how motivated one can become when a gun is pointed in their direction. A rule of thumb on the streets of Phoenix almost sounds like a scientific theory – the speed of a human being increases in relation to the velocity, direction, and number of lead projectiles launched at the said human's body. I found out how fast I was twice as a Phoenix Police Officer.

On one occasion my partner and I were on uniformed bicycle patrol at night in South Phoenix. While riding and minding our own business, a young gang member just down the street decided to increase his drug induced status among his peers by firing multiple rounds at us. Two things quickly got our attention – the bang of the gun and the bounce of the bullets off the street. I never knew I could ride a bike so quickly – this was a Tour de France performance. It's funny the location that gave us the best protection we so desperately needed was a neighborhood church we dove behind.

The other occasion of speed in relation to bullets was an emergency call another partner and I responded to at an apartment complex. The dispatcher advised us a tenant phoned in to report a fellow resident had shot a man in the courtyard over a dispute about a loud motorcycle. After we had arrived in front of the complex and approached the courtyard on foot, I looked over the gated entrance and saw an elderly man standing at the far end in front of his courtyard doorway. He had a shotgun in his hands. Lying at his feet was another man. Every once in a while radio calls were accurate.

Since we didn't know if the man on the ground was still alive and in need of emergency medical attention, my partner and I entered through the gate and into the courtyard to make contact and render aid. I began to speak to the shooter and was confident I could talk him out of the gun. My partner approached from the left, I approached along the row of apartment doors walking straight towards the shooter. As I was talking and walking forward, I was pressing up against the wall, taking advantage of the small amount of cover afforded by apartment doorways. My hope was to become one with the wall.

A series of events then began to fall together like dominoes in rapid, almost surreal succession. First, the shooter lifted up his weapon, began to point it at us, and said in the most unfriendly manner, "Let's get it on." Second, as the danger was just beginning to "amp up" to the highest level, the occupant of the apartment door I was "becoming one with" for some reason found it necessary to come outside into the courtyard at that very moment. Third, I pushed the exiting occupants back inside of their apartment at a speed I still marvel at to this day. Even more quickly than my push of people was my partner's trigger pull. I'd never seen anyone fire and reload as quickly and efficiently as my partner Ed. What prompted this speed? A homicidal nut with a gun who chose to point a weapon at us, chose to threaten us, and then chose to get one round off. He was dead before he hit the ground. It was finished so quickly I didn't even need to shoot. Sometimes the good guys win. Needless to say, the victim we were trying to rescue was dead. Lesson to be learned: noisy motorcycles in apartment complexes can get you killed.

I can only think of one thing faster than my blazing speed in the face of danger – how quickly twenty-five years went by as a Phoenix Police Officer. From the perspective of eternity, this quarter of a century was just a moment in time – the blink of an eye. I worked in various capacities in serving the citizens of Phoenix: uniformed patrol, public housing (*walking beat*), community action officer, neighborhood enforcement team, uniform and undercover drug enforcement, gangs, uniform and undercover vice enforcement, wiretaps, recruit training, and bicycle patrol. My areas of expertise in the law enforcement field included criminal and administrative investigations, media partnerships, public speaking, facilitating community projects and partnerships, non-profit group leadership, union negotiations, grievance/arbitration, ethics training, community based policing, administration, policing policies, and informant management. I was fortunate to be recognized as the top overall recruit in the Phoenix Regional Police Academy in 1987. Some of the awards presented to me throughout my career were Outstanding Performance of Duty, the Medal of Merit, the Police Chief's Unit Award, as well as the Protect & Serve Award. As a general instructor I produced and taught a variety of police instructional modules: a career survival class to new Phoenix Officers, police ethics in East Africa to Kenyan National Police Academy recruits, community based policing to college level students, and search and seizure to Saudi National Police Officers.

I loved doing police work. It took a lot of effort but was a lot of fun. Yet in the end, I gave up a great job of street level police work for the important job of union representation. My focus and task was to protect the protectors, help the helpers, and defend the defenders. It was a lot more comfortable being first through the door at a drug house during a search warrant than first through the door of the City Manager's office during a grievance. For fourteen years, even though I was a sworn certified Arizona police officer, I was also an executive board member of the largest police union in Arizona. For four of those years I was also the president of that union, the Phoenix Law Enforcement Association (*PLEA*). From a political point of view, PLEA was a liberal vehicle (*union*) which contained conservative passengers. The bulk of PLEA members were anti-tax, small government, pro-gun, rule of law Republicans.

During my tenure as PLEA President, our Association team was in the forefront, nationally and internationally, in dealing with the crime of illegal immigration. Six murdered and six seriously injured Phoenix Police Officers, all at the hands of people who shouldn't have been in the country in the first place, has a tendency to make one sensitive to the rule of law. Our Hispanic community in Phoenix (*which was roughly just 20 percent of the City's population*) was the subject of an alarming statistic: six out of ten homicide victims (*60 percent*) in Phoenix were Hispanic and three of the six were at the hands of illegal aliens. This shameful fact was met with silent indifference, and it was indifference which fueled the open border polices which burdened our state. In addition, our cops and community members were also carrying the blunt and dangerous end of a broken blind-eye Phoenix Police Department immigration policy. This police policy mandated an illegal alien commit another crime, cause more damage, and create another victim before officers could verify their immigration status. Why wasn't the same courtesy required by this political policy given to drunk drivers or prostitutes? Arizona Senate Bill 1070 (*SB1070*), which generated national controversy, legislative testimony, and a personal trip to the Attorney General's office in Washington DC, brought an end to policies like these in Arizona. SB1070 ensured Phoenix Police Officers were given the ability to make a discretionary phone call to ICE (*Immigration and Customs Enforcement*) when 1.) The person the officer contacted was connected to a crime and 2.) There was reasonable suspicion to believe the person was in the country illegally. The Phoenix Police Chief believed this phone call was a waste of resources and disingenuously labeled it as "routine immigration enforcement." Eighty percent *(80%)* of our members as well as tax-paying Arizona citizens saw it as common sense. Within a year of Arizona Governor Jan Brewer signing SB1070 into law in April 2010, crime in Phoenix plummeted to a thirty year low. Homicide investigators reported to PLEA that prior to SB1070, eighty-five percent *(85%)* of homicides in Phoenix involved illegal foreign nationals. After SB1070 that figure fell to five percent *(5%)* – so much for racism. Lesson learned: proactively addressing crime (*that's what illegal immigration is*) at its lowest level brings about deterrence.

PLEA shattered the myth of the rough uncaring demeanor placed unfairly on the shoulders of front-line police offices. Our Association was aggressive and effective in reaching out to the community and families in need. PLEA Charities, which was established during the first term of my PLEA presidency and was funded by our officers, reached out to a wide variety of groups and causes: Special Olympics, Sojourner Center (*domestic violence center*), St. Vincent DePaul (*poor and homeless*), River of Dreams (*outdoor adventures for persons with disabilities*), Sheriff's Youth Assistance Foundation, Downtown Urban Community Kids, Kids Street Park, Silent Witness, Apprenticeship to Jesus Community Garden, Cesar Chavez Foundation, Mothers Against Drunk Drivers, Espiritu NFL Charter School, Judicial Watch, Teleos Prep Academy (*inner city charter school*), NAACP scholarships, Parents of Murdered Children, and Camp Kesem (*children whose parents have cancer*) to name a few. It's easy to say "commitment" it's another thing to do it. That's why it was important for me, in an effort to encourage and serve our minority community partners, to join the NAACP (*founded by 40 white people*) and partner with the Anti-Defamation League. PLEA was able to unite with our minority partners more than once to protect the interests of the community from the politics of the indifferent.

Economically the PLEA team I served during my first presidential term negotiated the largest pay increase for our officers in the history of the Department. On the other economic bookend of the second term, the same PLEA team was able to prevent layoffs of junior officers when the economy tanked in 2009. PLEA's ability to work with both sides of the political aisle brought about unprecedented police labor legislation which provided protection to all law enforcement personnel throughout the State. We were able to bring about pension reform and saw the professional implosion of a self-absorbed police chief who was unable and/or unwilling to work with cops and our community partners.

The job of police work can go from slow and sluggish to fast and furious in a heartbeat. Police officers don't get paid for what they do but for what they might have to do. The variety, the danger, the authority and the discretion of the job make for a unique, high stress, frustrating and interesting occupation. When a plumber goes to work and makes a mistake, the floor gets wet with water. When a police officer goes to work and makes a mistake, the streets can run with blood. Police officers are one hundred percent responsible for the outcome of conduct that they are only fifty percent involved in. Remember, police officers respond to conduct others choose to engage in. The cop finishes the fight someone else starts. Police respond to decisions made by others. The outcome of these engagements can potentially result in a criminal indictment – of a police officer. It's not a game and it's nothing like Hollywood's portrayal.

Split second life and death decisions on a hot dark street behind a gun are armchair-quarterbacked for months from behind desks in air-conditioned well-lit offices by activists, media outlets, attorneys, and managers. The stress of the job doesn't come from the bad guy in front of you but from the manager to the rear. I know and expect and even understand what's going on in the bad guy's world. I'm trained to handle him physically and legally. He only causes five percent of the stress. The other ninety-five percent of the stress in the job originates from the police manager. I don't have a clue what he's going to do. There's no class in the police academy on how to adapt to the petty, personal, subjective standards of a short-sighted police manager whose authority can kill a cop's career. The baseline goal for some in police management is to minimize liability and sterilize public perception. Believe me, the "thin blue line," and the "wall of silence" were mostly myths in Phoenix. The slogan "Our Family Helping Your Family" was found on the sides of fire trucks not police cars. The atmosphere police management cultivated was "every man for himself" and "you never get in trouble for doing nothing." Now not all police managers were bad – just like not all sharks eat people. If you want to pet a shark, go ahead, I'll keep my distance – they're dangerous. I found there were always plenty of teeth, I mean managers, but so few leaders.

Principles about leadership are nothing new and certainly didn't originate with me. There is nothing new under the sun – how do you improve on truth? I believe a reasonable definition of a leader is a person who is committed to the success of others. I refer to this as servant-leadership. Managers do what's expedient, leaders do what's right – just look at Pilate's decision in regards to beating and crucifying a man he found no fault in. A leader knows where they're going and can motivate others to follow. One can determine if they're a leader by seeing if anyone chooses to follow them (*I wonder how many police chiefs are elected to their position by rank-and-file officers*). Many managers achieved their rank through the skill of test-taking and the benefit of the good-old-boy system; not the art and science of police work. In Phoenix, test-taking skills and exam scores still determine promotions not the needs of those who actually do the job. It was reported to PLEA by an inspections investigator that scores and ratings were changed and manipulated under order of police chiefs to facilitate the success of a few favorites. Unfortunately, some in upper-level police management lived for one of three things: sex, money, or power. Take sinful mankind and add police managers who embrace skewed priorities and expect frustrated communities and stressed out cops.

The joke was "I should have been a firefighter." While firefighters spray water, police officers spray lead. Everyone loves a firefighter – they rush to your house, carry you down the stairs, and rescue you from danger. Police officers kick down your door, grab you by the hair and drag you off to jail. Firefighters have dogs with spots; police officers have dogs with teeth. Firefighters have six-pack abs; police officers walk around with a keg. Police officers work from a car; firefighters work from a Lazy Boy. Remember, this was just a joke.

In the moment in time which consisted of twenty-five years, there were mundane radio calls, exciting search warrants, snitches, prostitutes, pimps, fights, bad bosses, good friends, broken bones, hurt feelings, fast food, low pay, long nights, hot days, drug dealers, illegal aliens, crime scenes, drunks, needles, traffic accidents, jury trials, dead bodies, suicides, homicides, sexual assaults, child abuses, police funerals, bookings, fingerprints, drug testing, depositions, range practice, internal affairs, complaints, polygraphs, contract negotiations, grievances, media interviews, tickets, reports, reports, reports, and more reports. All of this was a part of the law enforcement platform God allowed me to function in to address spiritual issues among my police peers. Paul was a tentmaker. Peter was a fisherman. I was a police officer.

Breaking down the twenty-five year blink of an eye leaves behind multiple units of smaller moments in time – minutes, hours, and days. Unfortunately, long-term memory is not a chit I have in my pocket. Unfortunately, the events and adventures (*moments in time*) I've forgotten outnumber the ones I remember. But even though some of the police work might be lost in the fog of years, my purpose in police work was clear and much broader than the rule of law. It was always evident to me my job was a platform from which I could have an eternal impact on my police peers.

I love police officers. Police officers work on the streets. The streets (*not the country clubs or council chambers*) of any city in America are reliable ethical indicators of what the lowest rung of a community looks like – and a community is rarely better (*or higher*) than the social, fiscal, political, moral, sexual, and spiritual standards of its lowest rung. Considering the danger, the liability, the stress, the disappointment, the lack of leadership, and the world of the lowest rung, I was, I am, and I will continue to be amazed and in awe of rank-and-file first responding police officers who choose to run to gun fights when normal people run away from them. Of all the professions mentioned in Scripture, only the police officer (*sorry pastors*) has a job which is ordained by God (*Rom. 13:1-5*). These men and women stand in the gap and walk point for the rule of law. They have alpha personalities with opinions to match. Most can out-swear a sailor and then beat him down in a fight. They risk their lives to save others. Many are on their second wife, some are on their third or fourth. They are consistently good people with high values. They are giving and generous. My personal and professional interaction with them has made me a better person. But sadly many of them are spiritually dead. In giving their lives to save others they tragically expose themselves to eternal separation from God. It was for this reason my request of God was simple: give those I had the opportunity to interact with a moment in time to be persuaded to exercise faith alone in Christ alone for eternal life. I thought the request was reasonable. You see, God loves police officers too.

My prayer was simple and the goal was clear. In order for me to address the spiritual dimension of life effectively, it was important to obtain the tools and skills to become useful to the Master. That's why God made seminary. Upon completion in 1993 I became a licensed pastor at Scottsdale Bible Church. I remember studying Greek and Hebrew vocabulary flash cards while patrolling the public housing projects as a Walking Beat Officer. The occasional gunshot was useful in breaking up the monotony of studies. Most pursue graduate degrees in theology to become pastors. I worked for mine to become dangerous. Can you think of anything more unsafe than bringing spiritual truth to the work place of the lowest rung? How many times was Paul beaten? What happened to John the Baptist when he challenged a morally corrupt political system? If you think biblical truth and practical Christian living are embraced with open arms by an imperfect pool of humanity, you're on drugs – sorry the police officer came out in me. The darker the place the brighter the light – and believe me, the practical application of biblical principles in the world of the lowest rung can make for unusual opportunities. When's the last time a pastor took the son of a drug addict, who was buying cocaine for him as an informant, to vacation bible school. When's the last time a pastor pointed a gun at someone or took a fight call in a topless bar? Police officers go places, see things, engage in conduct, and meet characters, few people, I mean pastors, do.

The smart man knows how much he doesn't know. The foolish king is unteachable (*Eccl. 4:13*). Left to my own devises, Proverbs 30:2 would be an appropriate life-verse for me: "Surely I am more stupid than any man, and I do not have the understanding of a man." A wife who loves my Maker and also loves me has been nothing but a generous encourager in our walk with God. I had another advantage in my spiritual journey. Sensible, Christ-centered parents and gracious seminary instructors took the time to "show and tell" (*2 Tim. 2:2*) me about God's person and purpose. I've been able to acquire and apply what I believe to be an effective, practical, and biblical world-view and evangelistic strategy. From this world-view and strategy God has allowed me to effectively impact the spiritual lives of the men and women I come into contact with. I'm just as certain the same opportunity exists for you. In addition to the investment of biblical instruction in my life, study, prayer, reading, failures, and successes have also been molding influences in the way I pursue friendship with God.

I've only wanted three things in my moment in time. One, to be God's friend. I've never wanted to be a spiritual giant, a "holy" man, or a "pillar of the assembly." I'm not sure I understand what those are or how to achieve them. But what I do know is how to be a friend. I don't feel God has many friends. I want to be one of the few. I can't think of anyone more important, interesting, kind, brilliant, fair, gentle, or compelling than Yahweh.

The second thing I've always wanted is peace in my heart. Peace is not an absence of conflict but knowing (*not feeling*) God is with me in the process. Having worked prostitution enforcement I learned the Beetles were wrong – you can buy love. Some women and men, for the right price, will value (*love*) you for a limited amount of time. What you can't buy is peace.

Third, all I've ever wanted in life is to see God change lives. Teaching and sharing my faith are the vehicles God has made available for me (*and all of us*) to see this happen. During my life, some moments in time have been a desperate search for truth. In the end, I always found Jesus when I found truth, and when I found truth I found Jesus. He is truth (*Jn. 14:6*). And if Christianity is true, and I'm convinced it is, a reasonable person (*the standard used in law enforcement*) might be persuaded the Judeo-Christian world-view is in line with reality when the evidence (*historic, scientific, and philosophic*) is fairly considered. Truth lights the fuse to dynamic and exciting change in a person's life. Truth sets people free (*Jn. 8:32*). I can't think of anything more exciting to witness than a changed life as a result of persuading a person to trust in Jesus Christ for eternal life. When this occurs, a huge positional paradigm shift takes place – spiritually dead to born-again (*"from above" / Jn. 3:3,7*).

Persuading people (*specifically Jews*) to trust in Christ for their eternal destiny (*evangelism*) was so important to Paul he said, "...for I could wish that I myself were accursed, separated from Christ for the sake of my brethren, my kinsmen according to the flesh (*Rom. 9:3*)." Paul was so intent in making evangelism a priority he allowed God to make radical changes in his own life so he could see spiritual changes in the lives of others. Paul wrote, " . . . I have become all things to all men, that I may by all means save some (*1 Cor. 9:22*)." A person demonstrates skill at living (*wisdom*) by patterning their life after Paul – "I exhort you therefore, be imitators of me (*1 Cor. 4:16*)." Engaging in dialogue with people about their eternal destiny is surely the most exciting and meaningful adventure one can experience.

Throughout the years God has graciously provided me moments in time to participate in evangelism with literally thousands of officers and people around the globe – from Kenya to Midland to Phoenix to Thailand. I can't remember a partner I rode with in a police car whom I didn't attempt to persuade to trust in Christ for eternal life. When the one you're relying on to save your life might be a whisper away from losing theirs eternally, it can be a motivator to proactively address spiritual issues. As a union rep, each officer I assisted with a labor issue or grievance was an opportunity to sit down with them to get their opinion on spiritual issues – code talk for engaging in evangelism. All of us know and have distinct contacts with people who are created in the image of God. Like police officers, they too are also a whisper away from eternal separation – Christ called it hell. God lets us enter the spiritual arena and engage in the eternal. Scripture is clear, as stewards we'll give account for what we did with the "platforms" He loaned us (*for example Mt. 25:14-30*). I would prefer to hear, "Well done good and faithful servant" in lieu of "Why did you exercise your right to remain silent when I told you to do the work of an evangelist?"

With confidence the biblical message is right, I believe it's vital to utilize biblical terminology to persuade people to trust in Christ for eternal life. The issue at hand is not about politics, economics, or social standards. The issue at hand is a spiritual one. Spiritual issues prompt me to use God's Word, encourage me to rely on my Partner (*the Holy Spirit*) and lead me to bow down in prayer. Our evangelistic efforts should be intentional and should be motivated out of love. In the end, a question needs to be asked of every person we're evangelizing: **Do you believe in Jesus Christ for eternal life?** Each person needs to be given a moment in time to trust in Jesus to secure their eternal destiny. God has allowed me to personally share my faith with thousands of people. Any success I've seen in my personal evangelistic efforts has absolutely nothing to do with the messenger. It unequivocally has everything to do with the message, the motive, and the means of communicating simple biblical truth. God allows each and every one of us to engage in the eternal. By applying the biblical patterns in Scripture, I'm confident Christ desires and will facilitate the spiritual multiplication efforts (*"work of an evangelist"*) of every believer to be both practical and powerful.

In the pursuit of changed lives, I believe the answers to the following questions provide the essential fuel to propel our Christian lives forward in a dynamic way:

1. How can I effectively share my faith?
2. Is my eternal destiny ever at risk?
3. Why work hard in the Christian life?

When I've had the opportunity to teach believers the biblical principles upon which the answers to these questions rest, many see their world-view and perspective of Scripture profoundly and positively altered. These three questions deal with three issues – *Eternal Life*, *Eternal Security*, and *Eternal Rewards*. Knowing what's involved in spiritual multiplication, operating with a safety net, and pursuing dividends from eternal investments give our lives purpose and perspective. A solid base in becoming an effective disciple and obtaining a launching pad for dynamic ministry is established as a result of acquiring an understanding of these simple yet profound issues. We all want our lives to count for something. So does God. John Mayer makes an insightful statement in his song "Homelife." He sings, "I refuse to believe that my life's going to be just some string of incompletes." We all want our lives to count. Not only do we want our lives to count, we want our lives complete – the knowledge of a job well done. The familiarity of the following truth doesn't' diminish its impact: It's not how well you start the race; it's how well you finish. Christ said, "It is finished." Paul finished the course. We have an opportunity to do the same. In order for believers to avoid a string of incompletes and put themselves in the good company of Christ and Paul, I'm convinced grasping the essentials of evangelism, eternal security, and eternal rewards can make all the difference in successfully completing the race set before us.

My thoughts on these pages are an attempt to make it clear that becoming a Christian is easy while becoming a disciple takes great effort; and the effort put into the process of becoming Christ-like will be compensated. You'll be reminded eternal life only requires child-like faith – it's simple to enter the Kingdom. As we look at the biblical text, it's interesting to note Christians are not called "obeyers" but "believers." Jumping up and down on my left leg had nothing to do with me becoming a husband. Since jumping up and down on my left leg had nothing to do with my marriage, I shouldn't look to see if I'm jumping with the left leg to determine if I'm a husband. The same thought process goes for our justification. Since our works (*Rom.*

4:4,5, 2 Tim. 1:9) and conduct (*Titus 3:5*) have nothing to do with our justification, we shouldn't look to them for assurance of salvation. Look to Christ for assurance. Some would say reliance upon Christ as one's only hope of heaven is wickedly inappropriate. My Catholic friends have committed this to print:

Council of Trent, Session 6, Canon 9: "If anyone says that the sinner is justified by faith alone, meaning that nothing else is required to cooperate in order to obtain the grace of justification, and that it is not in any way necessary that he be prepared and disposed by the action of his own will, let him be anathema."

I couldn't disagree more. Assurance is confidence in fact. Arrogance is confidence in fiction. To think I'm good enough for heaven or that God's grace is insufficient and needs my help is, in technical labor terms, "nuts." To think the Bible presents Christ (*the One who provides eternal life*) as God's sufficient solution for the world's imperfections (*sin*) and demonstrates that He's the only source of the free gift of eternal life is, in technical theological terms, "good news." What we'll see in the following pages is an alarmingly harmonious message from some Protestant pulpits and pages which appear to be in tune with this Catholic proposition from Trent.

When I'm convinced of the gracious simplicity in acquiring the free gift of eternal life, it impacts how I share my faith. When I'm confident this free gift can't be lost, it calms me down. I know there's room for failure in the Christian life. But yet where there's great grace, there's great accountability. When I'm certain Christ will reward, repay, and recompense me for what I do with this free gift, I'm motivated to "be holy" like He is holy. A grid of clarity can be generated when these issues are examined through the lens of biblical context – not an "a priori" theological system. Biblical clarity brings about powerful conviction from the Word. Linking that conviction from the Word with the Spirit's work in our lives is a means to a "well done good and faithful servant."

I believe when Christians grasp the simple yet powerful scriptural principles of justification and sanctification and the ability to distinguish between the two, life becomes an opportunity in which there is freedom to succeed or fail in our obligation of fulfilling the Great Commission. When we understand clearly how to obtain eternal life, that this free gift of eternal life is never in jeopardy of being lost, and understand the rewards for obedience, a solid foundation is established to work from in the task of spiritual multiplication.

- How does a person obtain eternal life? Faith alone in Christ alone for eternal life (*Eph. 2:8,9, Jn. 6:47, 1 Tim. 1:16, Rom. 4:4,5*).
- How can I have assurance of my eternal destiny? Trust Christ and His word (*1 Jn. 5:13, Rom. 8:31-39, Heb. 13:5, 2 Tim. 2:13*).
- Why should I obey? Besides *love* (*Jn. 14:15*), besides *fear* (*1 Jn. 2:28*), besides *duty* (*Lk. 17:7-10*), and besides *gratefulness* (*Heb. 12:28*), a common and repeated motive for obedience is *eternal rewards* and the opportunity to rule and reign with Christ in the Kingdom (*Rev. 22:12, 1 Cor. 3:12-15, 2 Cor. 5:10, Rom. 14:10, Mt. 6:19-24*).

In the Christian life there's room (*by the way, grace carries with it the meaning of "roomy"*) for victory and reward as well as room for defeat and loss.

Allow me to modify my political analogy of a police association and apply it to a theological framework. We all have a moment in time. The clock is ticking. When the vehicle of justification is confidently driven by believers towards the destination of eternal rewards, the moment in time called life takes on a deeper, richer, more meaningful purpose.

Know this—I'm not clever enough to trick anybody. When I walk into a room, I'm frequently reminded I'm not the smartest person in the place. My flaws haven't prevented God from allowing me to teach, interact, and provide presentations to small and large groups, Bible studies and weekend retreats. I've instructed pastors and lay leaders at conferences and seminars about issues of evangelism, assurance, and the doctrine of eternal rewards. My limitations haven't prevented me from seeing God's love and Word change peoples' lives (*1 Cor. 1:27 – God has chosen the weak things of the world to shame the things which are strong*). It's not rocket science. Greek and Hebrew are nice but unnecessary as long as you can read your English Bible. These presentations and seminars are the source of this book. The goal of this book is to encourage believers to entertain an idea and, after careful consideration, see them embrace it. Orthodoxy brings about orthopraxy – right thinking generates right living. Our interaction with the Bible has practical ramifications on how we think and how we live. Instead of relying on theological agendas and comfortable rhetoric, we need to trust the biblical text by means of appropriate context. Words have meaning and context impacts their meaning. We should not to let our theology drive the biblical text; let the biblical text drive our theology. Hopefully, by relying on the clear text of Scripture, you'll rediscover three biblical concepts which have made all the difference in my life and in thousands of others who handle God's Word with care and common sense: 1.) Eternal life is a free gift. 2.) This free gift cannot be lost. 3.) God's gracious response to obedience is eternal rewards. The following sections in this book will address evangelism, eternal security, and eternal rewards.

These written comments certainly aren't comprehensive. It provides an overview of basic principles found in a free grace perspective. What will become quickly clear on these pages is a grace-based theological system. Grace allows for failure. We can choose to fail and rebel in the Christian life with no risk to our eternal destiny. But it's important for us to understand that grace doesn't negate accountability – to whom much is given, much is required (*Lk. 12:48*). As a police officer I can assure you there are legal and physical consequences for lawlessness as a citizen. As a lay pastor, I can grant the same assurance that there are spiritual consequences for faithlessness as a Christian. But still the biblical evidence compels us to remember God's grace is greater than our failure. Grace saves us, grace keeps us, and grace brings us home.

Section 1: Issues in Evangelism

How Do I Share My faith?

CHAPTER 1

The Biblical Message Is Right

There isn't a ride at Disneyland that compares to a search warrant. If you're looking for two minutes of pure adrenaline, with guns drawn, punches thrown, shouting, running, and rummaging, then the ride to jump on is a search warrant. For the purpose of full disclosure that Hollywood doesn't share, the cost of admission for the two-minute search warrant ride is normally five hours of paperwork.

I still have copies of around one hundred search warrants in my attic that I wrote and served as a Phoenix Police Officer. Serving a warrant, though sounding chaotic, requires a plan in order to control the volatility of the event and to make a case that can be prosecuted. Each officer involved has an assignment. Someone is on the ram, someone has a specific window or door, someone is the "finder," and someone is first through the door. Depending on the situation, someone is assigned to break a window or insert pepper spray.

On one warrant my job was to ram the front door of a house. Remember, the guy on the ram isn't the first one through the door. His job is to make an opening so others can enter. In my eagerness to get inside, to be the first one on the Disneyland search warrant ride, I forgot the game plan. After ramming the door, instead of stepping aside, I dropped the ram and quickly ran through the door – first one in. But when I dropped the ram, I dropped it on my partner's foot. He wasn't happy and it didn't make it any better that he was my brother-in-law.

With an enthusiasm to match mine, I believe many Christians have a similar eagerness to participate in the Great Commission. I'm confident most believers want to share their faith. They want to have an eternal impact. They want to engage in the spiritual dimension of life. They have a love for people and want to persuade them. But frequently desire doesn't equate with reality. Unfortunately, from my contacts and interaction with believers, it seems they've been laid off from doing the "work of an evangelist." Spiritual multiplication is not taking place.

In their defense, please allow the union rep in me to explain why. First, it doesn't help that many Christians haven't been shown how to share their faith. A symptom of this failure takes the form of an assumption. The assumption is that evangelism is the job of "church staff" – they get paid to do that work. To aggravate this symptom, most Christians haven't seen personal evangelism demonstrated to them in the real world from the perspective of a layman. Second, when the message of evangelism is as varied as pastoral opinions from church to church, there is a lack of confidence as to what needs to be communicated. The mixed messages heard from the pulpit or from the radio or from bookstores do not translate well into a live conversation. Even the fool appears wise when he keeps his mouth shut—so why risk saying the wrong thing? Just don't say anything. Third, if you understand something profoundly, then you can communicate it simply. Issues, skills, and principles that are well understood are best passed on by those who grasp the subject matter inside and out. It's possible that believers haven't been taught and thus don't comprehend the simple, clear principles of evangelism. These principles are found consistently in the writings of the apostles and demonstrated in their evangelistic patterns and practices as found in the historical accounts of the life of Christ and the early church.

In order to determine believers' understanding of evangelism, I've asked the following questions to multiple groups of people. These questions and their answers demonstrate the lack of clarity as it pertains to the evangelistic message being communicated today. If we don't know how to communicate the biblical requirement to obtain eternal life, how is the non-Christian supposed to know? An error in the evangelistic message to the slightest degree can have eternal ramifications if it alters or subtracts from the simple truth of the Bible. This issue is important.

First I start off with three basic questions.

1. What is the last name of the current president of the United States? Regardless of the group of people (*and depending upon the sitting president*) the name was always 100 percent unanimous. ANSWER: Obama
2. Two plus two equals?
   Once again, I have yet to receive an incorrect or varied answer from any group this was presented to.
   ANSWER: Four
3. Mexico is (*choose one*) north, south, east, or west of Arizona. Again, I've never received an incorrect answer.
   ANSWER: South.

These questions are simple questions with singular, correct answers. Everybody was on the same page. But when it comes to question number four, watch out. This question should be no more complicated or any less singular to a group of Christians than the first three are to a room full of doctoral degrees.

4. What does a person have to do to obtain eternal life?
   ANSWERS:
   - Confess with their mouth and believe in their hearts that Jesus Christ is Lord
   - Put his faith in Jesus as the payment for his sins and giver of eternal life
   - Accept Christ as your Savior
   - Believe in God
   - Profess faith in Jesus
   - Believe in Jesus Christ and ask Him to be your Savior
   - Believe Jesus died in their place and repent and receive
   - Believe in Christ – accept His free gift of salvation
   - Die accepting Christ
   - Make Jesus Christ Savior and Lord of their life
   - Trust in Jesus as Savior. Repent or confess sins
   - Believe on the Lord Jesus Christ and accept His sacrifice for all to be saved. He died that we might live eternally

- Accept Jesus as his personal Savior and know He is God and ask for forgiveness of his sins
- Believe in Jesus – Lord of their life. Believe He died for us (*our sins*)
- Accept and believe Jesus as his Lord and Savior
- Accept Christ in his heart
- Accept Jesus as God's only begotten Son – believe He died and rose from dead
- Accept the Lord Jesus as their personal Savior and be forgiven of their sins
- Confess our sins and accept Jesus as my personal Savior
- Accept, believe, confess (*the ABCs of Christianity*)
- Believe in Jesus and His saving us on the cross
- Ask Jesus into their heart and confess their sins (*telling Him they are a sinner*)
- Believe in Jesus as Son of God
- Believe in Jesus
- Believe/repent
- Believe in Christ for eternal life
- Believe in Jesus Christ as my Savior
- Believe
- Believe in Jesus as God and Savior – be saved by Christ
- Trust in the Lord
- Accept Jesus as my Savior. Repent of my sin
- Accept Christ as Savior and Lord – die
- Repent—live
- Repent of my sins and believe/accept the gift of salvation of Jesus
- Believe God died for my sins and He rose from the grave
- Be right in the precepts of God, humble, believe
- Believe in Jesus, that He is who He says He is
- Faith in Christ for my salvation
- Believe in the work of Christ
- Believe – understand who Jesus Christ is and what He has done for you – change of mind
- Make Jesus Lord of your life
- Die

- Have faith in Jesus Christ
- Accept that God died for you and be willing to serve Him
- Have faith in Christ's gift of grace
- Believe in Jesus Christ as your Lord and Savior, that He died for your sins

This is called "a failure to communicate." This is called *not* being on the same page. If you want a picture of confusion, just look above. Presenting all of these to a non-Christian would breed catastrophic confusion. Is "Die" a wrong answer or is it the same answer as "Believe"? Is "Believe" the wrong answer? Believe what? Is there a difference between "Believe in Jesus as the Son of God," "Believe in Christ for eternal life," "Believe in the work of Christ," and "Believe – understand who Jesus Christ is and what he has done for you – change of mind"? Is "Make Jesus Lord of your life" the same answer as "Accept Christ in his heart"? How does one make Jesus the Lord of his or her life? Does accepting Jesus into one's heart mean the same to a forty-five year old as it does to a six year old? So many answers. So many problems.

The question wasn't any more difficult than the other three, yet it's eternally more significant. Why are there so many different answers? Remember, these are answers from long-time Christians at weekend retreats who attend independent, conservative, evangelical Bible churches. I'm confident a non-Christian would feel bad for us if we tried to tell him or her, "These are just different ways of saying the same thing." If that's the case, then "Washington" is the same as "Obama" because each answer has the letter "a" in it and each are real people who held a government job. A wrong answer won't fly in the first grade and a wrong answer won't fly in the Great Commission either. Houston, we have a problem.

Perhaps the problem is that we've let our theology get in the way of the simple message of the biblical text. Perhaps we enjoy making justification, a simple (*but no less grand*) concept difficult (*remember child-like faith – Luke 18:17 " . . . whoever does not receive the kingdom of God like a child shall not enter it at all"*). Maybe we prefer short-sighted rhetoric over the biblical text. Why don't we trust the Bible and the words God chose to use to communicate with? Maybe we just need to take a minute, open the New Testament, and see what the inspired written Word of God clearly says. Possibly by means of biblical context we could be prevented from adding to the biblical text and adding to the confusion. Perhaps this might aid us in overcoming a bad habit of altering the scriptural text to promote theological agendas.

In addressing the elements of biblical evangelism, we should remember the biblical message is right. The Hebrew Scripture tells us we can trust God and His Word.

> The law of the Lord is <u>**perfect**</u>, restoring the soul; The testimony of the Lord is <u>**sure**</u>, making wise the simple. The precepts of the Lord are <u>**right**</u>, rejoicing the heart; The commandment of the Lord is <u>**pure**</u>, enlightening the eyes. (*Psm. 19:7,8*)

Perhaps Peter, a godly man, forgot this. Paul tells us in Galatians 1:8,9 what happens when godly men alter God's Word.

> But even though we, or an angel from heaven, should preach to you a gospel <u>**contrary**</u> to that which we have preached to you, <u>**let him be accursed**</u>. As we have said before, so I say again now, if any man is preaching to you a gospel <u>**contrary**</u> to that which you received, <u>**let him be accursed.**</u> (*Gal. 1:8,9*)

By the way, this is the same Paul who said eternal life was a free gift (*Rom. 6:23*) and who publicly chastised Peter (*an apostle who God chose to write the inspired Word*) for adding religious expectations (*good works*) to the justification message. Paul recorded this historical confrontation in Galatians 2:11-14.

> But when <u>**Cephas**</u> (*Peter*) came to Antioch, I <u>**opposed him to his face**</u>, because he stood condemned. For prior to the coming of certain men from James, he used to eat with the Gentiles; but when they came, he began to withdraw and hold himself aloof, fearing the party of the circumcision.

> And the rest of the Jews joined him in hypocrisy, with the result that even Barnabas was carried away by their hypocrisy. But when I saw that they were **not straightforward about the truth of the gospel**, I said to Cephas in the presence of all, 'If you being a Jew, live like the Gentiles and not like the Jews, how is it that you compel the Gentiles to live like Jews?' (*Gal. 2:11-14*)

Paul clearly lets us know godly, well-meaning men (*Peter was one of Christ's three closest friends who actually walked on water*) can miss the mark in their presentation of the gospel and their understanding of the Christian life. This error was brought to Peter's attention:

> . . . nevertheless knowing that a man is not justified by the works of the Law but through faith in Christ Jesus, even we have **believed** (*notice it doesn't say turn from sin, baptism, confess, etc.*) in Christ Jesus, that we may be **justified by faith** in Christ, and not by the works of the Law; since by the works of the Law shall no flesh be justified. (*Gal. 2:16*)

It looks like Peter may have allowed his theology to drive the biblical text instead of allowing the biblical text to drive his theology. I wonder if this happens among well-intentioned, godly leaders today. I believe it does. Any alteration of the message is wrong. We can trust the text of Scripture in our efforts in evangelism.

In case you're wondering how Peter responded to Paul's reprimand, he shared his thoughts about Paul years later. Peter wrote,

> . . . just as also our **beloved brother Paul**, according to the wisdom given him, wrote to you, as also in all his letters, speaking in them of these things, in which are some things hard to understand, which the untaught and unstable distort, as they do also the rest of the Scriptures, to their own destruction. (*2 Pt. 3:15b-16*)

It sure looks like Peter was teachable and took this thing called "humility" seriously. Peter showed great intellectual courage. Believe it or not, I think Peter and Anthony Flew have a lot in common. Who's Anthony Flew? Christianity has Billy Graham. Atheists had Anthony Flew—until he changed his mind. Dr. Flew engaged in one of the greatest acts of intellectual courage I've seen. Dr. Flew showed incredible mettle when he changed his mind about his faith position of atheism. After looking at the evidence presented by the complex coding seen in DNA, he was compelled to take up the position of a deist (*one who believes in God*). This is documented in his book There Is A God (*New York, NY: Harper One, 2007*). Below is a list of some of the publications from Dr. Flew's pen.

God and Philosophy (*1966*)
Evolutionary Ethics (*1967*)
Body, Mind and Death (*1973*)
Crime or Disease (*1973*)
Thinking About Thinking (*1975*)
Sociology, Equality and Education: Philosophical Essays In Defense Of A Variety Of Differences (*1976*)
Darwinian Evolution (*1984*)
The Presumption of Atheism (*1976*).
Did Jesus Rise From the Dead? The Resurrection Debate (*1987*) with Gary Habermas
God, A Critical Inquiry (*1988*)
Does God Exist?: A Believer and an Atheist Debate (*1991*) with Terry L. Miethe
Atheistic Humanism (*1993*)
Does God Exist: The Craig-Flew Debate (*2003*) with William Lane Craig

I imagine Dr. Flew was heavily invested in his world-view. His decision to change his mind most likely had some serious financial ramifications. The writings above are just a handful of what he had written. And with published works come money. Many of his writings were in defense of atheism. By changing his mind he was, in essence, gutting the value of his work. This takes courage. In looking at his decision, one might ask if other well-published authors, be it secular or godly Christian men, have the same kind of courage to choose truth over money, conviction over compensation? I believe Dr. Flew chose truth. And I feel Peter's response to Paul's challenge took the same kind of wisdom, humility and courage. I'm hoping Peter and Anthony are helpful as we consider the writings of some godly men in comparison to the text of the Scripture. Hebrew wisdom literature instructs us:

> Every word of God is tested; He is a shield to those who take refuge in Him. **Do not add to His words** lest He reprove you, and you be proved a liar. (*Prov. 30:5,6*)

I'm confident God is smarter than I am. He's probably smarter than most people in pulpits, seminaries, or bookstores. To be honest with you, God is brilliant. For me to add anything to His Word, His principles, or His plans is sheer arrogance on my part. Less is often more and the absence of my input certainly isn't going to harm God's Word. Indeed, it might keep me out of trouble. I wonder if "adding to His words" is an acceptable practice readily embraced in Christian literature. I believe it is. Any alteration of the message is wrong. We can trust the text of Scripture when we share our faith. Paul wrote the following to a confused immature group of believers in Corinth:

> Now these things, brethren, I have figuratively applied to myself and Apollos for your sakes, that in us you might learn **not to exceed what is written**, in order that no one of you might become arrogant in behalf of one against the other. (*1 Cor. 4:6*)

I wonder if "exceeding what is written" is a common and comfortable practice heard from our pulpits. I believe it is. Being on the wrong end of Scripture is a dangerous place to be. Any alteration of the message is wrong. We can trust the text of Scripture in our soteriology (*theology of salvation*).

Even though specifically written to specifically address the prophetic writing of John in the book of Revelation, a broad truth can be gleaned which is consistent with what we've seen in the previous verses. Christ warned John's audience (*and us*):

> I testify to everyone who hears the words of the prophecy of this book: if anyone **adds to them**, God shall add to him the plagues which are written in this book; and if anyone **takes away from the words of the book of this prophecy**, God shall take away his part from the tree of life and from the holy city, which are written in this book. (*Rev. 22:18,19*)

Repetition is the mother of all learning. Any alteration of the message is wrong. We can trust the text of Scripture in our understanding of justification. God took the time to tell us we shouldn't go beyond what He inspired His authors to write. There seems to be a bold theme or command or pattern: "**Leave My Words alone**." It's almost as if God is communicating to believers His thought process and the written vehicle He chose to use to speak to us does *not* need our help. Since we can trust God's Word, and we have the ability and responsibility to understand the biblical text in context, a good question as it relates to issues in evangelism is: *What does the Bible say about how a person obtains eternal life?*

> Truly, truly, I say to you, he who **believes** [*"in Me" – Majority Text*] has eternal life. (*Jn. 6:47*)

In contrast, what does John Piper say? "These are just some of the conditions that the New Testament says we must meet in order to inherit final salvation. We must believe on Jesus and receive him and turn from our sin and obey him and humble ourselves like little children and love him more than we love our family, our possessions, or our own life. This is what it means to be converted to Christ. This alone is the way of life everlasting."[1]

See the difference? Perhaps Jesus meant for us to understand "believes in me" as Piper does. Or then again, maybe He doesn't. Can anyone say they have, are doing, and will continue to engage in Piper's good works to obtain eternal life? I honestly can't. I would be interested to see how Piper would communicate Christ's free gift of eternal life to a

---

1 Piper, John. Desiring God (*Sisters, OR: Multnomah Books, 1986*), pgs. 65-66

six year old boy who only wants to go to heaven. It appears Piper has gone beyond the biblical text. Like Peter, maybe Dr. Piper is in error. *What does the Bible say about how a person obtains eternal life?*

> And there is **salvation in no one else**; for there is **no other name** under heaven that has been given among men, by which we must be saved. (*Acts 4:12*)

In contrast, what did Billy Graham say? "And that's what God is doing today, He's calling people out of the world for His name, whether they come from the Muslim world, or the Buddhist world, or the Christian world or the non-believing world, they are members of the Body of Christ because they've been called by God. They may not even know the name of Jesus but they know in their hearts that they need something that they don't have, and they turn to the only light that they have, and I think that they are saved, and that they're going to be with us in heaven."[2]

See the difference? Perhaps like Peter, a godly servant of Christ can go beyond the biblical text and miss the mark of the "narrow" way Jesus spoke of. *What does the Bible say about how a person obtains eternal life?*

> And they said, "**Believe** in the Lord Jesus, and you shall be saved, you and your household." (*Acts 16:31*)

In contrast, what does John MacArthur say? "It's pretty simple. Anyone who wants to come after Jesus into the kingdom of God – anyone who wants to be a Christian – has to face three commands; 1) deny himself, 2) take up his cross daily, and 3) follow Him."[3]

See the difference? Perhaps well-known teachers today can go beyond the biblical text and make what's "pretty simple," like the free gift of eternal life, complicated and costly. How many of us can say we

---

2 HOUR OF POWER television program, "Say Yes To Possibility Thinking," #1426 Interview of Billy Graham by Robert Schuller. Part 1, an approximately 7-minute-long broadcast in Southern California on Saturday, May 31, 1997

3 MacArthur, John. Hard to Believe (*Nashville, TN: Thomas Nelson, 2003*), pg. 6

consistently adhere to all three of MacArthur's commands moment by moment, day by day. The moment I sin (*and John reminds us we do sin / 1 Jn. 1:8*) I fail to meet MacArthur's requirements for becoming a Christian. Like Peter, is it possible Dr. MacArthur is incorrect? *What does the Bible say about how a person obtains eternal life?*

> And the Spirit and the bride say, "Come." And let the one who hears say, "Come." And let the one who is thirsty come; let the one who wishes take the water of life **without cost**. (*Rev. 22:17*)

In contrast, what does J.I. Packer say? "In common honesty we must not conceal the fact that free forgiveness in one sense will cost everything."[4]

See the difference? Perhaps a loving best-selling author's theology drives off the cliff of logic and crashes into the wall of contradiction by going beyond the biblical text. What color is the number two? Do you have any square circles? Does it really make any more sense to say something free is costly? The fact is eternal life *is* free to the recipients. It appears the biblical text is pretty clear about this. The cost to God (*and it was great*) is not an expense to me. Free means free. Like Peter, is it possible Dr. Packer is mistaken? *What does the Bible say about how a person obtains eternal life?*

> For this is the will of My Father, that everyone who beholds the Son and **believes in Him** will have **eternal life**, and I Myself will raise him up on the last day. (*Jn. 6:40*)

Dr. Wayne Grudem comments on these words of Christ as recorded in John 6:40. He writes, "Here Jesus says that everyone who **believes in him** (*emphasis mine*) will have **eternal life** (*emphasis mine*)."[5] Dr. Grudem's comment is consistent with the biblical statement. But yet it

---

4 Packer, J.I. Evangelism and the Sovereignty of God (*Downers Grove, IL: InterVarsity Press, 1991*), pg. 73

5 Grudem, Wayne. Systematic Theology – An Introduction to Biblical Doctrine (*Grand Rapids, MI: Zondervan, 2000*), pg. 789

appears Dr. Grudem goes beyond the biblical text in his discussion of conversion. He states, "If there is no mention of the need of repentance (*defined by Dr. Grudem as heartfelt sorrow for sin, a renouncement of it, and a sincere commitment to forsake it and walk in obedience to Christ*[6]), sometimes the gospel message becomes only, 'Believe in Jesus Christ and be saved' without any mention of repentance at all. But this watered-down version of the gospel does not ask for a wholehearted commitment to Christ – commitment to Christ, if genuine, must include a commitment to turn from sin. Preaching the need for faith without repentance is preaching only half of the gospel."[7]

I'm confident John accurately quoted the words of Jesus. His words appear clear, complete and simple – lacking in nothing. The key word seems to be "believe." Not a whisper of "repentance" or "commitment" or "turning from sin." Perhaps there was a reason Christ refrained from utilizing these works of righteousness in regards to His gospel message. In contrast, Dr. Grudem is plainly requiring the addition of these good works to his (*small "h"*) gospel message. Like Peter, is it possible Dr. Grudem is deviating from the standard of justification salvation (*eternal life*) as presented by Christ?

A reasonable rule in understanding the Bible is to rely upon what is simple to understand what is complex. Most of Scripture is very clear. Parts of it are difficult. All of it is true. Trust the biblical text. Scripture doesn't need our theology to drive it. Leave the biblical text alone. God's Word should determine what our theology should be. Our theology should *not* define God's Word. Remember, He's God and we're not.

---

[6] Grudem, Wayne. Systematic Theology – An Introduction to Biblical Doctrine (*Grand Rapids, MI: Zondervan, 2000*), pg. 713

[7] Ibid, pg. 717

CHAPTER 2

The Goal Is Eternal Life

To be successful on the firing range, squeezing the trigger and focusing on the front site are crucial. Don't expect high scores on the range without these two skills. When riding a motorcycle or bicycle in a police capacity, riders are trained, "If you don't want to hit something, don't look at it. You'll hit what you look at." Here we see the same principle. You hit what you look at. On the range, hitting the target by looking at it works. On the freeway, you don't want to hit the large rock in the road. So the best way to avoid it (*and a subsequent crash*) is by *not* looking at it. If you want to hit the rock and crash, by all means look at it.

What's the goal or target in evangelism? Is it a changed life? Is it peace with God? Is it forgiveness? Is it repentance (*by the way, what is repentance*)? Is it to get Jesus into my heart? The goal appears to vary with the evangelistic tract in one's hand. The target always seems to be moving.

When I bought a 2010 Ford F150 pickup truck, I was having some problems with the console panel (*please try to refrain from brand name bantering and criticism – I bet you Jesus would have driven a Ford*). So in order to fix the problem, I went into the glove box of my wife's 2005 Kia Sorento and grabbed the manual for that vehicle in order to get input on how to fix the problem with my Ford truck. Surely the Kia manual would tell me where to locate the Ford fuse. They both had four wheels. They both had engines. They both were registered in Arizona. They both used gasoline as fuel. In reality, I didn't use the Kia manual for a Ford problem, but a Ford manual for a Ford problem.

There was specific literature produced to address a specific brand and model problem.

The same is true with the text of Scripture. There are specific texts to deal with specific problems and specific issues. All of God's Word is inspired but not all of God's Word deals with church discipline. All of God's Word is inspired but not all of God's Word deals with the Exodus generation. All of God's Word is inspired but not all of God's Word deals with the creation of the universe. All of God's Word is inspired but not all of God's Word deals with spiritual gifts. All of God's Word is inspired but not all of God's Word deals with the role of the husband in the family. Get the picture? All of God's Word is inspired but not all of God's Word deals with justification salvation or how a person obtains eternal life.

It can be a challenge to determine what the reason was behind the inspired books of the Bible. Sometimes it's spelled out clearly. Sometimes it takes multiple reads and a great deal of thought to find the underlying purpose. Each book was written with a purpose. The Synoptic Gospels (*Matthew, Mark and Luke*) were written to Christian audiences in order to communicate who Christ was, what He taught, and His expectations of believers. Each had a different audience, a different production date, a different author and/or source, a different layout, and a different style. When it comes to the Gospel of John, many in the evangelical community see the purpose statement in John 20:30,31.

> Many other signs therefore Jesus also performed in the presence of the disciples, which are not written in this book; but these have been written **so that** (*emphasis mine*) you may **believe** (*emphasis mine*) that **Jesus** (*emphasis mine*) is the Christ, the Son of God; and **that believing you may have life** (*emphasis mine*) in His name. (*Jn. 20:30,31*)

If you want to discover a clear and simple presentation on how to obtain eternal life, *don't* go to Numbers, *don't* go to Esther, *don't* go to Philemon, *don't* go to Jonah, and *don't* go to Matthew, Mark, or Luke. Those books weren't written for that reason any more than the Kia manual was written to deal with a Ford. Yes, the Kia manual contains truth. So do books outside of the Gospel of John. Yes, the Kia manual has some similarities with the Ford manual. So do books outside the Gospel of John. But for addressing the specific issue of how to obtain eternal life, leave the Kia manual behind and open the Gospel of John. That's the reason it was written – John said so. Let me suggest three reasons why John's gospel is worthy of our attention when it comes to evangelism.

- Paul was a brilliant theologian and God used him greatly to plant and shape the early church. God is still changing lives today by means of Paul's inspired words. The same is true with John's inspired writings. In considering a comparison of time, it's not unreasonable to believe the Gospel of John was written 20-30 years after Paul completed his manuscripts. Thus John had plenty of time to think about what he said in the context of what Paul had already presented. In addition to being inspired, John's writing had a great deal of time, experience, and theology behind it.
- Out of the twelve disciples, eleven of them were believers. Out of the eleven, three of them were in Jesus' inner circle (*Mt. 17:1*). Out of the three, one was really "tight" with Christ. That would be John (*Jn. 13:23, 19:26, 20:2, 21:7,20*). John thus had an incredibly unique relationship with the Creator of the universe and thus was well suited to address the issue of obtaining eternal life. John's writing seems to be influenced by a distinctive personal friendship with Jesus Christ.
- One way authors try to make a point is to use the same words again and again and again and again and again and . . . get the point? In John's gospel, the word "life" is used 36 times while the phrase "eternal life" is used 16 times. Life is the clear priority in John's gospel. The word "believe" or various forms of the word appear 98 times in the Gospel of John. May I suggest a radical goal in our evangelistic efforts? The goal of evangelism is eternal life. John was certainly qualified to address the issue of justification salvation with his audience, but the absence of the terms "justify" and "justification" indicate that, though important, the issue of "being declared righteous" didn't seem

to be John's focus. Thus, it might be wise for us to zero in on eternal life like John did.

In addition to his focus on eternal life, Paul, Matthew, and Peter presented similar concepts connected to John's goal of eternal life. Paul and Matthew used the term "regeneration" (*paliggenesia – Titus 3.5, Mt. 19:28*) and Peter utilized "born again" (*anagennao – 1 Pt. 1:3,23*). Spiritual death is a problem – eternal life, regeneration, or being "born from above" (*Jn. 3:3,7*) is the gift and/or solution men and women need access to.

Scripture tells us the cost of being imperfect (*sin is missing God's mark of perfection*) is death (*Rom 3:23, 6:23*). God is always fair (*Psm. 7:11*). He demands payment and won't compromise ("*The person who sins will die" – Ezek. 18:20*). In addition to always being fair, God is always loving (*1 Jn. 4:8*). God demonstrated His love by having Christ pay for the sins of the world (*Rom. 5:8*). Scripture is very clear that Christ did indeed pay for the sins of the world:

- Jn. 1:29 (*behold the Lamb of God who takes away the sin of the **world***)
- Jn. 3:16 (*for God so loved the **world***)
- Jn. 4:41,42 (*the Savior of the **world***)
- 1 Jn. 2:2 (*and He Himself is the propitiation for our sins; and not for ours only, but also for those of the whole **world***)
- 2 Cor. 5:15,18,19 (*He died for **all** . . . Christ reconciling the **world** to Himself, not counting their trespasses against them*)
- 1 Tim 2:1,6 (*gave Himself as a ransom for **all***)
- 1 Tim. 4:9,10 (*Savior of **all** men, especially of believers*)
- Titus 2:11 (*bringing salvation to **all** men*)
- Heb. 2:9 (*He might taste death for **everyone***)

Christ paid for all sin for everyone. He paid for the sins of the world. Even though the natural and personal consequences of disobedience remain, the judicial debt owed to God has been paid. A fair Creator has been satisfied at great expense to Himself. In police labor terms, it's what we call "a done deal."

But after looking at the biblical data, a valid question arises. If Christ paid for the sins of the world, why do people go to hell? The answer – because they lack eternal life; they are not "in Christ" (*Rom. 6:11,23, 1 Cor. 15:22*). Let's see, life 36 times, eternal life 16 times, and belief 98 times. In police work we call this a clue. John's clear focus was for a person to consider the evidence and believe in Jesus Christ for eternal life.

Even though a court declaration is real, it's of no consequence, whether good or bad, to a dead person. Yes, Christ paid the debt for everyone. But if a person refuses to believe in Jesus for the free gift of eternal life that only He can give them, Christ's payment has no eternal benefit for them, they remain "in Adam" *(Rom. 5:17a, 1 Cor. 15:22a).* Despite the fact the death penalty for sin has been paid, to say "no" to life (*Christ – Jn. 14:6*) is to choose death. Death is separation. Physically, death is separation of the body from the spirit. Spiritually, the spirit from God. Eternally, the spirit from God forever. Whether they are good or bad, selfless or selfish, kind or wicked, generous or greedy, those who refuse to exercise faith alone in Christ alone for eternal life will spend eternity separated from their Creator.

After twenty-five years as an inner-city police officer, I'm convinced most people, like the police officers who serve them, are good – in fact very good. If most people weren't good, there would be total chaos on the streets. What you see in most societies is that laws are generated and enacted to address the behavior (*or misbehavior*) of only ten percent of the population. Nine out of ten people get it – nine out of ten people are morally upright, law abiding, and cooperative. Just because none are perfect doesn't negate the efforts of the nine out of ten who are good and are trying hard. Having provided this picture of society, let's look at an important, unpleasant end-time event: the Great White Throne Judgment. The Apostle John wrote another book and picked up the theme of eternal life again in his prophetic product. This future event is found in Revelation 20:11-15 and John records the following:

> And I saw a great white throne and Him who sat upon it, from whose presence earth and heaven fled away, and no place was found for them. And I saw the dead, the great and the small, standing before the throne, and books were opened; and another book was opened, which is **the book of life** (*emphasis mine*); and the dead were judged from the things which were written in the books, according to their deeds. And the sea gave up the dead which were in it, and death and Hades gave up the dead which were in them; and they were judged, everyone of them according to their deeds. And death and Hades were thrown into the lake of fire. This is the second death, the lake of fire. And if anyone's name was not found written in **the book of life** (*emphasis mine*), he was thrown into the lake of fire. (*Rev. 20:11-15*)

Police officers consider themselves to be trained observers. Let's see what we observe in this passage. First, non-Christians appear at this event to give account for their deeds. We can see at least three books are opened from the phrase, " . . . and **the books** (*more than one and at least two*) were opened; and **another book** (*this additional book makes for at least three books*) was opened, which is the book of life." So given the information, we have at least three books.

Consider this—what if the first two books dealt with the conduct, deeds, or works of non-Christians? Paul seemed comfortable in dividing works into two categories – bad and good (*2 Cor. 5:10*). What if one book contained all their bad deeds, failures, and lawlessness and the other book contained their good works, generosity, and love? I'm confident when these books are opened, most men and women will have a "scorecard" which will show much more good than bad. They'll be able to say "I've done a pretty good job!" This is consistent with the ninety percent who get it. These books are nice and tallying the scorecard is exciting, but none of it matters in regards to eternal destiny. The sins of an imperfect and fallen world have been paid for so any books containing works would be moot. But the important book, when it comes to eternity, is that third book—the book of life. Notice it's *not* the book of forgiveness, or the book of repentance, or the book of baptism, or the book of communion, or the book of discipleship, or the book of perseverance, or the book of justification. No, none of those. It's the book of life. Life continues to be the issue. The payment for all the failures and sin found in the "bad book" does not place a person's name in the book of life. None of the successes or love found in the "good book" merit any traction when it comes to heaven or hell. The only thing that matters for a person in line at the Great White Throne Judgment is if their name is found in the book of life. Sadly, their presence at this venue indicates their name is absent. Did they have eternal life? At a moment in time, did they exercise faith alone in Christ alone for eternal life? How devastating to be in the ninety percent (*who get it*) and discover all the good works were good for nothing. Or the ten percent who failed miserably and find out all the sin issues had been dealt with and the only thing missing to benefit from this payment was the free gift of eternal life found in Christ. So many people are so close. But close doesn't count. There is a singular problem (*spiritual death*) which affects everyone and singular solution (*Jesus Christ*) available to everybody, along with a singular goal (*eternal life*) and a singular means/response (*faith*).

In the Arizona criminal justice system, citizens are provided multiple layers of protection through a legal concept known as lesser and included charges. This prosecutorial tactic provides additional tools in the courtroom for prosecutors. For example, to increase the level of deterrence, the crime of sexual assault can also bring about additional charges of kidnapping, an aggravated assault charge, and simple assault. Arizona is serious about protecting people from criminals and thus allows for the optional implementation of this charging strategy. The rule of law doesn't just stop with the original and most serious infraction; it can also address less severe violations also. If you have a sexual assault, you have the three other crimes too.

Back to the firing range analogy for a moment, front site is important but so is squeezing the trigger. When the trigger of a gun is squeezed, a chain of dynamic, powerful (*sometimes life-changing*) events is launched. A loud noise occurs ("*bang*"). The controlled explosion in the weapon causes the gun to recoil. A round travels down and out of the barrel. The projectile travels through the air faster than the speed of sound. And the bullet will eventually strike an object with a great deal of force.

Without the pull of a trigger, very little happens. With the pull of a trigger, watch out! In the spiritual dimension of life, believers are provided multiple blessings and standing with God by means of the "trigger" event of regeneration. The Bible presents God as being serious about the eternal destiny of men and women as well as their relational interaction and status with Him. Paul agrees with the message of John (*Jn. 20:30,31*)—God's gracious goal was to provide eternal life to all who would believe.

> . . . that, as sin reigned in death, even so grace might reign through righteousness **to** [*literally "with the goal of"*] **eternal life** through Jesus Christ our Lord. (*Rom. 5:21*)

Paul describes eternal life as a "free gift" (*Rom. 6:23*). A person's reception of God's goal, His free gift of eternal life, always "triggers" and commences numerous included blessings and wonders. Paul shares our justification is connected to the reception of eternal life.

> And the gift is not like that which came through the one who sinned; for on the one hand the judgment arose from one transgression resulting in condemnation, but on the other hand **the free gift** arose from the many transgressions **resulting in justification.** (*Rom. 5:16*)

If we have eternal life, we have the other blessings too. A change in positional standing and other included blessings which are attached to eternal life are far from optional – they're guaranteed. There's nothing "lesser" in the package, but the package is linked to the "trigger" event of being born-again. Some of the included blessings that come with eternal life (*being in Christ*):

- We benefit from propitiation (*receive forgiveness of sins – Acts 10:43*)
- We have peace with God (*Rom 5:1*)
- We were reconciled (*Rom. 5:10*)
- We are set free from sin (*Rom. 6:18*)
- We are set apart (*positional sanctification—Rom. 6:22*)
- We are sealed in the Spirit (*Eph. 1:13*)

Obtaining eternal life (*regeneration*) is the "trigger" event in our evangelistic efforts. As a result, a chain of blessings and positional changes bring about supernatural and powerful life-changing events. Justification, sanctification, forgiveness, adoption, freedom, and reconciliation are some of the many great and wonderful blessings that are all connected to the reception of eternal life. Remember, poor marksmanship can result in aiming at too many things. Aim is important in evangelism. With John's gospel as the contextual backdrop and blueprint for evangelism, the target or the goal is eternal life and the "trigger" event is the reception of the goal.

CHAPTER 3

Change Your Mind About Repentance and Forgiving

Let's talk briefly about repentance (*metanoia*) and forgiving (*aphiemi)*. First, the Greek term for repentance means "to change one's mind." It doesn't mean to feel sorry, remorseful or to turn from sin to God – all of which are good works.

- In Acts 26:20, Paul demonstrated that "repentance" and "turning to God" were not the same concept. He stated to Agrippa, " . . . that they should **repent** and **turn to God** . . ."
- In the Greek translation of the Hebrew Scriptures (*LXX – Septuagint*), this term is used consistently with the definition of "changing one's mind." Proverbs 24:32 says, "When I saw, I **reflected** (*repented*) upon it, I looked, and received instruction." By means of an anthropomorphism (*attributing human characteristics to God*), Amos 7:6 doesn't communicate the Creator had a sin problem. It tells us God repented; "The Lord **changed His mind** (*repented*) about this, 'It shall not be' said the Lord."
- Paul seems to present a distinction between "sorrow" (*lupeo*), "repentance" (*metanoia*), and "regret" (*ametameletos)* as if they were three different concepts which, even though related at times, are not one and the same. We learn sorrow sanctifies (*saves from the power of sin*) Christians by generating numerous good works in their lives – earnestness, vindication, indignation, fear, longing, zeal, avenging of wrong, AND repentance.

> For the **<u>sorrow</u>** that is according to the will of God **<u>produces</u>** a **<u>repentance</u>** without **<u>regret</u>**, leading to salvation (*sanctification*), but the sorrow of the world produces death. For behold what earnestness this very thing, this godly sorrow, has produced **<u>in you</u>** [*Christians in the context*]: what vindication of yourselves, what indignation, what fear, what longing, what zeal, what avenging of wrong! In everything you demonstrated yourselves to be innocent in the matter. (*2 Cor. 7:9,10*)

- The goal of John's historical account of Christ's life seems clear: " . . . that believing you may have life in His name . . ." (*Jn. 20:31*). Yet the terms "repent" or "repentance" are absent in the Gospel of John. John had access to the word "repent" because he chose to use it twelve times in the Book of Revelation, eight times when addressing Christians in the church in Revelation 2 and 3. It seems believers needed to "change their mind" about sinful conduct they were engaged in.
- There are certainly times in the biblical text where "repent" is used in an evangelistic context. Examples would be Acts 2:38, 17:30,34, 20:21. In those cases, the meaning stays the same but the context makes repentance synonymous with faith. People "changed their minds" about who Christ was and what they were trusting in for their eternal destiny.

Second, the Greek term for "forgive" can mean to leave, divorce, reject, produce, or to forgive. The term, as it is used to communicate "forgiveness," is used twice in John's gospel as it relates to mankind's sin. It occurs two times in one verse near the end of the historical account (*Jn. 20:23*). Like "repent" John had access to the word "forgive" and used it twice in 1 John as it relates to mankind and God. He didn't use it at all with this meaning in Revelation. Trusting in Christ for eternal life establishes God as our Father – a relationship which is eternally secure (*Jn. 1:12*). Judicially, Christ's payment (*Col. 2:13,14*) cancelled our debt "to the court." Police officers understand forgiveness is not an issue in a court of law, acquittal (*justification – Rom. 5:1,9, Gal. 2:16*) is. Justification is a forensic issue. Forgiveness is a familial issue. Forgiveness is crucial in maintaining fellowship with God (*1 Jn. 1:5-10*). Jesus set the terms required to be His friend: "You are My friends if you do what I command you to do (*Jn. 15:14*)." When I sin, and I do, in order to restore fellowship with My Father I need to "confess" my sin to Him and agree I missed the mark and ask for forgiveness. This situation is somewhat similar with life in the physical world (*acknowledging that all illustrations fall short*). Tom Spencer, my biological father, gave me life for free at no cost to me. There is nothing I can do to *not* make him my father. But if I wanted to make Tom Spencer my friend, I needed to obey the rules of the house. Tom Spencer will always be my father. Tom Spencer is *not* always my friend. Likewise, God is always my Father. But my conduct determines if He'll be my friend (*or better yet, if I'll be His*). Forgiveness and confession are critical in maintaining this fellowship whereas faith alone in Christ alone for eternal life is critical in establishing the relationship. Forgiveness and eternal life are complimentary but separate issues and shouldn't be blended or confused. The blessing of forgiveness is reliant upon the reception of eternal life.

CHAPTER 4

Use Biblical Terms

I'll never forget one seminary assignment (*yes that's right – just one*) in a Greek class, I got lazy (*frequently synonymous with stupid*) and cut and pasted comments and statements from the commentary works of others. My professor reminded me this was inappropriate and certainly an unwise and unacceptable method for a student of God's Word to gain a proper understanding. I needed to do my own work and not rely on others. He referenced the crowd's response to Christ's teaching in what we refer to as "Sermon on the Mount" found in Matthew 5-7. Matthew 7:28,29 says:

> The result was that when Jesus had finished these words, the multitudes were amazed at His teaching; for **He was teaching them as one having authority**, and not as their scribes. (*Mt. 7:28,29*)

A teaching method of the day took the focus off the text of Scripture and relied upon on the quotes of others, and the quotes about other's quotes, and so on and so on and so on. Jesus was original. He did His own work; He relied upon Himself – the author of Scripture. In this section we'll see that perhaps we've fallen into the habit of the scribes of Jesus' day. Remember, words have meanings and God took the time to choose His words carefully. I can't offer anything to improve them. So let's invest the time to look at His biblical text.

Many concepts and words in evangelistic presentations today appear to fall short of the biblical mark. They're not based or sourced in the Bible. If the words of the Lord are perfect, why wouldn't I use them? Why deviate and change? Why say something else? Many terms bandied about in evangelism today are not UNBIBLICAL, just NON-BIBLICAL. They're inventive human rhetoric which has no foundation in the biblical text. Unfortunately, many today rely upon the quotes and thoughts of others when the words and ideas of the author of Scripture are easily accessible and understood in the Bible right in front of them. Jesus was very clear on how to obtain eternal life:

> Truly, truly, I say to you, he who **believes** [*"in Me" – Majority Text*] has eternal life (*Jn. 6:47*).

The following evangelistic phrases are commonly heard, used, and seen in books, from pulpits, and in tracts today. How do they compare with the words of Christ?

- Follow Jesus
- Forsake all
- Pray a prayer
- Put Jesus on the throne of your life
- Promise to live for Jesus
- Get your life turned around
- Turn away from the world toward God
- Surrender your life to Christ
- Make Jesus Lord of your life
- Invite Jesus into your life
- Turn from your sins
- Be willing to turn from your sins
- Keep the 10 commandments
- Give up your life
- Admit you're a sinner

Don't get me wrong, none of the phrases in the list should be described as bad. These are all good things. But that's the problem; they're good things, commonly referred to as good works. The biblical text does not generate confusion when it comes to the role works play in justification salvation.

> But if it is by grace, **it is no longer on the basis of works**, otherwise grace is no longer grace. (*Rom. 11:6*)

When the terms in the list are examined closely, questions can arise. What does it mean to follow Jesus? How long do I have to follow Him? Where do I have to follow Him to? Does the "all" in "forsake all" really mean "all?" Can anyone say they've forsaken all? Just one sin proves that's not the case. Where is a historical account in the text of Scripture in which praying a prayer was given to us as the biblical pattern in evangelism? Did Jesus or Paul or James or John or any of the apostles ever ask anyone to pray a prayer? Isn't making Jesus the Lord of my life or putting Him on the throne an obedience issue? Is obedience required to obtain eternal life? Which is it – turning from my sin or just a willingness to turn from my sin? By the way, isn't turning from sin a work of righteousness? The questions which jump out of this Pandora's Box are as many as the day is long. Confusion replaces clarity and subjectivity replaces simplicity when we go beyond the text of God's Word.

A phrase I grew up with and which is utilized to this day in evangelistic efforts is the concept "ask Jesus into your heart." This phrase is comforting and common but is it consistent with the context and content of the Bible? In Revelation 3:20 John quotes Jesus:

> Behold, I stand at the **door** and knock; if anyone hears My voice and opens the **door**, I will come in to him, and will **dine with him**, and he with Me. (*Rev. 3:20*)

This comment was offered up by Christ to the church of Laodicea. It's a square peg of a picture that doesn't need to be rammed into the round hole of literalism (*similar to parables*). But yet there is still a specific issue and a specific truth. This church had become useless to the Master and their conduct was offensive to Christ. Let's see if the context of the biblical text will shed light on what Christ said and how to use His words appropriately and as intended.

First, Christ is talking to Christians – people who already had eternal life. Since the words are directed to a specific believing church and the audience is described as "those whom I love," it seems reasonable the audience in mind consisted of those who already had eternal life. To use this verse as an evangelistic tool is not evil or wicked, it's just out of context; thus inappropriate. Christ's words were not directed to get people to trust in Him for eternal life but to get Christians who already had eternal life to obey and embrace fellowship with Him. If He didn't use them with an evangelistic focus, should I?

Second, hearts don't have doors. Churches do. To equate the door Christ was knocking at as somehow connected to "a person's heart" is unwarranted and going beyond the biblical text. Christ is talking to a group of believers who He loves but who are disobedient. Hot water is useful. Cold water is useful. They were "lukewarm"—a picture of uselessness. That's why Christ spits them out. It's not a loss of eternal life but a loss of fellowship. Remember, being useful is a good work and good works are not required for justification salvation. Christ desired fellowship with them. He presents a picture of Himself standing outside of their assembly and knocking on the door, initiating the desire to renew personal friendship. He is encouraging them to obey and become useful. To further paint the picture of fellowship, Christ wants to not only come in but also wants to dine with them – a marvelous portrait of friendship (*Psm. 23:5-6*).

To use this verse out of context with an evangelistic intent shows confusion. To equate "the door" as the door to the heart confuses the means with the results. The biblical text tells us once a person trusts in Christ for eternal life, Christ comes in to their life. Remember, the goal is eternal life, not to get Christ into my heart. We become children of God when we receive/believe/have faith in Christ for eternal life (*Jn. 1:12, Gal. 3:26*). Three passages illustrate that subsequent to conversion, Christ comes into the life of the Christian. Galatians 2:20 says, "I have been crucified with Christ; and it is no longer I who live, but **Christ lives in me** . . ." Galatians 4:6 states, "And because you are sons, God has sent forth **the Spirit of His Son into our hearts** . . ." Paul writes in Col. 1:17 "…to whom God willed to make known what is the riches of the glory of this mystery among the Gentiles, which is **Christ in you**, the hope of glory." Scripture seems to indicate Christ comes into the life of the believer following regeneration or being "born again."

To use Revelation 3:20 out of context can confuse children. As a parent, it's easy to see young kids can have a difficult time grasping abstract principles. They think in concrete terms. So to ask a child to have Jesus come into their hearts, the picture in their young mind is a 5'9" Jewish guy who wears sandals somehow shrinking down and getting inside of their chest. It is both reasonable and possible for a child to exercise childlike faith to obtain eternal life. But causing childlike confusion by using Scripture out of context should be criminal. In addition to using verses out of context, another way of going beyond the biblical text is to ascribe powers and adjectives to the issue of faith.

The Bible is clear that the means of obtaining eternal life is through faith. Time and again we hear the Disney-like motif "You've just got to have faith" as if the act of believing is what solves the problem. Christ is the solution (*the object*) to the problem of spiritual death. Faith is the means in which the solution is applied. A house is on fire. What puts it out, the water or the hose? Don't think too hard about this one. In reality it's the water that puts out the flames. The hose is just the means by which the solution gets to the problem. The hose doesn't put the fire out and faith doesn't provide us eternal life – Christ does.

Faith is simply trust, confidence, persuasion or belief in a person, principle, or object. In Greek lexicons (*except the recently revised Bauer lexicon – no reason given for the change in the definition of faith from the previous version*), the term "pistuo" (*believe*) and "pistis" (*faith*) do not give any indication or perception of obedience or commitment. It looks as if the biblical text provides a reasonably clear definition of faith:

> Now faith [*daily living faith*] is the **assurance** [*being sure*] of things **hoped** for, the **conviction** of things not seen. (*Heb. 11:1*)

Hope treats unseen things as reality. Faith is our ability to be certain of the things of God that can't be seen. It's *not,* "If I believe hard enough it will happen." Faith isn't limited to just the spiritual dimension of life. I trust when I squeeze the trigger it will go off. The reason I believe this is because of the evidence. The gun has gone off every time I've pulled the trigger in the past, and past history is a good indicator (*or evidence*) of future performance. I exercise faith when I set an appointment in ten minutes and the address is five miles away. Why did I make the appointment? Not because I'm a fast runner. I made the appointment because the car is in the driveway and it has started for me the past three years without fail. I don't have to get into the car and start it prior to scheduling a date on my calendar. Believing the car will start and actually starting the car are two different things. Believing the chair will hold me up and actually sitting in it are two different things. I don't have to commit or yield my rear end to the chair to believe it will hold me up. I believe the earth is round and orbits the sun because scientific facts compel me to. I believe George Washington was the first President of the United States because the historical evidence is reasonable. I believe citizens have the right to remain silent (*I would never talk to the police*) because I've been exposed to case law and the Constitution. Faith isn't mystical or magical, it's practical. A world full of non-Christians exercises faith every day.

The Hebrew concepts of "love" and "hate" as seen in Romans 9:13 (*"Jacob I loved, but Esau I hated"*) communicate the idea of God making a choice. A western mindset which uses the English language might be tempted to incorrectly impose the issue of emotions on this biblical text. Context keeps this from occurring. In the same way, caution should be exercised when defining or understanding the Greek term for faith by means of a thought process based upon a Latin frame of mind and/or an English dictionary. Police officers refer to this as "apples and oranges." When it comes to faith, it appears unreasonable to impose the three progressive Latin concepts of "noticia" (*knowledge*), "assensus" (*intellectual acceptance*), and "fiducia" (*trust/obedience*) on the Greek terms for faith and believe. This thought process can lead to a non-biblical focus on the type of faith instead of the biblical object one puts their faith in – Jesus Christ. This in turn can create an unreliable and unreasonable expectation by some that a "changed life" is an indicator of a person who has "truly believed." In addition, others teach incorrectly faith in Christ for eternal life is not a choice but a gift from God. There's a reliance upon Ephesians 2:8 to support this thought process.

> **For by grace you have been saved through faith**; and **that** not of yourselves, **it** is the gift of God. (*Eph. 2:8*)

The Greek construction of this sentence indicates "**that** (*Greek – neuter*) not of yourselves, **it** is the gift of God" can *not* be **faith** (*Greek – feminine*), but "**that**" refers to the entire provision "by grace you have been saved through faith." The difference between "dog" and "God" is just two letters but the meaning and implication behind the change is enormous. Context is crucial. When scripture is mishandled, even in the slightest degree with a small word like "that," serious errors with eternal implications can arise. In addition, if faith is a gift from God, why is a person held liable for failing to meet God's required means of faith in Christ if God didn't give Him faith in the first place? If this is fair and this is love then we're in trouble – call the police union for help!

In a historical account of the life of Christ, Jesus provided us a wonderful picture of what faith is. In John 6:47 Jesus says, "Truly, truly, I say to you, he who **believes** [*"in Me" – Majority Text*] has eternal life." A good teacher will engage in the practice of restatement to get a point across. This is what Jesus did in John 6:54 during the same teaching session. Jesus said, "Truly, truly he who **eats My flesh and drinks My blood** has eternal life." This word picture offended some who heard it. They missed the point. Belief is like eating and drinking. Faith is passive appropriation. No one would ever equate it with work no more than one would equate drinking or eating with work. It's doing something, but that something is not work. It's confidence or trust. When a guy asks a girl out on a date, he doesn't ask her to help him change the oil in his car (*work*) but to go out to dinner (*eating and drinking*). He's asking her to do something but nothing that would be related to work.

Our act of faith does not provide eternal life. Faith is just the means which passively appropriates (*believes in*) Jesus Christ for the free gift of eternal life. Many are tempted to source justification salvation in faith instead of the Person. This is seen by the use of many common non-biblical descriptors of faith.

- Spurious faith
- Counterfeit faith

- Intellectual faith
- False faith
- Insincere faith
- Pseudo faith
- Emotional faith
- Head faith
- True faith
- Authentic faith
- Saving faith
- Personal faith
- Real faith
- Efficacious faith
- Heart faith

Each word in front of the term faith is an adjective. None of these adjectives as it pertains to faith is found in the text of Scripture. When the emphasis becomes the type of faith instead of the Person in whom we have faith in (*Christ*), statements that go beyond the biblical text are bound to spring up. They sound good but they're simply not true. Case in point: A fellow seminary graduate stated from the pulpit to a large group of people about the need for the correct type of faith in order to be justified. To drive his point home he stated, "A person can miss heaven by 18 inches, that's the distance between the head and the heart. If you don't have heart faith you don't have eternal life."

There are several problems with this statement. First, faith doesn't provide eternal life, Christ does. This teaching places an incorrect emphasis on faith as if it's the object instead of the means. Second, there is no biblical support for the concept of "head faith" and "heart faith." There's a clear inference in his words that the "mind" is inferior to the "heart." Scripture appears to provide a different picture. At times, the head (*mind*) and the heart are presented as synonymous: Psm. 26:2" . . . test my **mind** and my **heart** . . . ," Prov. 17:20 " . . . he who has a crooked **mind** (*i.e. heart*) finds no good . . . ," Heb. 8:10 " . . . I will put My laws into their **minds**, and I will write them upon their **hearts** . . ." In other places, the biblical text shows the mind is what's crucial – 1 Cor. 2:16 " . . . we have the **mind** of Christ . . . ," 1 Pt. 1:13 " . . . gird your **minds** for action . . . ," Rom. 12:2 " . . . be transformed by the renewing of your **mind** . . ." Third, can anyone really make a distinction between "head belief" and "heart belief?" Do you believe 2 + 2 = 4 with your head or your heart or does it really matter? Do you believe with your head or your heart that if you jump out of a plane with no parachute from three miles up you'll die upon landing? Do you believe in the concept of "head faith" verses "heart faith" with your head or your heart? Some might call making distinctions in faith as "thinking too hard." Some might just feel better calling it non-biblical. Others would call this making the simple complex. Personal subjective descriptors of faith are common ways non-biblical terms are utilized to go beyond the biblical text.

The use of biblical terms and the concepts they communicate are crucial in addressing the eternal destiny of the men and women we come into contact with. It's wrong to "wing it" and the use of reckless rhetoric is alarmingly insufficient in adhering to the biblical message and the biblical patterns of evangelism. We can do better.

CHAPTER 5

The Method Is to Persuade

As in any occupation, there were always a few officers whose goal every shift was to do as little work as possible. Some worked so hard at dodging reports it would have been easier to take the report in the first place. But that's just how they did their job. Yes, there was a third shift officer who would bring a pillow to work and "dock" his police car in a secluded parking lot known as "the bat cave." He showed up to work, but how he did it was a little questionable. And then there was the lieutenant who never let his on-duty police management job get in the way of his personal real estate business. "How" we do our work is just as important as "why" we do it. Not doing work, sleeping on the job, personal business on-duty – these are clearly strategies and tactics, but are they the right ones for effective police work? As a taxpayer (*you know, the boss*), what do you think? Misguided policing methods can make for unhappy and frustrated citizens.

I wonder what God thinks of "how" we do the work of evangelism. Is it consistent with the biblical pattern He's provided us? Do our approaches irritate Him? Do our tactics discourage, offend, or confuse the one on the listening end? If there's frustration in evangelism, perhaps the problem is not the message but how we're delivering it. Do we engage in evangelism by yelling, shouting, pointing fingers, or whacking people over the head? Or do we do nothing at all? I wonder if our methods resemble those employed by Jesus and Paul.

How we shoot a gun impacts our score. There's a huge difference between "jerking" the trigger and "squeezing" it. In the same way, if we're misguided about the method of evangelism, disappointment, like a poor shooting score, is sure to follow. If we're doing the right thing the wrong way we might be spinning our wheels. And one of the best ways to avoid frustration is to disengage from the activity that's causing it. Maybe this is a reason evangelism isn't a consistent dynamic part of the Christian life. But evangelism doesn't have to be an offensive, fearful, or frustrating chore. It can and should be an exciting and fulfilling opportunity.

The method ("*how*") of evangelism is to persuade people. Belief and persuasion are twin sons of different mothers. Belief is the biblical response—persuasion is the biblical method in prompting the response. Evangelism is utilizing a moment in time to convince or sway a spiritually dead person to exercise faith alone in Christ alone for eternal life.

There is a line in the sand. On one side is spiritual death. A good term for this is a "broad way that leads to destruction." Most people, according to the Bible, are on this dead side of the line. What we see in the world seems to verify this biblical observation—works oriented religion is a wide avenue which fails a multitude of men and women. On the other side of the line is eternal life – the narrow way which leads to life. According to Jesus, few people are on this side of the line (*Mt. 7:14*). We can see the life and death lines in the sand in various passages of the biblical text.

- "He who believes in the Son has **eternal life**; but he who does not obey the Son shall not see **life**, but the wrath of God abides on him." Jn. 3:36
- "But whoever drinks of the water that I shall give him shall never thirst; but the water that I shall give him shall become in him a well of water springing up to **eternal life**." Jn. 4:14
- "Truly, truly, I say to you, he who hears My word, and believes Him who sent Me, has **eternal life**, and does not come into judgment, but has passed out of **death** into **life**." Jn. 5:24
- "I am the bread of **life**. Your fathers ate the manna in the wilderness, and they died. This is the bread which comes down out of heaven, so that one may eat of it and not **die**." Jn. 6:48-50

- "Therefore, just as through one man sin entered into the world, and **death** through sin, and so **death** spread to all men, because all sinned." Rom. 5:12
- " . . . that, as sin reigned in **death**, even so grace might reign through righteousness to **eternal life** through Jesus Christ our Lord." Rom. 5:21
- "For the wages of sin is **death**, but the free gift of God is **eternal life** in Christ Jesus our Lord." Rom. 6:23
- "And you were **dead** in your trespasses and sins." Eph. 2:1
- "...even when we were **dead** in our transgressions, made us **alive** together with Christ (by grace you have been saved)." Eph. 2:5
- "And when you were **dead** in your transgressions and the uncircumcision of your flesh, He made you **alive** together with Him, having forgiven us all our transgressions." Col. 2:13
- "And yet for this reason I found mercy, in order that in me as the foremost, Jesus Christ might demonstrate His perfect patience, as an example for those who would believe in Him for **eternal life**." 1 Tim. 1:16
- " . . . but now has been revealed by the appearing of our Savior Christ Jesus, who abolished **death** and brought **life** and immortality to light through the gospel." 2 Tim. 1:10
- "And the Spirit and the bride say, 'Come.' And let the one who hears say, 'Come.' And let the one who is thirsty come; let the one who wishes take the water of **life** without cost." Rev. 22:17

The "name of the game" (*in evangelism*) is to move spiritually dead people to life. It's to get them over the line – not by a yard or a mile, but by the slightest degree. Remember, the smallest about of faith (*like the size of a mustard seed – Mt. 17:20*) can solve the biggest problem (*like the lack of eternal life*). It's not to get them from pagan to Paul. It's not to get them from death to disciple. It's not to get them from Darwinism to creationism. It's not to get them from vile to virtue. It's not to see them transformed into an "obeyer" but, by means of regeneration, a "born-again believer." Being an imitator of Paul as an obedient disciple is an important issue in the Christian life. But it has nothing to do with passing "out of death into life."

How do we get non-Christians across the line? Persuasion. Better yet, gentle, well-reasoned persuasion. The means of moving unbelievers across the line from death to life is seen in the brilliant biblical pattern of evangelism as demonstrated by Jesus and Paul throughout the New Testament. No examples of altar calls. No one was asked to pray a prayer. Paul went out of his way to let his audience know "Christ did not send me to baptize . . . (*1 Cor. 1:17*)" but to preach the gospel. What Jesus and Paul demonstrated in their evangelistic strategies was personal interaction with people through the use of persuasion. There was simple and clear face-to-face dialogue with questions and answers. Dialogue, questions, and clarity are key ingredients in the art and science of persuasion. Just because evangelism addresses a spiritual issue doesn't mean people shouldn't be challenged to reason and to think – to engage their minds.

When Jesus was persuading and communicating with Nicodemus in John 3, there was dialogue, there were questions, and there was clarity. Jesus spoke to Nicodemus in a context he understood. Christ understood the concept of regeneration profoundly and was able to communicate it clearly. No request for yielding or lordship, just belief in Him for eternal life (*Jn. 3:16*). Christ persuaded by presenting evidence to Nicodemus that He was the only giver of eternal life and was worthy of his confidence for his eternal destiny.

> Now there was a man of the Pharisees, named Nicodemus, a ruler of the Jews; this man came to Jesus by night and said to Him, "Rabbi, we know that You have come from God as a teacher; for no one can do these signs that You do unless God is with him." Jesus answered and said to him, "Truly, truly, I say to you, unless one is **born again** [*literally "from above"*] he cannot **see** [*in the context – synonymous with "enter"*] the kingdom of God." Nicodemus said to Him, "How can a man be born when he is old? He cannot enter a second time into his mother's womb and be born, can he?" Jesus answered, "Truly, truly, I say to you, unless one is born of **water** and the **Spirit** [*wind*] he cannot **enter** into the kingdom of God. That which is born of the flesh is flesh, and that which is born of the Spirit is spirit. Do not be amazed

> that I said to you, 'You must be **born again** [*from above*].' The **wind** blows where it wishes and you hear the sound of it, but do not know where it comes from and where it is going; so is everyone who is born [*out*] of the **Spirit** [*wind*]." Nicodemus said to Him, "How can these things be?" Jesus answered and said to him, "Are you **the teacher of Israel** and do not understand these things? Truly, truly, I say to you, we speak of what we know and testify of what we have seen, and you do not accept our testimony. If I told you earthly things and you do not believe, how will you believe if I tell you heavenly things? No one has **ascended** into heaven, but He who **descended** from heaven: the **Son of Man**. As Moses lifted up the serpent in the wilderness, even so must the **Son of Man** be lifted up; so that whoever **believes** will in Him have eternal life. For God so loved the **world**, that He gave **His only begotten Son**, that whoever **believes** in Him shall not perish, but have eternal life." (*Jn. 3:1-16*)

"*The* teacher of Israel" should have seen the prophetic connection between his conversation with Christ and Proverbs 30:4.

> Who has **ascended** into heaven and **descended**? Who has gathered the **wind** in His fists? Who has wrapped the **waters** in His garment? Who has established all the ends of the **earth**? What is His name or **His son's name**? Surely you know! (*Prov. 30:4*)

Jesus was trying to persuade "a man of the Pharisees" to trust in Him for eternal life. His dialogue was brilliant and a lesson for all of us. In the end, Christ was able to persuade Nicodemus and get him across the line (*Jn. 12:42,43, 19:38,39*). Not that evangelistic tracts are wrong, but don't you believe Jesus demonstrated people are worth the time for face-to-face interaction instead of a quick, "Here read this" and leave?

When Jesus spoke to "a woman of Samaria" at a well (*Jn. 4*), again we see persuasion by means of dialogue, questions, and clarity. Eternal life was the issue and persuasion was the method. The fact of the woman's imperfection (*sin*) was discussed but yet there was no request or command on the part of Christ to have her stop sinning. Moving (*persuading*) the woman from death to life by means of belief in Him was the method. And Jesus showed us she was moved (*persuaded*) in her understanding of Him from being a Jew (*vs. 9*) to being a prophet (*vs. 19*) to finally being the only giver of eternal life – the Messiah (*vs. 29*). The end result of this evangelistic interaction: "And many more **believed** because of His word." (*Jn. 4:41*)

Jesus' contact with the man who was born blind (*Jn. 9*) followed a similar strategy of persuasion but this time with the addition of meeting a real, physical need in order to facilitate the solution to the spiritual one. In this historical account we see the man's perception and understanding of Christ move (*persuasion*); it moves from Jesus as a man (*vs. 11*), to a prophet (*vs. 17*), to a God-fearer (*vs. 31*), and then once again, to the only giver of eternal life – the Son of Man, the Messiah (*vs. 35*). The end result from the man, "Lord, I **believe**." (*Jn. 9:38*)

When Lazarus died (*Jn. 11*), the historical account of the interaction between Martha and Christ shows the real hurt and valid expression of grief in both of their lives (*remember, Jesus wept / Jn. 11:35*). Again, we see dialogue, questions, and clarity. Jesus makes a bold statement:

> I am the resurrection and the life; he who **believes** in Me shall live even if he dies, and everyone who lives and **believes** in Me shall never die. (*Jn. 11:25-26a*)

John records, under the inspiration of the Holy Spirit, the important issues in an evangelistic conversation – "life," "death," "never die (*eternal*)," "belief," "believes in Me." And once again, we see a call to answer a simple question, "Do you believe this (*Jn. 11:26b*)?" No call for confession or communion or commitment or baptism. No demand or hint at turning from sin to God; simply faith alone in Christ alone for eternal life. It's clear from Martha's response she had been persuaded to believe in Christ for eternal life prior to this tragic event. Her brother was dead and cold in a tomb but she had still seen and heard enough to believe.

> She said to Him, "Yes, Lord; **I have believed** that you are the Christ, the Son of God, even He who comes into the world." (*Jn. 11:27*)

The time and talk of Christ had ultimately convinced (*persuaded*) her to believe in Him to get her across the line – to move from death to life. In addition to John's record of Christ, we see Luke's historical account of the evangelistic efforts of Paul. Like Christ, the pattern and method used by Paul was to "persuade."

- And some of them were **persuaded** and joined Paul and Silas, along with a great multitude of the God-fearing Greeks and a number of the leading women. Acts. 17:4
- And he was reasoning in the synagogue every Sabbath and trying to **persuade** Jews and Greeks. Acts. 18:4
- And he entered the synagogue and continued speaking out bolding for three months, reasoning and **persuading** them about the kingdom of God. Acts 19:8
- You see and hear that not only in Ephesus, but in almost all of Asia, this Paul has **persuaded** and turned away a considerable number of people, saying that gods made with hands are no gods at all. Acts 19:26
- And King Agrippa replied to Paul, 'In a short time you will **persuade** me to become a Christian.' Acts 26:28
- And when they had set a day for him, they came to him at his lodging in large numbers; and he was explaining to them by solemnly testifying about the kingdom of God, and trying to **persuade** them concerning Jesus, from both the Law of Moses and from the Prophets, from morning until evening. And some were being **persuaded** by the things spoken, but others would not believe. Acts 28:23,24

Paul engaged in evangelism by means of constructive dialogue – persuasion. A common ingredient of this dialogue process was the use of reason (*so much for the superiority of "heart faith" over "head faith"*). Religious questions in a non-threatening environment are an evangelistic strategy I believe are consistent with the biblical pattern. Dialogue, questions, and clarity once again are key ingredients in the art and science of persuasion. I've found dialogue generated by religious surveys foster meaningful communication about spiritual issues in a manner which does not create a defensive atmosphere or attitude. The survey (*it's really the questions in the survey*) I use I borrowed from Campus Crusade for Christ (*now known as Cru*). The multiple questions are clearly designed to address the spiritual dimension of life. I honestly want to know what the person I'm sharing my faith with thinks. Their opinion is of great value to me. In order to assure them of this value and cultivate open dialogue, I explain two personal expectations. First, I advise the person, "Don't be nice, be honest." We're not there to stroke my ego. The second request I make is for them to give me ***their*** opinion, *not* what they think their mother would want them to say. I assure them I'm not going to talk to their mothers about their answers and opinions.

I've utilized the aforementioned survey and the questions within it hundreds and hundreds of times. Evangelistic dialogue revolves around the following questions:

1. What is your spiritual background (*i.e. church, denomination, religion, etc.*)?
2. Of the following, how would you rank each in terms of importance? (*1 – not important, 5 – very important*)

	1	2	3	4	5
FAMILY					
WORK					
MARRIAGE					
RELIGION					
EDUCATION					
FRIENDS					
HEALTH					
LUCKY BREAKS					

3. Do you think that there is a God and how do you know?
4. How much of the Bible have you read?

5. If your young child asked you the following questions, how would you respond?
   a. *What makes something right and what makes something wrong?*
   b. *Why do people die and what happens to them when they die?*
   c. *Why should I live and not commit suicide?*

6. In your opinion, how does a person get to heaven?
7. In your view, what is a Christian?
8. Would you give me your opinion on four basic principles of Christianity?

The key question in this survey is number 6: **In your opinion, how does a person get to heaven?** What's being asked is what they think is required to obtain eternal life. This is the line in the sand. The answer to this question has eternal ramifications. We can tell what a man or woman is entrusting their eternal destiny to by means of this question. Let me share with you some actual answers to this query:

- I don't believe in Hell. There is no alternative to heaven.
- Be fair and just in this world. Your body of work will be judged.
- Do more good than bad.
- Believe in God, confessing sins, hoping for forgiveness.
- Having a personal relationship with God and living that way. Not religion or doing certain things. Know what God's expectations are of us and living accordingly.
- Accept Jesus Christ as your savior and then do the best you can. Be Christ-like.
- Being the best person you can be. When you make mistakes ask for forgiveness. Live the best life you can. Realize you're not perfect.
- Doing righteous deeds. Obeying God's and man's law. Not purposefully causing harm to others.
- If people do go to heaven they get there by living a good, honest, healthy life and being a good person.
- Being a good person and doing the right things with no short-cuts.

- Follow what God has told you to do.
- Living life the right way. Caring for others. Putting forth the best effort to do the right thing.
- Reading the Bible. Doing good deeds.
- Take Jesus as savior. Ask Him to forgive sins. Try to be a good person and continue to improve yourself.
- Person has to have a relationship with God. Serve God. Do God's work.
- Soul goes through purgatory then judgment day. As long as you ask for forgiveness. There's got to be a place for the problem kids.
- Believe in God – Supreme Being. Live a good life that He would approve of. Do nothing that you would have to hide or be accountable for.
- Accepts Christ as savior, repents, and asks for forgiveness.
- Accept Jesus Christ as savior. More than that; live by moral guidelines.
- By believing in a power greater than yourself.
- Accept Jesus as savior – that's all.

Every person, and many, many more that I've asked these questions to were good, moral, kind, successful, intelligent, educated people. The bulk of them were police officers. Some of them were media professionals. Some were homosexuals. Some held world champion black-belt titles. Some were community activists. Some were engaged in adultery or sex outside of marriage. Some battled alcoholism and some struggled with internet pornography. Some were bitter at their churches. All of them were very honest and open.

When we take these answers and compare them to the standard of Christ's words, alarm bells should go off. What even generates more concern is many of these answers closely resemble inappropriate rhetoric espoused by popular authors found on the bookshelves in our church bookstores today. In stark contrast, Jesus and Paul made it clear:

> Truly, truly, I say to you, he who **believes** [*"in Me" – Majority Text*] has eternal life. (*Jn. 6:47*)

> For by **<u>grace</u>** you have been **<u>saved</u>** through **<u>faith</u>**; and that not of yourselves, it is the **<u>gift</u>** of God; **<u>not as a result of works</u>**, that no one should boast. (*Eph. 2:8,9*)

The clear New Testament standard for justification: Faith alone in Christ alone for eternal life. This small sample of survey answers demonstrates what appears to be a natural desire to incorporate works, deeds, or conduct as a necessary ingredient to secure one's eternal destiny. It's possible these American professionals provided these answers because this is what they hear and see all the time in their culture. But is it really a problem of culture or is it a problem of concept?

One day I had the opportunity to sit down with three Muslim students on the campus of Arizona State University. I began to share my faith with them and asked them what was required for them to enter Paradise. They quickly and corporately told me one's good deeds have to outweigh their bad deeds when Allah puts them on his scales. I then asked them, "How do you know if you've done enough." Their response still rings in my ears to this day – "That's the hell of it; you never know if you've done enough." Here we have a completely different culture but the concept which relies upon works for one's hope of heaven is the same.

There is a consistent theme in all of these answers—the ones from the Americans and the ones from our Muslim friends. What's consistent is the flawed concept which says personal effort (*works*) impacts eternal destinies. The thought process is flawed because it falls short of the clear, simple, biblical standard required to obtain eternal life. Any reliance upon works says Christ is an insufficient object to provide eternal life – it takes more than Him. A works-oriented thought process says faith alone is an inadequate means of obtaining eternal life – it takes more than that. Works, performance, or lifestyle are crucial – Christ's payment on the cross is not enough to move a person out of death into life.

The teacher asks, "What is two plus two." Even though 3.99999999 and 4.00000001 are close, they're incorrect. The answer to the question is highly specific: 4. Call me narrow-minded but there is only one answer to the question. If my opinion deviates from reality (*truth is that which is consistent with reality*) then my opinion is of little value. Dilution of the truth to the smallest degree results in falsehood. People aren't "kinda pregnant" and answers aren't "kinda true." Truth (*reality*) has a tendency to be rigid. Reality (*truth*) can be somewhat narrow. That's life. When it comes to eternal life, Peter was either right or wrong when he said of Jesus (*while being filled with the Holy Spirit*):

> And there is **salvation in no one else**; for there is **no other name** under heaven that has been given among men, by which we **must be saved.** (*Acts 4:12*)

Apparently Peter learned well from Christ about the narrow way. Yes, it's narrow but it's available to ALL – anyone can come. Paul was convinced faith alone was a sufficient means (*not to mention the only means*) in obtaining eternal life. He was clear again and again when he said:

> For we maintain that a man is **justified by faith** apart from works of the Law. (*Rom. 3:28*)

Any addition of any works misses God's clear and required means: 4.00000001 is just as wrong at 4,688. Any reliance upon or injection of works clearly implies Christ is not worthy of my trust and God is wrong when He only requires faith as the means. This is a dangerous position to be in. The wrong object or incorrect means has eternal consequences.

In a marketplace full of competing ideas, it can appear to be a daunting challenge to persuade someone to abandon their life-time reliance on the flawed concept of works-based justification and rely solely upon the grace of God. Elijah found himself in a daunting position when taking on the 450 prophets of Baal (*1 Kgs. 18*). The odds were 450 to 1 . . . plus God. Guess which side won that day? In the same way, even though dialogue, questions, and clarity are key ingredients in the art and science of persuasion, we're not selling a car but saving a soul. That's why it's important to always remember evangelism is a spiritual issue.

CHAPTER 6

Evangelism Is a Spiritual Issue

Up to this point we've seen the biblical text is right when it comes to the clear concept of justification – faith alone in Christ alone for eternal life. We've seen through context, simplicity, and repetition the authors of the Bible seemed to make it quite clear eternal life is the goal in evangelism. I've shared with you my belief, knowing the biblical text is right, that it only makes sense to use biblical terms in our evangelistic presentations. The method of our evangelistic presentations is to persuade people to trust in Christ for eternal life—to move them from death to life.

Good cops are good actors (*that doesn't necessarily mean they're good looking*). There are times when you don't care but you need to act like you do. There are times when you care a great deal but you need to act completely disinterested. The "drama" of police work is seen in the "good cop, bad cop" approach presented to suspects. Although the strategy might be old, it works. One partner leverages ill-will, bad feelings, and harsh consequences against the kindness and care of his "merciful" counterpart. This approach usually meets with success as it solicits the results (*technically we call this a confession*) needed to make a successful case. There was one time when I acted like I wanted to step up and start a fight (*bad cop*) with a drug dealer. I began to charge the suspect while my partner stepped in between us and had to fight and push me back (*pre-planned good cop intervention*) in order to protect the unlicensed pharmacist (*politically correct way of saying drug dealer*). Even though there were no Academy Awards, the acting was brilliant and the outcome was stunning – we got inside of his apartment.

A good partner (*regardless of his/her acting role*) is crucial in effective police work. Two sets of eyes, heads, guns, and hands are better than one. No one can effectively police without partners. The action is too fast and certainly the stakes are too high to go it alone. In interacting with people (*be it a victim or suspect*), the ability to have support outside of one's self is nothing but beneficial. Since I've had two different partners save my life on two different occasions, the concept of partnership has taken on a new and deeper meaning to me.

Police work is the here and now; evangelism is the "there" and "then." When it comes to evangelism, it's even more crucial to have a partner – can anything be more important than the eternal destiny of a person created in the image of God? The biblical pattern shows without the Holy Spirit involved, our efforts in sharing our faith will be for naught. The Spirit's critical role and involvement (*"power"*) is as important in our evangelistic efforts today as it was in the early church (*Acts. 1:8*). As I touched on before, selling a car is not a spiritual issue and thus I would be hard-pressed to provide Scriptural support for the role of the Spirit in this endeavor. The art and science of persuasion (*and a customer's good credit rating*) are enough to see the goal of a new car payment come forth. Persuasion is important in our evangelistic efforts. But our Partner (*the Holy Spirit*) and our prayer are just as crucial. A Partner and prayer are essential in seeing a person move from spiritual death and cross the line into eternal life. In John 16:8-11 Christ shares with us the role of His Spirit in evangelism. He states:

> And He, when He comes, will **convict the world** concerning sin and righteousness and judgment; concerning sin, because they do not believe in Me; and concerning righteousness, because I go to the Father, and you no longer behold Me; and concerning judgment, because the ruler of this world had been judged. (*Jn. 16:8-11*)

What we see in this passage is the role of the Holy Spirit as it pertains to convicting non-believers (*" . . . convict the world . . . . they do not believe in Me"*) *not* Christians. Along with regenerating (*Titus 3:5*), sealing (*Eph. 4:30*), identifying (*baptizing*) a believer with the Body of Christ (*Eph. 4:4-6*), producing spiritual fruit (*Gal. 5:22,23*), communicating to the

Father we are His children (*Rom. 8:16*), and distributing spiritual gifts (*1 Cor. 12:11*), another ministry of the Holy Spirit in the lives of believers today is illumination. We can see this in the following passages:

- "I pray that the eyes of **your** [*in the context believers*] heart may be **enlightened** . . ." (*Eph. 1:18a*)
- "For to **us** God **revealed** them through the Spirit . . ." (*1 Cor. 2:10*)
- "Now **we** have received, not the spirit of the world, but the Spirit who is from God, that **we** might know the things freely given to **us** by God, which things we also speak, not in words taught by human wisdom, but in those **taught by the Spirit** . . ." (*1 Cor. 2:12-13b*)
- "And there is no creature hidden from His [*literally "its" – the word of God*] sight, but all things are **open and laid bare** to the eyes of Him with whom **we** have to do." (*Heb. 4:13*)

Believers have a phenomenal advantage in life in that they have access to understanding and application when it comes to God's Word. There is no need to rely upon a subjective internal feeling which many would say is the Spirit convicting. Non-Christians have the same thing and they call it a conscience. Our Mormon friends value a "burning in the bosom." Superior to a subjective experience, a more certain (*yet supernatural*) means of moral direction exists; the Spirit illumines the Word of God in our lives. This is what convicts us of God's biblical standards and principles. Illumination of the truth of the Bible is what notifies us of acceptable and unacceptable conduct. The Spirit exposing reality from Scripture provides a foundation for application of biblical truth.

The non-Christian, besides being spiritually dead and deeply loved by God, has another disadvantage when it comes to the biblical text and spiritual issues.

> In whose case the god of this world has **blinded the minds of the unbelieving**, that they might not see the light of the gospel of the glory of Christ, who is the image of God. (*2 Cor. 4:4*)

This is why it's important to be reminded that a sharp argument, though useful in persuading, won't make the difference in moving a person across the line. The key is the Holy Spirit's conviction. God doesn't drag anyone into the Kingdom, He "woos" (*draws*) them (*Jn. 6:44, 12:32, Acts 16:14*). It would be wise of us to follow His example and love people across the line.

In John's historical account, Christ lays out three areas of conviction His Spirit addresses in the lives of non-believers. First, He convicts the non-Christian of sin – the sin of not believing in Christ for eternal life. An unbiblical and unwise reliance upon works is pointed out by the Spirit. Second, He convicts the non-Christian of righteousness. He highlights Christ is a worthy object of trust. Lastly, He convicts the non-Christian of judgment. He calls the question: choose who you will believe. It appears from Scripture that the Spirit takes our efforts of evangelistic persuasion and communicates to the hearer, "What they're saying is true. You had better believe it." This seems consistent with additional insight provided by Christ about His Spirit. In John 15:26, 27 we can see another example of how important a partnership is with Christ's Spirit.

> When **the Helper** comes, whom **I will send to you** from the Father, that is the Spirit of truth, who proceeds from the Father, **He will bear witness of Me**, and you will bear witness also, because you have been with Me from the beginning. (*Jn. 15:26,27*)

A powerful biblical principle which has successfully shaped the evangelistic strategies of many has been, "Share your faith in the power of the Spirit and leave the results to God." This emphasizes the crucial role our partner the Spirit plays in our spiritual multiplication efforts. It also provides relief to the one sharing their faith. A "no" response is not the fault or the responsibility of the evangelist. The faithful Christian who engages in the Great Commission didn't provide the free gift of eternal life – he/she gets no credit. The same Christian also did not provide the response to his/her gospel presentation – he/she gets no blame. Our partnership with the Creator of the Universe can be a source of great comfort. This same partnership provides us with a great advantage in addressing the eternal.

Guns and badges are given to a select few in our society to address the rule of law. In order to successfully accomplish this unique but crucial mission, a cooperative team effort is vital. Surprises aren't fun in police work. Communication certainly helps at reducing the "Ooops-factor" which frequently accompanies unplanned events. Law enforcement communication takes on many forms. Reports, radio calls, mobile computers, memos, training, citations, search warrants, affidavits, verbal testimony, and at times even hand signals on the street. In Phoenix, an officer holding up four fingers to their partner at a traffic stop imparts a good concept. The same officer holding up his/her index finger signals a completely different message – this is bad news. Both hand signals are communication techniques used to accomplish the mission – enforcing the law. Interaction between parties clarifies intentions and goals; among law enforcement it assists in keeping everyone on the same page by utilizing the strengths of each team member. Without communication one can expect an ineffective policing effort.

Evangelism is a unique and sacred task entrusted by God to a few in the world – those who are born-again. And because expectations are quite low for spiritually dead people, it's not a mission God demands Buddhists, Muslims, atheists, Darwinists, Hindus, communists, or other participants of man-made religions to successfully complete. Dead people aren't reliable. For believers to successfully accomplish their mission, called the Great Commission, communication still remains a vital concept. This interaction between partners, the Holy Spirit and the Christian, fosters success by playing to the strengths of those involved. We have a function and so does the Holy Spirit. Evangelism is a team effort. Since everyone has a dynamic role, an effective outcome hinges upon each partner's ability to get their job done. I'm confident the weak link in the team is *not* the Holy Spirit—it's me. That's why I believe there's wisdom in remembering our important obligation of prayer – spiritual communication. Without prayer, one can expect an ineffective evangelistic effort.

Scripture says when our desires match our Father's desires, we can expect answers to prayer. Let's consider the following chain of reasoning through a short list of biblical references.

- God wants us to fulfill the Great Commission – Matt. 28:19,20.
- God provided us a biblical pattern to follow in fulfilling the Great Commission seen in the documented history of the early church – Acts 1:8.
- God reaffirmed through Paul's last words that we are to multiply ourselves spiritually and we're to do the "work of evangelism" – 2 Tim. 2:2, 4:5.

At a point in my career I worked second shift (*swing shift*) hours when I was assigned to public housing. After briefing one day, I realized I had left my ballistic vest at home (*wait until you forget and leave your gun in the jail locker and hit the street with an empty holster – such a hollow feeling*). Like communication, body armor is also essential in accomplishing the mission of police work. I was in a panic because, even though I could have gone on-duty without it (*Phoenix has an optional wear policy*), there was no way I was going out exposed. I wore my vest more for the ability to take a punch than for blocking bullets. Like any smart husband, I called my "smarter" wife at home to have her bring it to me. Shannon got in the car and rocketed down the freeway to the precinct. Like me, she understood and was committed to the principle that my vest was an important part of the equation in effective police work. As she was driving at warp speed on the road, a Department of Public Safety Officer (*DPS – Arizona State Highway Patrol*) pulled her over for excessive speed. When he approached the driver's side window of her car, Shannon showed him my vest and explained I was a Phoenix Police Officer and she was enroute to make sure I had my vest on before I hit the street. Like me and like Shannon, the DPS officer was also committed to the principle my vest was an important part of the equation in effective police work. Without issuing a ticket, he encouraged her to take off and get to the precinct as quickly as she could. By the way, Shannon has gotten out of several tickets by exercising executive privilege – "My husband is going to be so mad. He's a police officer." You can't say I married a dummy.

I believe God's mission and objective for us is clear – evangelism. If Christ came to seek and to save the lost (*Lk. 19:10*), surely we should at least consider this as a focal point in our lives too. To take the desire of God's heart and the powerful partner of His Spirit but to leave prayer behind is like doing police work without a vest. Doing a "shift" without prayer will cause us to miss out on an important part of the equation of effective evangelism. Does the biblical text bear out the importance of prayer when it comes to evangelism? I believe it does.

> **"Please Lord help me share my faith."**
> And if we know that He hears us in whatever we **ask**, we know that we have the requests which we have asked from Him. (*1 Jn. 5:15*)
>
> **"God, will you give him or her a moment in time to be persuaded to trust in Your Son for eternal life?"**
> **Ask**, and it shall be given to you; **seek**, and you shall find; **knock**, and it shall be opened to you. For everyone who **asks** receives, and he who **seeks** finds, and to him who **knocks**, it shall be opened. (*Mt. 7:7,8*)
>
> **"Jesus, please help me not to go beyond the biblical text when I share my faith."**
> If you **ask** Me anything in My name, I will do it. (*Jn. 14:14*)
>
> **"God, please use me to move him or her from death to life."**
> You did not choose Me, but I chose you, and appointed you, that you should **go and bear fruit**, and that your fruit should remain, that whatever you ask of the Father in My name, He may give to you. (*Jn. 15:16*)
>
> **"Father, will you give me an opportunity to share my faith with someone this week?"**
> If you abide in Me, and My words abide in you, **ask** whatever you wish, and it shall be done for you. (*Jn. 15:7*)

In the above verse (*Jn. 15:7*), to abide in Christ is defined as obeying His commandments (*Jn. 15:10, 14*). In 1 John we see other terms used to express a Christian's obedience to Christ, terms like "fellowship" (1:6), "know" (*2:3*), "keep His commandments" (*2:4*), "in Him" (*2:5*), "abide in Him" (*2:6*), "walk in the same manner" (*2:6*), and "in the light" (*2:9*). We need to invest specific and deliberate prayer to be consistent with the biblical pattern and to be obedient to the Scriptural mandate provided in the biblical text.

CHAPTER 7

Time to Evaluate

The following set of instructions comes from an evangelistic tract I found in a church I had visited years ago. The instructions are as follows:

> 1. Admit you are a sinner. See Romans 3:10
> 2. Be willing to turn from sin (repent). See Acts 17:30
> 3. Believe that Jesus Christ died for you, was buried and rose from the dead. See Roman 10:9-10
> 4. Through prayer, invite Jesus into your life to become your personal Saviour. See Rom.10:13
>
> ***WHAT TO PRAY***
>
> Dear God, I am a sinner and need forgiveness. I believe that Jesus Christ shed His **precious blood** and died for my sin. I am willing to turn from sin. I now invite Christ to come into my heart and life as my personal Saviour.

In light of what has been presented, and with the goal of instruction in mind, please allow me to evaluate the material. The evangelistic tract's instructions are not unbiblical; they just appear to be non-biblical. The following issues rise to the forefront.

1. Nowhere in this set of instructions is belief/faith in Christ mentioned. It does mention belief in historical events in regards to His death, burial, and resurrection. But a historical event doesn't provide eternal life, a historical person does. The death, burial, and

resurrection are proofs that Christ is a worthy person to entrust one's eternal destiny to. Belief in a person is different than belief in a proof.

2. The issue of life is nowhere to be seen. If the goal of evangelism is eternal life, how is this goal accomplished without even mentioning it? Remember, even John made it clear forgiveness is a fellowship issue not a matter of justification.
3. This set of instructions promotes good works. Admitting I'm a sinner is a good thing to do. Being willing to turn from sin (*a poor definition of repentance*) is a good work. Prayer is a good thing, but in the historical pattern of evangelism presented in the Bible, prayer isn't utilized as a means of expressing faith. By the way, is being willing to turn away from sin the same as actually turning away from sin? How willing do you have to be? And if I sin, does that mean I'm really not a Christian or does it just mean I'm being disobedient?
4. This doesn't even utilize the finest evangelistic document which God provided for us in the New Testament – the gospel of John is missing.
5. Scripture is used out of context. Inviting Christ into one's heart is not a biblical mandate but appears to be based upon a call to the church at Laodicea to reestablish fellowship with Christ (*Rev. 3:20*).

Many of the phrases, comments, requests and verses are familiar to us. But sadly, with a person's eternal destiny at stake, we should consider moving out of our comfort zone and away from the rhetoric which permeates it and move back towards the biblical pattern that is found in the text of Scripture. Deviations from the biblical text can have drastic spiritual consequences. People are worthy of biblical precision.

Following is another section of a gospel tract found near the end of an evangelistic publication. It means no harm but is it really helpful in providing a clear, consistent, biblical message of evangelism? It reads as follows:

> **To Our Guests...**
> *We're glad you're here!*
>
> We frequently have many guests in our services who have questions about church membership. That's great, because we have some answers!
>
> **How do I become a Christian?**
>
> **Repent** - Turn away from your sin to follow God's new direction for your life. (Rom. 3:23; Acts 3:19)
>
> **Believe** - Trust in Jesus Christ, God's only Son, for eternel life. (Jn. 3:16)
>
> **Confess** - Acknowledge Jesus as the supreme authority over your life. (Rom. 10:9, 13)
>
> **Receive** - Accept God's free gift of salvation. (Rom. 6:23, Jn. 1:12)

It seems faith alone in Christ alone for eternal life is insufficient to secure a person's eternal destiny; there are at least two other requirements.

- The good work of turning away from your sin. This requirement generates some questions. Which sins must I turn away from? How long do I have to turn away from them? If I turn back to the sins does that mean I never was a Christian, I lost my salvation, or I'm just a disobedient believer? Isn't following God's direction the same as obedience (*a good work*)?
- The good work of confessing Jesus as the supreme authority over one's life. This requirement also generates some questions. Who has to hear this confession? When do I have to make this confession? If I sin, does that mean I never was a Christian? Does sinning indicate Jesus is not the supreme authority over my life? Or does sinning just indicate I'm a disobedient child of God? Additionally, it's probable Romans 10:9,13 is being used

out of context as a justification issue when indeed it deals with sanctification for believers (*See section: Psssst. I've got A Secret*).
- In addition to two good works, there appears to be a distinction made between believing (*defined as trust*) in Jesus Christ for eternal life and receiving God's free gift of salvation. This issue generates some questions. Is it possible to believe in Christ for eternal life and yet not receive God's free gift of salvation? Are these meant to be two distinct concepts or just a restatement of faith as the sole requirement for justification salvation? John 1:12 seems to equate the two terms as synonymous.

> But as many as **received** Him, to them He gave the right to become children of God, even to those who **believe in** His name. (*Jn. 1:12*)

To add good works to justification is obviously in conflict with Paul (*Gal. 1:8,9, 2:16*). Once again, people are worthy of a clear and consistent biblical presentation. Confusing and unclear works-oriented presentations like these might upset the faith of some (*Gal. 1:7, Titus 1:11*).

CHAPTER 8

Evangelism by the Numbers

A Christian living by faith is like police officer doing their job. It's exciting. It's meaningful. It makes a difference. It's hard. And like police work, living by faith requires courage. An officer with a belt and a vehicle full of tools is useless without courage. But that's still not quite enough. Training is needed to temper the blunt end of courage and make it surgically precise and effective. God has given us truth, all the tools (*Eph. 1:3*), the pattern, and the greatest Partner to accomplish the mission. Do we have the courage (*not to mention the compassion – Mt. 9:36*) to share the gospel with those who are spiritually dead—those who risk eternal separation from the Creator of all things? Does our world-view compel us to engage in evangelism so men and women, who are created in the image of God, might have a moment in time to put their confidence in Christ as their only hope of heaven? If a lack of confidence and a lack of courage is the disease, training is frequently the cure. Training is an effective method of overcoming fearful hesitation in not only police officers, but in believers as well. Let me share with you the basic framework I use in sharing my faith with others.

Remember the three requirements to obtain eternal life: 1.) Believe 2.) In Jesus Christ 3.) For eternal life. In my evangelistic efforts, this is what I'm trying to persuade people to do. After praying for them, I talk to them. I ask them if I can get their opinion about four basic principles of Christianity.

Principle number one is God loves them and wants them to live forever. I like good news. Most people are attracted to good news. I start out with good news. I'm confident God has a wonderful plan for people's lives, but that's a difficult concept to find in the gospel of John and link with the issue of justification. John's focus was eternal life. Two verses from John's gospel which emphasize principle number one:

> For God so loved the world that He gave His only begotten Son, that whoever **believes** in Him should not perish but has **eternal life.** (*Jn. 3:16*)

> . . . I came that they might have **life**, and might have it abundantly. (*Jn. 10:10b*)

Some people have an image of God as a crabby old man waiting to whack the guy who steps out of line. Others perceive Him as a disengaged senior in a rocking chair not paying attention. Both perspectives are inconsistent with the Bible. God loves them and wants them to live forever.

Principle number two is spiritual death is a problem. Death is separation. Physical death is the separation of the spirit from the body and eternal death is the separation of the spirit from God forever. A lot of people would call that hell and I believe they'd be correct.

> For all have **sinned** and fall short of the glory of God. (*Rom. 3:23*)

The word "sin" was a Greek archery term. The Greek archer would shoot an arrow at a target with the goal being the middle mark – the bulls-eye. If the arrow hit outside of the center, they would count how many "sins" or sections he missed the mark by. God's mark or standard in our lives is perfection. There is no doubt people are good but no one is perfect. Whether it be a little white lie or an armed robbery, sin is sin, missing the mark of perfection is missing the mark. Whether it be a little impatience at a left hand turn light or molesting a child – sin is sin and missing the mark of perfection is missing the mark. You might be better than me but goodness is not the issue. Perfection is. Everything has a cost and the cost of imperfection (*sin*) is death.

> For the wages of sin is **death.** (*Rom. 6:23a*)

The cost of a double cheeseburger is a dollar. The cost of a nice car is $100,000. The cost of being imperfect is death – separation from God. Many people think being good, not being bad, being religious, baptism, communion, education, being a good parent, being successful, not smoking, not chewing, not drinking, will pay the death penalty for their imperfection. Don't get me wrong, these are all good things. But they're good for nothing when it comes to paying a death penalty. They're good for nothing when it comes to providing eternal life. The cost of sin is spiritual death, not being good. How does a person pay a death penalty (*the response to this question is interesting*)?

God is always fair and the penalty must be paid. There is no probation or parole with God. The cost of being imperfect is death. God won't compromise on the cost – He demands payment. But God is always loving. Because of that, He had His Son, Jesus Christ, pay the penalty for the entire world.

Because no one is perfect, everyone has a problem.

Principle number three is Jesus Christ is the solution. How do I know God loves me? Scripture tells us.

> But God **demonstrates His own love towards us** in that while we were yet sinners (*imperfect*) Christ died for us. (*Rom. 5:8*)

The reason Christ had to die on the cross was because the penalty of sin was not being good and not 20,000 push-ups and not being religious – the cost was death. Just ask anybody on death row if they know what it takes to pay a death penalty.

Over 2,000 years ago Christ made a bold statement. He said:

> I am the **way** and the **truth** and the **life**; no one comes to Father, **but through Me.** (*Jn. 14:6*)

That's a pretty bold statement to make unless it's true. Here's a proposition: If a person gives me $20, I can guarantee their eternal destiny. I have yet to have a person take me up on my offer. No one ever does. The reason they don't trust me is because I can't prove what I just said. Police officers make a living off of a thing called evidence. We have to prove our case in a court of law. Jesus proved He was the only giver of eternal life through a thing called "resurrection."

> For I delivered to you as of first importance what I also received, that Christ **died for our sins** according to the Scripture, and that **He was buried**, and the He was **raised on the third day** according to the Scripture, and that **He appeared** to Cephas, then to the twelve. After that He appeared to more than five hundred brethren at one time, most of whom remain until now, but some have fallen asleep; then He appeared to James, then to all the apostles; and last of all, as it were to one untimely born, He appeared to me also. (*1 Cor. 15:3-8*)

A police officer can wreck a life with just his eyewitness testimony. Add another eyewitness and the case is closed. Add an additional 499 eyewitnesses and, in legal court terminology, "game over." It's a worthy challenge to find an ancient historical event more well-documented and testified to than the death (*proof– He was buried*) and resurrection (*proof– He appeared*) of Jesus Christ.

The Bible tells us God loves us and wants us to live forever. Scripture has communicated spiritual death is a problem. God's Word points out Jesus Christ is the only solution. These are great truths but truth without application is pointless. How does a person apply these three biblical or basic principles of Christianity? The answer—principle number four.

Principle number four states, at a moment in time, we must exercise faith alone in Jesus Christ alone for eternal life. Jesus repeatedly made it clear any person could place their trust or confidence in Him as their only hope of heaven.

> Truly, truly, I say to you, he who hears My word, and **believes Him who sent Me, has eternal life**, and does not come into judgment, but has passed out of death into life. (*Jn. 5:24*)

> For this is the will of My Father, that everyone who beholds the Son and **believes in Him, may have eternal life**; and I Myself will raise him up on the last day. (*Jn. 6:40*)

> Truly, truly, I say to you, **he who believes** [*"in Me" – Majority Text*] **has eternal life**. (*Jn. 6:47*)

> Jesus said to her, "I am the resurrection and the life; **he who believes in Me shall live even if he dies**, and everyone who lives and **believes in Me shall never die**. Do you believe this?" (*Jn. 11:25,26*)

Paul appeared quite convinced faith alone in Christ alone for eternal life was how any person could guarantee his/her eternal destiny.

> . . . and after he brought them out, he said, "Sirs, what must I do to be saved?' And they said, "**Believe in the Lord Jesus, and you shall be saved**, you and your household." (*Acts 16:30,31*)

> For **by grace** you have been **saved through faith**; and that not of yourselves, it is the gift of God; not as a result of works, that no one should boast. (*Eph. 2:8,9*)

Grace can be defined as unmerited favor – getting something for free. We do it all the time at Christmas when we buy presents. Paul mentions "saved." Saved from what? Eternal separation from God. Faith is simply trust or confidence in a person, thing or proposition. In whom does a person have to place their trust in to be saved from an eternal death penalty? In whom does a person have to have confidence in to obtain eternal life? Answer – Jesus Christ. To restate the verse within the given context, "For by God's unmerited favor you've been saved from eternal separation from God by trusting in Jesus Christ for eternal life; and that not of yourselves, it is the gift of God; not as a result of works, that no one should boast."

Based upon these four principles, *do you believe?* Do you believe in Jesus Christ for eternal life?

During my twenty-five year moment in time, I have found utilizing the aforementioned four principles is consistent with the biblical pattern of evangelism. The terms are biblical. The principles rely upon the truth of Scripture. The goal is eternal life. The method is to persuade. Men and women are created in the image of God. They have incredible value. Each person should be given a moment in time for the Holy Spirit to use the biblical text to convict (*expose*) spiritual needs. I feel utilizing these four principles will allow God to give us a moment in time to rise above the rhetoric and dynamically engage in the eternal and watch Him change lives. The purpose of addressing these principles in evangelism is to obtain a biblical perspective and better understanding of the "vehicle" of justification. My goal is to encourage us to biblically and confidently use the platforms God has provided us to give those people in our lives a moment in time to believe in Jesus Christ for eternal life.

In our pursuit of purpose and perspective, let's move from issues of spiritual multiplication to principles of eternal security and assurance. We know the Bible tells us the gift is free but is it forever? How do I know I have eternal life? What, if any, are the indications a person is justified? Does God give us a safety net or should our failures in the Christian life be a cause of concern? We know what's biblically required to obtain eternal life. We know how to communicate this good news in a manner consistent with the biblical text. But is it presumptuous to think our faithlessness won't impact our future?

Take Christ at His word when He says He freely gives the gift of eternal life to those who trust in Him as their only hope of heaven. Let me sum up the next section in five words: Look to Christ for assurance.

Section 2: Issues of Assurance

Is My Eternal Destiny at Risk?

CHAPTER 9

Eternal Security Is a Biblical Fact

It's not unheard of or unusual to see police officers or their departments fail. This can be expected when recruitment is done from the pool of humanity. This pool is imperfect so outcomes and results in law enforcement are not always stellar. Yes, we've had on-duty school resource officers accidentally print out pornography from their work/ school computer to the principal's secretary's desk. Yes, we've had on-duty officers go from one precinct to another and pick up prostitutes while being monitored by their peers. Yes, we've had on-duty officers smoke crack cocaine in uniform in a marked police car. Yes, we've had officers steal hundreds of dollars of merchandise from stores they were employed at in an off-duty capacity. Yes, we've had on-duty detectives steal thousands of dollars from drug dealers and stash the cash in a trash barrel outside of the precinct. Yes, we've had police detectives enter property rooms and exchange prescription drugs for aspirin to fuel their addiction to pain killers. Yes, we've had police managers falsify and manipulate scores, ratings, and statistics to obtain federal funding to boost their salary or to further a good-old boy system. Yes, we've had police chiefs obtain compensation in violation of state pension statutes. Yes, we've had police departments ignore the rule of law to pursue political agendas and pacify political correctness. In the context of thousands upon thousands of police interactions, transactions, and contacts each month decade after decade, to see failure several times a year is not unusual or surprising. But neither should it be tolerated, condoned, excused, or accepted. In a brief four year period as the PLEA President, the Association facilitated the departure (*translation – get out or get fired*) of over thirty of our members – police officers. There's a standard the community expects, deserves, and pays for. PLEA felt a practical way to serve our citizen partners and our members was to keep the bar high.

The battle PLEA constantly faced was the Chief's office would routinely lower the bar (*police ethical standards*) to minimize management misconduct. One lieutenant had an allegation of untruthfulness that was unresolved by the Department's Professional Standards Bureau (*internal affairs*). The reason it was unresolved, according the Police Chief, was the lieutenant believed what she was saying was true. Even with three witnesses stacked against her, she was not held liable for lying. Subsequently, any officer who believed they were telling the truth in administrative investigations, even though they weren't, was not held accountable for a lack of veracity. How do you prove a person believed what they were saying was untrue? This is called making the simple complicated. Some call it moral suicide. I call it corruption.

In one aspect, police work is simple. Enforce the law while obeying the law. But, as I've just shared with you, a bad habit that pops up out of the imperfect pool of humanity is to make the simple complicated. We not only see this in the police world, we see this in the Christian world too. What could be simpler than child-like faith in Jesus Christ to secure our eternal destiny? Assurance of salvation appears to be one of the simple biblical issues made complicated by religious rhetoric. How can a person be sure if they have eternal life? How can a believer be sure of their eternal destiny? How do I know I'm going to heaven? Technically, these questions focus on eternal security and issues of assurance. When rhetoric takes precedence over the biblical text, the simple and free gift of eternal life is needlessly complicated. In this section, please allow me a moment in time to look at eternal security and how a person can be certain of his/her eternal destiny and his/her eternal relationship with God.

The Supreme Court said police officers can lie. In the course and scope of their duty, police officers can use deception. How do you think undercover work is completed? The drug dealer asks, "Are you a cop?" And the undercover detective replies, "Well, since you asked, I honestly have to tell you yes, I'm a police officer." *Not*! At times, effective police work relies upon the ability to deceive.

Our Neighborhood Enforcement Team (*NET*) in the Central City Precinct would receive complaints from neighborhood groups of drug houses in their community. From a uniformed patrol strategy, the best way to shut them down and arrest the dealers was through an activity warrant. An activity warrant demonstrates to a magistrate there is enough activity (*probable cause*) consistent with narcotic sales to allow police officers to forcibly enter the location and search it and any listed occupants (*as listed on the search warrant*) on the premises. Probable cause is a legal concept in which a reasonable person would believe a crime has been or is being committed. Information needed in an activity warrant at a specific location which demonstrates probable cause would/should include: 1.) location (*high drug area*), 2.) complaints from neighbors of activity about the specific address, 3.) narcotic enforcement experience and training, 4.) documented drug related activity at the specific address, 5.) drug arrests of people seen visiting the listed location, and 6.) information from arrestees of activity and persons inside and at the specific address. Our NET squad got to a point where we could crank out an activity warrant in a day – watching, writing, serving, arresting, booking and then at times doing reversals (*posing as drug dealers and selling fake dope to willing customers*).

From places of concealment our squad would watch the activity at the complaint location. If a car would stop and the vehicle's occupant would get out and approach the house, go inside for several minutes, and then leave the area, that type of activity was consistent with narcotic sales. Watch several vehicles and their passengers engage in this conduct and probable cause is starting to build. Foot traffic at the location with brief visits was another indicator drugs were being sold. When it came to vehicles and foot traffic, we would stop these visitors of the drug house when they had left the area.

In contacting vehicles, it was important to make sure there was a traffic violation in order to engage in what the courts call a "pre-textual stop." Pre-textual stops are loathed by defense attorneys but approved by the bench. A pre-textual stop utilizes traffic codes to enforce narcotic statutes. These stops are nice because no one drives perfectly, certainly not people who visit dope houses. In the same vein, people who visit dope houses struggle to keep their driving privileges legal. In contacting the driver, there was a chance he/she would be suspended or have an outstanding arrest warrant. If this was the case, they would be placed under arrest. Their persons along with the vehicle would be searched incident to arrest. The goal was to find drugs in their possession or in their constructive possession (*immediate access and control of*) inside of the vehicle. If they were in possession of drugs, they'd be advised of their Miranda rights and we would try to obtain information on the drug location and on the sellers. This information then became a part of the search warrant affidavit used to get a judge's permission to knock the door in and search the occupants and the structure.

When it came to those visiting the drug house on foot, traffic violations weren't a readily available tool. Deception was. When a person under observation was engaged in conduct consistent with narcotic sales (*time of day, length of visit, location*), once again we would contact them after they had left the area. Upon contact I would advise the pedestrian I had some worries and would appreciate it if they talked to me. I made it very clear to them they did *not* have to talk to me and were *not* under arrest (*it's not a crime to visit a drug house*). People who visit drug houses usually aren't up to speed on their constitutional rights. They're quick to forget they don't have to talk to police officers. What aggravates their forgetfulness even more is when you're nice to them.

With sad eyes and a heartfelt tone I would explain to them I was concerned they were visiting a drug house. I told them I wasn't mad at them. I didn't think they were the problem. The vendors at the location selling drugs were the problem. I then was untruthful with them. I told them they were in a federal drug enforcement location which mandated they cooperate in taking a drug test as a result of their conduct and whereabouts. The untruthfulness continued. If this test indicated even the smallest amount of narcotics was in their system, there would be federal ramifications. With all the sympathy available to me, I told them we all have problems and struggles – I certainly did, and if they struggled with narcotics, it was my preference to handle it informally. I told them I was very worried they had drugs in their pocket. I continued to be disingenuous. I informed them if what they said was in their system deviated from what the federal blood test revealed, there could be serious consequences.

I finally told them the truth. If they were in possession of drugs, and they voluntarily gave them up, I would not book them into jail—they would not be arrested. I kept my word on this issue.

Eight out of ten pedestrians would comply and give up their dope. Remember, intelligence is not a requirement in the illegal narcotic business. Once again I made it clear upon their surrender of the drugs in their possession they were *not* under arrest. I would then talk to them about how many times they had been to the drug location, what they bought there, how long they had been using drugs, who was inside selling, if there were weapons in the sellers' possession, where the drugs were located at the address, and the names and descriptions of the sellers. After this discussion they were released. Later in the shift, I would impound the drugs they had voluntarily given to me and then I would write a criminal report listing them as a suspect and requesting criminal charges for possession of narcotic drugs be filed. Recall, I told them I wouldn't book them into jail ***that*** night. I didn't say I wouldn't get an arrest warrant issued and book them ***another*** day. A combination of three "drug house visitor" stops consistently provided enough probable cause to get a warrant and knock down a door. This was the job and the job was fun.

This book isn't being written to discuss ethical theory and the moral ramifications of my conduct. But let's go down a quick bunny trail just to explain why I could sleep at night without a guilty conscience. Is dishonesty in the capacity of a police officer sin? I don't think so. Who would have thought I can do something God can't. And there are some things God cannot do. One of them is lying (*Titus 1:2*). Joseph accused his brothers of wrong-doing by alleging they were spies (*Gen. 42:9 – LXX Greek translation of Hebrew Scripture*). Yet Rahab is praised in the Bible for welcoming spies in peace – spies sent by God into her house (*Heb. 11:31*). Spying sounds like a clever but disingenuous strategy (*like undercover police work*) for God's people to engage in. In weighing the need for truth with evil men against the need to protect innocent life, life for the innocent takes priority over truth for the wicked. If the Nazis came to your Paris door in 1942 and asked if you were hiding Jews, is it a moral failure to provide inaccurate information to the Gestapo about the Hebrew family tucked away in your attic? No. Is it offensive to God? No. Keeping innocent Jews alive takes priority over keeping evil Nazis accurately informed – the higher ethic takes precedence. The same is true in police work. When it comes to protecting the lives of our community and their wellbeing, the need to protect innocent life outweighs the need to tell evil lawless men the truth (*Ex. 1:15-22, Acts 5:29*). Thus, was I untruthful? Yes. Did my actions offend God? No. I slept like a baby and made a ton of overtime at court. This is what graded absolutism looks like in the world of law enforcement.

So what's the point of all this drug talk? The Bible makes it clear faith alone in Christ alone for eternal life secures a person's eternal destiny. This is the truth. As I've demonstrated, I can lie. God can't (*Num. 23:19, Titus 1:2, Heb. 6:18*). His word is true. Jesus was blatantly honest – "Truly, truly, I say to you, he who **believes** [*"in Me" – Majority Text*] has eternal life." Here's where I find churches and godly teachers today making the simple and clear complicated and confusing. If I trusted in Christ for eternal life and thus met the biblical requirement to secure my eternal destiny in the kingdom and in heaven, do I not possess the free gift of eternal life? What about "eternal" don't we understand? If eternal is not forever, then what is it? And if Christ knowingly used the term eternal when it came to life, and the authors of the inspired biblical text did the same, shouldn't we take God at His word. In addition to quantity, eternal life also addresses the quality of the Christian life – full, meaningful, effective and appreciated. Don't trust me – trust Jesus Christ. Paul's words smacked of confidence when it came to his eternal destiny. The same Paul who realized he could be "disqualified" (*1 Cor. 9:27*) and suffer the loss of eternal rewards was more than assured of his possession of the free gift of eternal life.

> For this reason I also suffer these things, but I am not ashamed; for I know whom I have **believed** and I am **convinced** that He is able to guard what I have entrusted to Him until that day. (*2 Tim. 1:12*)

In light of the confidence John exuded, what would cause a believer to disbelieve Scripture and not take Christ at His word when it comes to their eternal (*there's that word again*) destiny?

> These things I have written to you who **believe** in the name of the Son of God, in order that you may **know** that you have **eternal life.** (*1 Jn. 5:13*)

There would be times when an officer would overhear a parent in a restaurant with a misbehaving child say, "If you don't behave, I'm going to have that officer take you away." This is one of the quickest ways to offend a cop. More than one parent has been advised by a "throw-down" officer of the following pointers. First, don't pass the burden of your poor parenting skills onto an innocent police officer. Second, don't be untruthful to your child. Learn to train your child in the realm of reality. Lastly, what value is added to a priceless child by needlessly cultivating in them uncertainty about those paid to protect them? Police officers will safeguard a child regardless of their conduct. Kids in trouble need to be taught to run as quickly as they can to a police officer. This child-rearing strategy does nothing but increase the danger for a child in a dangerous world. The ends of a trained child don't justify the foolish means of falsehood and fear.

What value does uncertainty and doubt bring to the table of a child of God? In the Bible, doubting or debating is a picture of instability (*Jms. 1:6-8*). How does a Christian's speculation of possessing eternal life facilitate their role in fulfilling the Great Commission? Where in the biblical text is doubt identified as a valued character trait in a spiritually mature believer? Notice the tense of the action words in the following verses. When the possession of eternal life is presented in the realm of reality as a completed action (*past tense*), our eternal destiny as Christians is what is technically known as a "done deal."

> Truly, truly, I say to you, he who hears My word, and believes Him who sent Me, has eternal life, and does not come into judgment, but **has passed** out of death into life. (*Jn. 5:24*)

> Christ **redeemed** us from the curse of the Law, having become a curse for us – for it is written, "Cursed is everyone who hangs on a tree." (*Gal. 3:13*)

> For He **delivered** us from the domain of darkness, and **transferred** us to the kingdom of His beloved Son. (*Col. 1:13*)

> And when you **were dead** in your transgressions and the uncircumcision of your flesh, He **made you alive** together with Him, having forgiven us **all** (*not "some"*) our transgressions. (*Col. 2:13*)

In addition to the ideas of "eternal" and "done deals," there are three other concepts Scripture utilizes when addressing the issue of security and assurance: No one, nothing, and never.

1. No One:

Jesus made it clear in John 10:28, "...and I give eternal life to them, and they shall **never** *(ou me—Greek double negative*) perish; and **no one** shall snatch them out of My hand." The Greek double negative in the English word "never" is an example of a "litotes." It communicates a hyper-positive idea – "you're absolutely going to live!" Combined with this positive idea is further encouragement – "no one shall snatch them out of My hand." Even though eternal, God is someone. When it comes to created beings, Satan is someone. I am someone. You are someone. Only "no one" can snatch a believer out of the hand of Jesus. Can you think of anyone who is "no one?" Everybody is somebody and nobody is "no one." So when Christ said "no one," perhaps He meant "no one."

2. Nothing:

Paul wrote of the concept of "nothing" separating a believer from the love of the Creator. In Romans 8:38,39 he wrote;

> For I am convinced that **neither** death, nor life, nor angels, nor principalities, nor things present, nor things to come, nor powers, nor height, nor depth, **nor** any other created **thing**, shall be able to separate us from the love of God, which is in Christ Jesus our Lord. (*Rom. 8:38,39*)

Is there anything that is "nothing?" Everything is something and only "nothing" can separate us from the love of God. Let's take a look at how roomy grace really is. Is cheating on my wife something or nothing? Is impatience something or nothing? Is homosexuality something or nothing? Is armed robbery something or nothing? Is a little impatience in a left-hand turn lane something or nothing? Is pride something or nothing? Is indifference something or nothing? Is drug addiction something or nothing? Is child pornography something or nothing? Is apostasy something or nothing? Is materialism something or nothing? Is atheism something or nothing? Is failing to persevere something or nothing? Which of these sins did Christ's death on the cross *not* pay for? Which of these things or actions is "nothing?" Is there anything that falls outside of Paul's list? They are all "something" and only "nothing" can separate us from the love of God.

3. Never:

Jesus said in John 6:37, "All that the Father gives Me shall come to Me, and the one who comes to Me I will **certainly not** ("*never*") cast out." As in John 10:28, the term "never" is a double negative in the Greek (*ou me*) to emphasize the impossibility of an event from occurring. It doesn't mean "highly unlikely" but "never." In reading the book of Hebrews, it's not a far stretch to see the author was writing to Jewish believers who were contemplating going back to Judaism in order to relieve the pressure their Christian faith was bringing to their lives. The overall tone of the book is to exhort and encourage. In Hebrews 13:5 a portion of this encouragement can be seen:

> Let your character be free from the love of money, being content with what you have; for He Himself has said, 'I will **never** desert you, nor **will I ever** ("***never***") forsake you.' (*Heb. 13:5*)

The author of Hebrews used this double-negative three more times (*8:11, 8:12, 10:17*). In these verses we see twice God will "**never**" remember our sins and in the kingdom there will "**never**" be a need to teach each other because all "shall know" God in the kingdom.

In his prophetic production, John used this Greek double negative to teach us that "**never**" will anything unclean or anyone who practices abomination and lying come into the New Jerusalem but only those whose names are written in the Book of Life (*Rev. 21:27*). Peter told his audience as long as they "practiced" (*pursued and applied*) the goals of faith, moral excellence, knowledge, self-control, perseverance, godliness, brotherly kindness, and love they would "**never**" stumble and miss out on the eternal reward Christ would provide them (*2 Pt. 1:11*). Paul used the term at least five times in his letters. In these passages we learn:

- A man whose sin the Lord "**never**" takes into account is blessed (*Rom. 4:8*).
- A willingness on Paul's part to "**never**" eat meat if it offends a struggling Christian (*1 Cor. 8:13*).
- When we walk by the Spirit we will "**never**" carry out the desires of the flesh (*Gal. 5:16*).
- Believers who are alive at the Rapture will "**never**" precede dead brethren in meeting Christ (*1 Ths. 4:15*).
- Non-believers left behind after a day of the Lord will "**never**" escape the pending destruction (*1 Ths. 5:3*).

Outside of the three occurrences in Acts (*13:41, 28:26 X 2*) we see the Greek double negative "never" used in the historical gospel accounts nearly 63 more times. Heaven and earth will come and go but the words (*as well as the letters and parts of letters – Mt. 5:18*) of Christ will "**never**" pass away (*Lk. 21:33*). Jesus said unless a person's righteousness surpassed the scribes and Pharisees, they would "**never**" enter the Kingdom of God (*Mt. 5:20*). Peter said he would "**never**" deny Christ (*Mk 14:31*) but yet he did. If "never" doesn't really mean "never" then why was Peter held liable for his betrayal. By the way, when fallible men like me and Peter, all of us members of the pool of fallen humanity, use the term "never" in a selfish moment of faithlessness, take care in giving our words much weight.

As we've just seen, eternal security is a simple and clear Scriptural fact. There is **no one** and **nothing** which can jeopardize our eternal destiny. God will **never** abandon us or revoke His free gift of eternal life.

Assurance is confidence in this fact. The moment a person believes in Christ for eternal life, they have assurance. They just trusted in Jesus for their eternal destiny and wouldn't have done so if they weren't certain about the person of Christ and the outcome. Theologically speaking, assurance is the essence of this act of faith. Assurance may come and go in the life of believer. Security remains a fact. Reality is what it is, with or without us. We make nothing true. Our confidence or questions, successes or losses, understanding or ignorance don't make anything true or false. We don't determine reality, we only respond to it. The Bible clearly demonstrates the reality of eternal security. It's a fact. The principle is true.

The words of Christ are clear about His unending commitment to us. And even though the biblical pattern directs us to look to Christ for assurance, some would have us look to our faith for confidence. As we've seen previously, faith doesn't save, Christ does. Faith is the means, Christ is the object. Unwise, unbiblical, and unnecessary doubt is generated when a person's focus goes to his/her faith for assurance instead of focusing on Christ. The long list of non-biblical adjectives linked to the word faith certainly doesn't help but only aggravates the situation. All analogies fall short, but in an attempt to clarify the connection between the means (*faith*) and the object (*Christ*), please indulge me.

Two men were on different sides of the same lake when a freak winter storm hit. On the west side of the lake a 300 pound man stood on a 10 foot high pier. The ice at the bottom of the pier he was on was 1/8 of an inch thick. On the east side of the lake a 150 pound man stood on another 10 foot high pier. At the bottom of his pier the ice was a solid 8 feet thick. The 300 pound man had 100 percent faith when he jumped off the pier the ice would hold him. The 150 pound man only had 2 percent faith if he jumped off his pier the ice would hold him. Both men jumped at the same time – what happened to each man?

I've presented this illustration to hundreds of people. Have you ever seen a dog turn his head sideways after being presented with something which doesn't compute? I often encounter the same type of reaction with this illustration. For years people have heard the Disney motivator – "You just gotta believe!" Disney's about to let them down. After the question there is usually a slight pause as they work through it. Ultimately the answers are the same. The 300 pound man gets wet. The 150 pound man stays dry. When challenged as to why the 300 pound man got wet when he had 100 percent faith, the answer is consistently "thin ice." When asked why the 150 pound man stayed dry when he only had 2 percent faith, the answer is consistently "thick ice." The lesson—it isn't how much faith a person has, what matters is the object in which he/she places their faith in. You can be sincere (*like many of our Muslim friends*) but be sincerely wrong. A little bit of faith (*the means*) in the right object (*Christ*) for eternal life (*the goal*) solves the problem (*spiritual death*). The words of Christ are clear about His unending commitment to us.

Even though the biblical pattern directs us to look to Christ for assurance, a loud opinion from pulpits today is that a person's works (*lifestyle*) are the primary indicator of one's regeneration. The fruits of the Spirit can possibly be a secondary indicator a person is born-again, but not the main crucial gauge. Believers are instructed to look to conduct or a changed life for assurance. This dependence upon works, fruit, and obedience as the source of assurance launches a valid question: If works had nothing to do with my justification, why would I look to works to see if I'm justified? If eternal life is a free gift provided without any act of obedience, why would I look for obedience to see if I have eternal life? When works become the basis for our assurance, expect to be turned into fruit inspectors in determining who is and who is not a believer. Get ready to embrace subjective standards which have no support from the biblical text. What does the biblical text say about works, justification, and eternal life?

> Because **by the works of the Law no flesh will be justified** in His sight; for through the Law comes the knowledge of sin. (*Rom. 3:20*)
>
> Being **justified as a gift by His grace** through the redemption which is in Christ Jesus. (*Rom. 4:24*)

> For we maintain that a man is **justified by faith apart from works** of the Law. (*Rom. 3:28*)

> Now to the one who works, his wage is not reckoned as a favor, but as what is due. But to the one who does not work, but believes in Him who justifies the ungodly, his **faith is reckoned as righteousness**, (*Rom. 4:4,5*)

> Who will bring a charge against God's elect? **God is the one who justifies**. (*Rom. 8:33*)

> Nevertheless knowing that a man is **not justified by the works of the Law but through faith in Christ Jesus**, even we have believed in Christ Jesus, that we may be justified by faith in Christ, and not by the works of the Law, since by the works of the Law shall no flesh be justified. (*Gal. 2:16*)

> Now that **no one is justified by the Law** before God is evident; for, 'The righteous man shall live by faith.' (*Gal. 3:11*)

> For by **grace** you have been saved through **faith**; and that not of yourselves, it is the gift of God; **not as a result of works**, that no one should boast. (*Eph. 2:8,9*)

> Who has saved us, and called us with a holy calling, **not according to our works**, but according to His own purpose and **grace** which was granted us in Christ Jesus from all eternity. (*2 Tim. 1:9*)

> He saved us, **not on the basis of deeds** which we have done in righteousness, but according to His **mercy**, by the washing of regeneration and renewing by the Holy Spirit. (*Titus 3:5*)

In order to understand unclear and difficult verses, it's reasonable to use clear and uncomplicated verses – like these. It seems clear from the text of Scripture works, deeds, and conduct do not provide eternal life – faith alone in Christ alone for eternal life is the singular requirement for justification. If works, deeds, the Law or works of the flesh fail at producing eternal life, if none of these justify, why would or should we look to them as the primary indicator of our justification salvation. It appears works are ineffective and, when the biblical text is taken in context, works are also an unreliable gauge in determining one's spiritual standing and eternal destiny. Don't look to faith for assurance, look to Christ. Focus on the fact that eternal life is sourced only in Him.

CHAPTER 10

Wolves, Sheep, & Mere Men

Conduct is everything in law enforcement. It's unlawful conduct which injures people and property. Compliance with the rule of law is directly related to conduct. That's why there are no "thought police." During the debate over the crime of illegal immigration, there was an unfounded suggestion that Phoenix Police Officers would engage in racial profiling and biased policing. There was clearly an insinuation police officers who wanted to partner with federal law enforcement personnel in addressing the crime of illegal immigration were tainted with racism; and this without any history of civil rights violations anywhere in the State of Arizona.

A probing question asked by critics of Arizona Senate Bill 1070 (*SB1070*) in an attempt to link the statute to racism was; "What's an illegal alien look like?" The idea was immigration enforcement efforts, due to our southern Arizona border with Mexico, would unfairly focus on the Hispanic community. To counter this false belief, the answer to the question was another question; "What's a person look like with two rocks of crack cocaine in their pocket?" You can't tell by looking. You can only tell by observing conduct which generates suspicion. The point of the second question was to demonstrate crime is based upon conduct *not* skin color or culture. Just like I needed conduct along with reasonable suspicion to get into someone's pocket, so officers needed conduct and reasonable suspicion to get into someone's immigration status.

From the Scripture we've been exposed to up to this point, determining who's a criminal and determining who's a Christian have nothing in common. The determination method of criminals and Christians is far beyond apples and oranges – it's at the level of night and day. You see, crimes are tied to conduct (*Paul would call them works*) while justification is based on Christ. Actions are a crucial component in the sanctification process but fruit and works have nothing to do with being born-again (*justification salvation*). Or do they? Here's what some godly men are saying about justification, assurance, and how crucial works are to obtain eternal life.

- "Woven throughout the New Testament is the insistence that a **transformed life** (*emphasis mine*) is evidence of and necessary for salvation."[1]
- "True saving faith is a repentant faith in Jesus Christ, and that produces **good works** (*emphasis mine*). If that's not there, it doesn't matter what you say."[2]
- "Saving faith is no simple thing. It has many dimensions. 'Believe on the Lord Jesus Christ' is a massive command. It contains a **hundred other things** (*emphasis mine*)."[3]

There is no doubt in my mind a goal godly men like these hope to see in the church is mature, obedient believers with a deep, abiding fellowship with their Creator and a positive impact on their world. But the ends don't justify the means. To employ a theology which relies upon works, fruit, and changed lives for assurance and justification falls short of the simple biblical standard. To employ a theology which doesn't allow for failure falls short of clear examples in the biblical text. Statements like these create more problems than they solve – one of them being doubt. How does fostering doubt in the life of a Christian make him or her a more useful and dynamic spiritual multiplier? What wisdom is there in looking to someone or something other than Christ for assurance? If I'm looking beyond Christ for assurance, the implication is Christ is

---

1 Schreiner, Thomas R. / Caneday, Ardel B. The Race Set Before Us (*Downers Grove, IL: InterVarsity Press, 2001*), pgs. 283,284 (Thomas R. Schreiner & Ardel B. Caneday, 2001)

2 MacArthur, John. Hard to Believe (*Nashville, TN: Thomas Nelson, 2003*), pgs. 104

3 Piper, John. Desiring God (*Sisters, OR: Multnomah Books, 1986*), pg. 65

insufficient in providing eternal life. Watch the honest questions which flow from the belief that works, conduct, commitment, or a changed life are crucial to justification and assurance.

1. Define a transformed life?
2. I used to watch on-line pornography five times a week. I've cut back to one time a week. Is that a transformed life?
3. Who has to see this transformation in my life?
4. What time frame is required to transform a life?
5. If my life is transformed, but I revert back in forty years, did I really have a transformed life to begin with?
6. What is repentant faith?
7. What good works need to be produced?
8. How many good works need to be produced?
9. Who do these good works need to benefit?
10. Besides belief in Christ, what else is needed for my soul to reach heaven?
11. Why is faith alone in Christ alone for eternal life insufficient to secure my eternal destiny?
12. Where did Christ get it wrong?
13. What was Paul thinking?
14. If saving faith requires a hundred other things, could you tell me what number 67 is?
15. What's number 53?
16. What's number 33 – that's my lucky number?
17. What other works do our Catholic, Muslim, and Mormon friends rely upon that we might be missing?
18. What is it about child-like faith that is difficult?
19. How does grace fit in with good works, a transformed life, and a hundred other things?

The phrase "the thin blue line" communicates a minority position when it comes to the small amount of people willing to risk their lives to protect others. I'm confident the grace-based teaching presented in this book is perceived by some in the evangelical community as a minority position – a "thin grace line." As a result, harsh criticism from godly men is sometimes launched against those who maintain eternal life is free and eternal security is real. The following statement from a popular Christian teacher is telling about the schism in the church regarding the free gift and eternal security. J.I. Packer stated:

"The pastoral effect of this teaching [*grace theology*] can only be to produce what the Puritans called 'Gospel hypocrites'—persons who have been told that they are Christians, eternally secure, because they believe that Christ died for them, when their **hearts are unchanged** (*emphasis mine*) and they have **no personal commitment** (*emphasis mine*) to Christ at all. I know this, for I was just such a Gospel hypocrite for two years before God mercifully made me aware of my **unconverted state** (*emphasis mine*). If I seem harsh in my critique of [*Dr. Zane*] Hodges' [*grace-based theology advocate*] redefinition of faith as barren intellectual formalism, you must remember that once I almost lost my soul through assuming what Hodges teaches, and a burned child always thereafter dreads the fire."[4]

Let me try my best to translate this comment. "Imagine the gall! Hodges thinks a person is a Christian simply because they exercised faith in Christ. How dare him! Let's be clear. Without *our* commitment, Christ's sacrifice and God's grace are ineffective. Without *our* involvement, *our* work, and *our* effort, justification just won't happen. It obviously takes more than child-like faith in Christ for eternal life to secure one's eternal destiny."

An expectation is a requirement on the back end. An expectation goes like this: "Here, it's free. You can have it. ***But*** I'd better see [*insert – "changed heart, personal commitment, transformed life, good works, a hundred other things, denial of self, taking up cross, following Christ*]." If this is free, I'd hate to see costly. "But" is a small word and a huge "negator." God bless our Catholic friends. At least they're upfront and honest in their theology about the works required to secure one's eternal destiny. There's little room for doubt what the Muslim is required to do to enter paradise. The Mormon makes mandatory conduct clear as to what it takes to become a god and/or a spirit wife. It appears the up-front requirements of obedience, fruitful discipleship, and a visibly

---

4 Packer J.I. Tabletalk, *(P.O. Box 547500, Orlando FL 32746, Ligonier Ministries, Inc.)*, May, 1991.

changed life are moved and shuffled to the back of the justification equation as expectations in the misguided rhetoric of some godly teachers in the evangelical church. Changing the location of a work doesn't change what it is. Scripture remains clear and compelling. Truth has a tendency to be consistent and pristine. The Bible teaches fruit and works have nothing to do with providing eternal life, either up front or on the back end; either as a requirement or an expectation. Thus they have nothing to do with eternal security. Jesus seemed to verify this in Matthew 7:13-23. In this section of the Sermon on the Mount, Christ instructed His disciples about end-time events, wolves, and false prophets. The passage reads as follows:

> **Enter** through the narrow gate; for the gate is wide and the way is broad that leads to destruction, and there are many who enter through it. For the gate is small and the way is narrow that leads to **life**, and there are few who find it. **Beware of the false prophets**, who come to you in **sheep's** clothing, but inwardly are ravenous **wolves**. You will know them by their fruits. Grapes are not gathered from thorn bushes nor figs from thistles, are they? So every good tree bears good fruit, but the bad tree bears bad fruit. A good tree cannot produce bad fruit, nor can a bad tree produce good fruit. Every tree that does not bear good fruit is cut down and thrown into the fire. So then, you will know **them** by their fruits. Not everyone who says to Me, 'Lord, Lord,' will enter the kingdom of heaven, but he who **does the will** of My Father who is in heaven will enter. Many will say to Me on that day, 'Lord, Lord, did we not prophesy in Your name, and in Your name cast out demons, and in Your name perform many miracles?' And then I will declare to them, 'I never knew you; depart from Me, you who practice lawlessness.' (*Mt. 7:13-23*)

Christ begins this section with a command – "**Enter** through the narrow gate . . ." This command is important because the narrow gate of faith alone in Christ alone (*Jn. 14:6*) for eternal life is the only requirement to secure one's eternal destiny. In this passage (*Mt. 7:21*) "Enter[*ing*] through the narrow gate" is the "will of the Father." Abstaining from sexual immorality is the will of God in the context of 1 Thessalonians 4:3. In contrast, "enter through the narrow gate" is ***the*** command which distinguishes Christianity from every other world religion and philosophy. Works-oriented world-views are "broad" and "lead to destruction" and "many" are destroyed and dominated by it.

Following this command, Christ offers a second – "**Beware** of the false prophets . . ." The subject of the rest of the passage and the focus of Christ's teaching until verse 24 are not believers but false prophets. In describing these false prophets, Jesus describes them as wolves in sheep's clothing. On the outside they look, sound, smell, and act just like sheep. Inside they are wolves. Externally they act like believers but internally (*spiritually*) they are non-Christians, those who will not "enter the kingdom of heaven" (*vs. 21*). This is a picture of a person engaged in Christian conduct on the outside (*good works, transformed life, etc.*), but who is spiritually dead. Christ then uses another analogy of trees and fruit. Christ tells us "you will know **them** by their fruits." The "them" in the context hasn't changed; it's still the false prophets. The fruit of a false prophet or a misdirected teacher is *not* their conduct (*they act just like sheep*) but their teaching. Christ touched upon this concept again in Matthew 12:33-37:

> Either make the tree good and its fruit good, or make the tree bad and its fruit bad; for the tree is known by its fruit. You brood of vipers, how can you, being evil, **speak** what is good? For the **mouth speaks out of that which fills the heart**. The good man brings out of his good treasure what is good; and the evil man brings out of his evil treasure what is evil. But I tell you that every careless **word** that people **speak**, they shall give an accounting for it in the day of judgment. For by your **words** you will be justified, and by your **words** you will be condemned. (*Mt. 12:33-37*)

A false prophet's teaching will be in direct contrast to the command of Christ – **enter** by the narrow gate. If we want to know who a "false prophet" or a "misguided" (*unbiblical* – 2 Pt. 2:1) Christian teacher is, just ask them the following question – "In your opinion, how does a person obtain eternal life?" Their answer to that question will sound like a wolf howling if they incorporate or require any form of works in justification salvation. It's sadly interesting to see these false prophets relied upon Christian conduct and good works in their failed attempt to obtain eternal life. These "wolves" (*false prophets*) were confident their prophecy, exorcisms, and miracles (*sounds like conduct one would engage in at church*) would produce positive eternal results. Since they disobeyed by ignoring the narrow way but instead chose to rely upon their works, they wound up being eternally separated from Christ.

"Fruit inspection" which focuses on conduct is not encouraged by or patterned after the biblical text. This passage is frequently used out of context to link a person's relationship with God to their conduct. That dog won't hunt. It's the criminal dimension of life that is linked to conduct – let's call them works. The born-again (*spiritual*) dimension of life is based upon faith.

We now move from wolves to mere men. Paul shares with us there were Christians who acted just like unbelievers, in fact worse. Paul tells us there were believers in the Corinthian church whose conduct would embarrass a pagan. Their sexual relationship with their father's wife was in violation of even civil law provisions of the day. Paul writes to rebellious, disobedient believers in 1 Corinthians 3:1-3:

> And I, **brethren**, could not speak to you as to spiritual men, but as to men of flesh, as to babes in Christ. I gave you milk to drink, not solid food; for you were not yet able to receive it. Indeed, even now you are not yet able, for you are still fleshly. For since there is jealousy and strife among you, are you not fleshly, and are **you** [*brethren*] **not walking like mere men**? (*1 Cor. 3:1-3*)

Paul seemed aware a Christian's (*brethren*) conduct is not a reliable (*and certainly not the sole*) indicator of whether the person has eternal life. There are believers who act like "mere men." He continues in 1 Corinthians 5:1:

> It is actually reported that there is **immorality among you** [*believers in the context*] and immorality of such a kind as

> does not exist even among the Gentiles, that someone has his father's wife. (*1 Cor. 5:1*)

Once again we see a Christian's ("*you*") practice is not guaranteed to line up with their position in Christ. Paul reiterates the certainty of position (*justification*) and the option of practice (*sanctification*). He says in Eph. 2:10,

> For we are His workmanship, created in Christ Jesus for **good works**, which God prepared beforehand, that we **should** walk in them. (*Eph. 2:10*)

It doesn't say "will" but "should." The mood of the Greek verb in this passage is subjunctive. The context and the grammatical use of the term "walk" doesn't seem to move the mood beyond probability to certainty. Thus, maybe we will walk in His good works for us, maybe we won't. God has good works lined up for those who obtained eternal life by grace through faith in Christ. It's our choice to walk in them or not. If we don't, our relationship (*justification*) with God will still be secure, but our fellowship (*sanctification*) with Him will be impaired. Prior to Paul's writings, James referred to this as "dead" (*useless*) faith (*Jms. 2:17,20,26*).

In the end, Paul relied upon his apostolic authority to deal with and discipline the immoral Christian in the aforementioned specific passage. He writes in 1 Corinthians 5:5:

> I have decided to deliver **such a one** [*believer in the context*] to Satan for the destruction of his flesh, that **his spirit may be saved** in the day of the Lord Jesus. (*1 Cor. 5:5*)

There is no reason to equate the destruction (*Rom. 9:22, 1 Cor. 11:30, 1 Ths. 5:2,3, Heb. 12:5-13, 1 Jn. 5:16*) of one's flesh as hell but only as an aspect of God's discipline. This passage deals with the destruction "of his flesh" not the eternal destiny of the spiritual dimension of his life. The context tells us the ultimate condition of this believer's spirit – "saved."

In my brief twenty-five year moment in time on the Phoenix Police Department, I've seen more Christian law enforcement personnel chewed up and spit out by the harsh police environment than I've seen grow spiritually. One peer, prior to becoming a police officer, was a youth pastor at a church. He was married, fresh, and excited about combining his faith with his job. As his time wore on as an officer, his usefulness to the Master eroded. He left his wife, began to abuse alcohol, started living with another woman, and communicated in a foul-mouthed manner which would embarrass a sailor. In other words, here was a believer who looked (*engaged in conduct*) just like the "brethren" in Corinth. My police peer was a Christian who was walking like "a mere man" – an unbeliever. I've seen pastors fail also: cheating on their wives, cheating on their wives again, abusing drugs, knowingly using Scripture out of context, and stealing money from petty cash boxes after removing the hinges of the door the cash box was locked behind. I know homosexual Christians who are battling immune deficiency issues, believers who are in prison for statutory murder (*Christ raised the bar and defined murder as unjustified anger – Mt. 5:21,22*), born-again men who struggle with pornography, believers who are addicted to illegal narcotic drugs, and Christians who are doing time for federal theft convictions. I'm not condoning or minimizing the conduct. But the biblical fact is Christ paid for each and every one of these sins. The conduct of these Christians had absolutely nothing to do with their justification. Yet, to deny failure in the Christian life exists is to deny reality. Paul failed (*Rom. 7:7-24*). Peter failed (*Jn. 18:25-27*). I fail too (*1 Jn. 1:10*).

Wolves act like sheep, false prophets look just like believers, Christians walk like mere men, and conduct can be deceiving. Perhaps conduct is better tied to discipleship (*sanctification*) than justification and eternal security. John documented an important statement from Christ;

> Jesus therefore was saying to those Jews who had believed Him, 'If you abide in My word, then you are truly **disciples** of Mine.' (*Jn. 8:31*)

There seems to be a distinction between belief and abiding (*obey*). Becoming a Christian involves faith. Becoming a disciple involves faithfulness. Jesus repeated this idea by saying,

> By this is My Father glorified, that you bear much fruit (*obeying*), and so prove to be My **disciples.** (*Jn. 15:8*)

Even after the great struggles in the Corinthian church (*immorality, favoritism, misuse of the Lord's Supper, abuse of the gift of tongues, suing one another in court, insensitivity, favoritism*), Paul never questioned their eternal destiny or relationship with God. Between his two letters to Corinth, he refers to them as "brethren" 32 times, "saints" 5 times, and twice considered them "temples" of the Lord (*1 Cor. 3:16, 6:19*). In police work we call these clues. Their positional justification didn't seem to be an issue. But their practical conduct was. Paul admonished the Corinthians they needed to be concerned about their obedience and choices. They needed to address their practice because of their position. That's what was frustrating to Paul – their position in and life from Christ deserved (*not required*) obedient practice. They had been "bought with a price (*1 Cor. 6:20*)." Frequently, "whistle-blowers" are attacked. This is what happened to Paul. With great irony and sarcasm he defended his own conduct and motives from Corinthian accusations. Paul pointed out their disobedience and disingenuous intentions by saying:

> Test yourselves to see if you are **in the faith**; examine yourselves! Or do you not recognize this about yourselves, that Jesus Christ is in you – unless indeed you **fail the test**? (*2 Cor. 13:5*)

Some in the church were "seeking proof" and challenging Paul's apostolic authority (*2 Cor. 13:3*). Did Christ really work in and through him? Paul's response: Don't throw stones in glass houses. "Test yourselves to see if you are in the faith; examine yourselves!" Paul had used the phrase "in the faith" in the past. It was connected with obedience and orthodoxy (*correct thinking*) – " . . . stand firm **in the faith** . . ." (*1 Cor. 16:13*) and " . . . reprove them severely that they may be sound **in the faith** . . ." (*Titus 1:13*). He finishes 2 Corinthians 13:5 with what appears to be a shot of scorn that's dripping with sarcasm – "You, yes you, have got all the answers. You've got it all together. No problems in your church. Christ is clearly working in you. Who am I? I'm just an apostle. I'm the one who's short. I'm the problem. Unless I'm right and you're wrong and you aren't living up to Christ's standards of obedience—unless indeed you fail the test." The concept of "failing the test" is the Greek term "adokimos." It can mean "depraved" (*Rom. 1:28*). It can also mean "disqualified" (*1 Cor. 9:27*). Paul used the term in this manner concerning himself. As a believer who was eternally secure, he was concerned he might be "disqualified" and forfeit an eternal reward. And at the end of this letter to the Corinthians he used it three times in row in 2 Corinthians 13:5,6,7. Within this passage, it's defined as "unapproved" in verse seven. There's no indication in this context that it pertains to anything more than disobedience. With apostolic authority, Paul was clear, "If I come again, I will not spare anyone (*2 Cor. 13:2*)." It seems the issue was the faithlessness of these disobedient Corinthian Christians.

The context in all three passages doesn't seem to be justification but an admonition to sanctification. It's a call to obedience. Why would Paul refer to them as "brethren" and then tell them to make sure they are "brethren?" Paul was consistent and smart. He understood it's not what we do for Him, it's what He's done for us. Don't look to conduct or good works for assurance, look to Christ. He's the sole source of our justification salvation.

CHAPTER 11

More Sheep, Coins & Prodigals

Believers are of great value to God. He loves us dearly. Christ illustrated the Father's love for lost things in well-known parables about sheep, coins, and sons. In these touching stories, the truth of our Father's tender love clearly stands out. What we see in these parables is Christians (*sheep, coins, and sons*) can become lost and separated from fellowship with their Master. The parables, which are presented one after the other, are found in Luke 15:1-31.

> Now all the tax collectors and the sinners were coming near Him to listen to Him. Both the Pharisees and the scribes began to grumble, saying, "This man receives sinners and eats with them." So He told them this parable, saying, "What man among you, if he has a hundred **sheep** and has **lost one of them**, does not leave the ninety-nine in the open pasture and **go after** the one which is lost until he finds it? When he has found it, he lays it on his shoulders, rejoicing. And when he comes home, he calls together his friends and his neighbors, saying to them, 'Rejoice with me, for I have found **my sheep** which was **lost**!' "I tell you that in the same way, there will be more joy in heaven over **one sinner** [*believer in the context*] who repents than over ninety-nine righteous persons who need no repentance. Or what woman, if **she has ten silver coins** [*drachma – one day's wage*] and **loses one coin**, does not light a **lamp** and **sweep** the house and search carefully until she finds it? When she has found it, she calls together her friends and neighbors, saying, 'Rejoice with me, for I have found **the coin which**

I had lost!' In the same way, I tell you, there is joy in the presence of the angels of God over **one sinner** [*believer in the context*] who repents. And He said, "A **man** had **two sons** [*believers in the context*]. The younger of them said to **his father**, 'Father, give me the share of the estate that falls to me.' So he divided his wealth between them. And not many days later, the younger son gathered everything together and went on a journey into a distant country, and there he squandered his estate with loose living. Now when he had spent everything, a severe famine occurred in that country, and he began to be impoverished. So he went and hired himself out to one of the citizens of that country, and he sent him into his fields to feed swine. And he would have gladly filled his stomach with the pods that the swine were eating, and no one was giving anything to him. But when he **came to his senses** [*good example of repentance*], he said, 'How many of my father's hired men have more than enough bread, but I am dying here with hunger! I will get up and go to **my father**, and will say to him, "Father, I have sinned against heaven, and in your sight; I am **no longer worthy** to be called your son; make me as one of your hired men."' So he got up and came to his father. But while he was still a long way off, his father saw him and felt compassion for him, and ran and embraced him and kissed him. And the son said to him, 'Father, I have sinned against heaven and in your sight; I am no longer worthy to be called your son.' But the father said to his slaves, 'Quickly bring out the best **robe** and put it on him, and put a **ring** on his hand and **sandals** on his feet; and bring the **fattened calf**, kill it, and let us eat and **celebrate**; for **this son of mine was dead** and has come to life again; **he was lost** and has been found.' And they began to celebrate. Now his older son was in the field, and when he came and approached the house, he heard music and dancing. And he summoned one of the servants and began inquiring what these things could be. And he said to him, 'Your brother has come, and your father has killed the fattened calf because he has received him back safe and sound.' But he became angry and was not willing to

> go in; and his father came out and began pleading with him. But he answered and said to his father, 'Look! For so many years I have been serving you and I have **never neglected a command** of yours; and yet you have never given **me** a young goat, so that I might celebrate with **my** friends; but when this son of yours came, who has **devoured your wealth with prostitutes**, you killed the fattened calf for him.' And he said to him, 'Son, you have always been with me, and all that is mine is yours. But we had to celebrate and rejoice, for this brother of yours was dead and has begun to live, and was lost and has been found.'" (*Lk. 15:1-32*)

This parable is worthy of a dissertation but please allow me a brief comment. In the broad context, Matthew was writing to Jewish believers to provide them information about their Messiah and His teachings. With this broad context as a backdrop, it would have been important for Matthew's Christian audience to know how much God loved them, even if they were "sinners" and became "lost." Sheep, coins, and sons are all pictures of things of great value and things which can become lost – just like the believers whom Matthew was writing to.

Believers are consistently referred to and presented as sheep in the New Testament (*Mt. 10:16, 25:32,33, Jn. 10:16, 21:16, Acts 20:28, 1 Pt. 2:25, 5:2*). The term is never used in the biblical text to describe an un-believer. In this parable, it appears the owner of the sheep (*"my sheep"*) is a picture of Christ. Sheep are not the smartest creatures in the world. Sometimes they get lost and separated from the safety of the flock. But even when this happens, they still remain sheep and ownership doesn't change. What a fantastic picture of a faithless Christian ("*sinner*"), a faithful Shepherd, and the fact of eternal security. Christ proactively maintains and desires us to have deep and abiding fellowship with Him.

The term "drachma" (*coin*) appears only two times in the New Testament – both times in this parable (*Lk. 15:8*). A sheep could be bought for one drachma. Thus the value and representation of the coin is similar to the preceding picture of a sheep – that of a Christian. This silver coin was worth a day's wage. Because it was of great value, anyone who lost one (*like the woman in the story – another picture of Christ as an owner of something valuable*) would become panicked and by means of great effort use a "lamp" and "sweep" the house in order to find it. Coins, like Christians, can become lost and wind up in dark and dirty places. And even though coins and Christians can go missing and forego investment opportunities their Master has for them, they still remain valuable coins and priceless children. A "lost coin" maintains value, but if it's lost it's useless. The "lost coin" is another picture of the reality of failure in the lives of believers, the security of their relational position to God, and Christ's passion for their friendship and involvement in His plans.

Lastly, Christ shares the famous story of the prodigal (*wasteful and reckless*) son. Seeing Matthew was writing to born-again men and women, there doesn't seem to be a good reason to view this parable with an evangelistic frame of reference. The story line is clearly conduct driven and we know eternal life and justification have no relation or connection with one's works or conduct. Perhaps a better application of this parable is to relate it to sanctification and fellowship.

The players in Christ's parable are a man (*God the Father*) and "two sons" (*believers*). Christians are routinely referred to throughout the New Testament as children of God (*Jn. 1:12, Rom. 8:16, Eph. 5:1, 1 Jn. 3:1*) while non-Christians are never presented or pictured in this manner. This story matches reality – our selfish short-sightedness can cause us to be shockingly insensitive to our heavenly Father. We see this in the boy asking for his inheritance early. The backhanded flavor of this request tasted like a death wish. "I can't wait for you do die, Father, so give me what's mine." How disruptive this had to have been on the father's assets and financial portfolio. In contrast to this selfishness, God responds selflessly. God in His sovereignty gives us our freedom (*and allows us to sin*) and He gets nothing out of the deal. Like the father in the parable, He allows His children to go off to a "distant country."

Sinful, selfish decisions always carry a consequence for disobedient believers. This truth is framed for us by means of the famine and desperate situation the son was in. It's only when he "came to his senses" and regained perspective of the value of the fellowship (*friendship*) he had with his father that he moved in the right direction. The wasteful and reckless son changed his mind and went back home. Again we're hit with another wonderful picture of our heavenly Father. He sits on the front porch, looking down the road, and waits for disobedient, faithless children (*"sinners"*) to come home. He values and desires fellowship with us. Even though the father didn't know why the son was returning in the story, it's just like God to leap at the chance to lovingly embrace us for any movement toward Him. It should be noted that even though it would have been culturally undignified for a man with the father's status and stature to run, he sprinted to his boy. God condescends to love us and to repair the fellowship we've broken.

Once the wasteful son returned home, he was put in a position to earn rewards again. His father gave him a robe, a ring, a fattened calf, and a celebration to go with it. At no time during his absence did the son ever stop being a son. Even though the son felt he "was no longer worthy," feelings don't change facts. The fact is, at no time while the son was in a distant country did the father ever stop being his father. The father defined "dead" as "lost." In the context of this story, death is separation – a loss of fellowship (*friend/son*) due to sinful choices. Their relationship (*father/son*) never changed. This is an incredible picture of eternal security and the power of grace.

In the final scene, sadly we're given another picture of another son. The response of the other son to his brother's return was shameful. Arrogance makes it comfortable for self-righteous believers to think they "have never neglected a command" of God. Selfish Christians are quick to lose sight of the big picture and eternal obligations. The use of personal pronouns, as in a "goat for **me**" and a "feast for **my** friends," provides us a picture of the older son's problem. Additionally, self-righteous believers can be quick to impugn the character of others – Christians included. The older brother, without any evidence, maligned the character of his younger sibling by insinuating sexual immorality. He told his father his brother "devoured your wealth with prostitutes." Not true. No evidence whatsoever. Once again, shameful.

These parables are fantastic snapshots of the depth of God's love and the value of people He created in His image. Christians can and do fail. When they do they're called "sinners" (*Jms. 5:19,20*). In spite of our faithlessness, He remains faithful. God is the champion of grace. Because of this, we can know our eternal destiny is secure.

CHAPTER 12

Residents & Citizens, Christians & Disciples

To determine if a person is born-again by conduct is like determining a person's citizenship by where they live. There's a relationship between residency and citizenship but the two certainly aren't synonymous. Are all residents of Arizona citizens? No. There are many residents in Arizona who are in the country illegally. At any given time, 20 percent of the jail inmates in the Maricopa County jail in the City of Phoenix are in the country illegally. Nationally, 25 percent of all immigration holds in the United States originate from this same jail. Are all citizens Arizona residents? No. Some residents reside overseas due to business, family, military commitments, and faith-based ministries. It's not an unreasonable assumption a resident would be a citizen, and a non-resident would not be a citizen, but assumptions aren't facts. The fact is residency and citizenship are two different critters. Let's modify the analogy to see if we can draw out a theological connection with a similar thought process.

Are all Christians disciples? No. This is confirmed from Paul's interaction with the Corinthian believers. Clearly not all Christians are obedient. Not all Christians are bearing fruit. Thus not all Christians are disciples. Remember, Christ's requirement for a Christian to be a disciple is obedience and fruit. He made the challenging and difficult discipleship mandate clear in Luke 9:23:

> And He was saying to them all, "If anyone wishes to **come after Me**, let him **deny** himself, and **take up** his cross daily, and **follow Me.**" (*Lk. 9:23*)

If this discipleship requirement doesn't sound like a free gift the reason is because it's not. It's a sacrificial lifestyle on behalf of Jesus Christ. Denying, taking up a cross, doing this daily, and following are what theologians, police officers, and rocket scientists call good works. And good works aren't required for justification salvation, just discipleship. But one question remains.

Are all disciples Christians? I believe a historical event in the life of Christ and His own group of followers (*disciples*) will help to shed light on this question. Throughout the gospels we see the historical interaction between these twelve men and Jesus. Out of the twelve disciples, one of them was not a believer – Judas (*Jn. 6:69-71*). This suggests sometimes God's plans allow for failure. But time and again, Judas was referred to by the writers of the inspired biblical text as a disciple and even an apostle. So, perhaps not all disciples are Christians. What does the biblical text say?

> And having summoned His **twelve disciples** (*which included Judas*), He gave them (*which included Judas*) authority over unclean spirits, to cast them out, and to heal every kind of disease and every kind of sickness. Now the names of the **twelve apostles** (*which included Judas*) are these: the first, Simon, who is called Peter, and Andrew his brother; and James the son of Zebedee, and John his brother; Philip and Bartholomew; Thomas and Matthew the tax-gatherer; James the son of Alphaeus, and Thaddaeus; Simon the Zealot, and **Judas Iscariot** (*told you so*) the one who betrayed Him. These **twelve** (*which included Judas*) Jesus sent out after instructing **them** (*which included Judas*), saying, "Do not go in the way of the Gentiles, and do not enter any city of the Samaritans; but rather go to the lost sheep of the house of Israel. And as **you** (*which included Judas*) go, preach, saying 'The kingdom of heaven is at hand.' Heal the sick, raise the

> dead, cleanse the lepers cast out demons; freely **you** (*which included Judas*) received, freely give." (*Mt. 10:1-8*)

There is nothing in this biblical text or others (*Mk. 3:14-19, 14:17-21, Lk. 6:12-16, 22:14-23*) which would lead a reasonable police officer to disbelieve or deny Judas was *not* a follower (*disciple, apostle*) of Christ. He spent time with and hung around Christ; going where He went. If that's not the definition of a follower or a disciple, I don't know what is. We have a saying in police work – if it looks like a duck, and sounds like a duck, and walks like a duck, it's probably a duck. This rule of thumb was helpful in identifying drug dealers, prostitutes, and Police Chiefs.

In Arizona, our public safety pension system has a rule; once you retire you can't come back in the same position. This prevented what is known as "double-dipping." In other words, on Friday you can't retire from job X and then the following Monday, while you're collecting a pension for having done job X, come back and get paid for doing the same job X. State legislators thought this was fiscally and morally unhealthy for the pension system. Jack Harris, the former Phoenix Police Chief, is worthy of recognition seeing he invested nearly four decades of his life in the Phoenix Police Department. He retired in 2007. Less than a month later, the City Manager hired him back, not as the Police Chief but as the "Public Safety Manager." But recognition of Harris' service doesn't negate the rules. PLEA saw a duck, I mean a chief, but the City wanted to call it a "Public Safety Manager." Let's see, Harris wore the same Police Chief uniform, he wore the same four-stars on his collar, he wore the same Police Chief badge, he worked out of the same Police Chief's corner office in the police building, he was called the Police Chief, he was identified as the Police Chief at functions and on letterhead, and had the same span of authority he did prior to retiring as Police Chief. In fact, several years into his "Public Safety Manger" job the City Manager published a letter assuring Chief Harris he was indeed the Police Chief (*even though he was paid as the Public Safety Manager*). When Judicial Watch (*a non-profit conservative government watchdog group which fights corruption*), on behalf of taxpayers and officers, sued the City and the Police Chief for violating the "same job" provision of the pension laws, the City's defense was, "No, he's not the Police Chief. He's the Public Safety Manager. We gave him a few additional duties and those make it a different job." That's like taking a Ford truck, attaching a U-Haul trailer to it, and then calling it a Chevy because it has additional payload. This is what happens when government attempts to alter reality and break the rules to justify a corrupt good old boy system. Facts are helpful in determining what a person is. The facts point out Judas was a disciple of Christ every bit as much as they point out Jack Harris was the Police Chief. The rules about ducks apply to both disciples and chiefs. Quack!

The documentary evidence of Matthew 10:1-8 is pretty clear – not all disciples are Christians. In addition, based upon the historical accounts, one might also be compelled to believe Judas engaged in extraordinary, unique, and Christ-directed ministry experiences which met with success. I don't know about you, but I've never cast out a demon, I've never healed a sick person, I've never cleansed a leper, I've never raised the dead. But it sure looks like Judas may have. You think he would have caught on in the end. So perhaps there are disciples who are not believers. Is there any other biblical support to lend credence to this theory?

At a point in Christ's ministry, He had a large gathering of followers (*disciples*) beyond the twelve. These disciples reacted to Christ when He said, "He who eats my flesh and drinks My blood has eternal life, and I will raise him up on the last day (*Jn. 6:54*)." John recorded the response and reaction of the crowd (*disciples*) in John 6:60-71:

> Many therefore of **His disciples**, when **they** heard this said, "This is a difficult statement; who can listen to it?" But Jesus, conscious that **His disciples** grumbled at this said to **them**, "Does this cause **you** to stumble? What then if **you** should behold the Son of Man ascending where He was before? It is the Spirit who gives life; the flesh profits nothing; the words that I have spoken to **you** are spirit and are life. But there are **some of you** [*disciples in the context*] **who do not believe**." For Jesus knew it from the beginning who **they** were **who did not believe**, and who it was that would betray Him. And He was saying, "For this reason I

> have said to **you**, that no one can come to Me, unless it has been granted him from the Father." As a result of this **many of His disciples** withdrew, and were not walking with Him anymore. Jesus said therefore to **the twelve**, "**You** do not want to go away also, do **you**?" Simon Peter answered Him, "Lord, to whom shall **we** go? You have words of eternal life. And **we have believed** and have come to know that You are the Holy One of God." Jesus answered them, "Did I Myself not choose **you, the twelve**, and yet **one** of you is a devil?" Now He meant **Judas** the son of Simon Iscariot, for **he**, **one of the twelve**, was going to betray Him. (*Jn. 6:60-71*)

The group which heard Christ's comments consisted of: 1.) His disciples and 2.) The twelve. Specific names mentioned were: a.) Simon Peter and b.) Judas the son of Simon Iscariot. The larger group of disciples found Christ's statement offensive. They "grumbled" and they "stumbled." Christ identified there were some (*not "all"*) of His disciples in the larger group "who did not believe." Repeatedly in the context of the gospel of John, belief in Christ for eternal life is an obvious theme. A clear statement of this purpose by Christ is in John 6:47; "Truly, truly I say to you, he who **believes** [*"in Me" – Majority Text*] has eternal life." The restatement of these words in picture form (*eat and drink*) was given by Christ is John 6:54. This is what some disciples were offended by. After being confronted by Christ, many of His disciples, who did not believe, were not walking with Him anymore (*a pretty good definition of an ex-disciple*). It appears a person can be a disciple and not be a Christian (*believer*).

The second group in the account is identified as the twelve. We know who this was. Peter clearly indicated they had believed in Christ for eternal life. John documented this as far back as the wedding at Cana (*Jn. 2:11*). John goes out of his way to clarify that out of the twelve, Judas was not a believer. In fact, Christ refers to him as "a devil." Not very nice but true. To reaffirm, we again see in a smaller group of disciples, not everyone was a believer. Once again, it appears a person can be a disciple and not be a Christian. So to utilize discipleship requirements of obedience or commitment or fruit or good works as the standard for assurance or to inspect fruit is to employ a faulty, defective, non-biblical criterion. Don't look to works or a changed life for assurance. Like Peter, look to Christ. Jesus Christ has "the words of eternal life."

In a zeal for purity in the church, which is of great value, a thought process among some believers is to make NO distinction between being a disciple and becoming a Christian. There's a blending of sanctification and justification. There's no differentiation made between God as our friend and God as our Father. Works and faith have become the tandem means to justification. Blending sanctification and justification brings a "fall from grace" (*Gal. 5:4*) and creates disruption in the lives of believers (*Gal. 5:10*). "Falling from grace" is something. Only "nothing" can separate us from the love of God. "Falling from grace" is to willfully step aside from the truth of the gospel and rely upon a works oriented religious system. Rhetoric forces what is free to become costly. But grace makes no demands in the reception of the gift.

To inject a little works or a little sanctification into the faith-based issue of justification has a broad, damaging, confusing, and biblically inconsistent impact. I can remember asking suspects a question which aided in convictions. I would ask a person if they had a little or a lot of drugs in their system. If they said a lot, there's an admission to drug use. If they said a little, there's an admission to drug use. The only answer which was beneficial to them was telling me they wouldn't have any drugs in their system. The same is true for works. We can say "faith alone" but when we add just a little bit of good works or expectations, or a "hundred other things," either way there's reliance upon effort to assist Christ in providing eternal life. Paul might have responded – "Anathema!"

One can't say "I'm the Police Chief" to maintain authority and then say "I'm not the Police Chief" to avoid a pension infraction. One can't say "eternal life is free" to agree with the biblical text and then say "it will cost you everything" to advance a theological agenda. Both are nonsensical contradictions. Eternal life is free to the recipient. It's costly to the giver; our justification cost God His only begotten Son. Personally, I wouldn't give my boy up for anyone—the cost is too high for me. Like godly authors of today, believers in Galatia had "fallen from grace" too. Paul spoke to them about the injection of works into the gospel. His harsh tone ("*you foolish Galatians, who has bewitched you" / Gal. 3:1*) emphasized his concern about combining works (*the "Law"*) and faith. Paul wrote:

> For in Christ Jesus neither circumcision nor uncircumcision means anything, but faith working through love. You were running well; who hindered you from obeying the truth? This persuasion did not come from Him who calls you. **A little leaven** [*reliance upon works*] leavens the whole lump of dough. (*Gal. 5:6-9*)

God made it clear eternal life is a free gift (*Jn. 4:10, Rom. 3:24, Eph. 1:6, 2:8, 3:7, Rev. 21:6, 22:17*). Because we freely accepted His gift of eternal life which He freely gave, we don't owe Him anything (*Rom. 4:4,5, Col. 2:9-11*). Even if I could pay Him for it, I don't believe He's impressed with my work. The words of Isaiah to the nation of Israel hold relevance for us today. What does God think of our performance?

> For all of us have become like one who is unclean, and all our righteous deeds are like a **filthy garment**; and all of us wither like a leaf, and our iniquities, like the wind, take us away. (*Is. 64:6*)

The "filthy" rag is a Hebrew idiom for a used article of feminine hygiene. Offensive – that's what Yahweh thinks of the good things I do. I wonder how my sin comes across to Him. We can't work for eternal life. He doesn't allow, ask or want us to work for it. So why look to works to see if the gift has been accepted. Look to Christ for assurance.

CHAPTER 13

Just Because It Can't Be Seen Doesn't Mean It's Not Real

A good cop has a good nose. There are many things I can't see which are real. I might not have seen the drunk driver who vertically parked his car on the support wire of a telephone pole consume alcohol, but I can smell it on his breath. I didn't see him drink but I know he did. Even though I can't see someone smoking marijuana, the unique and identifying odor of burning cannabis is a court-approved means to probable cause. Just because I can't see the crime being committed, my sense of smell confirms the reality of a violation of a state drug offense in process. The nose wins again. Scripture, like our nose, also confirms many things I can't see – certainly positional spiritual changes in a believer's life. Just because I can't see a changed life doesn't mean it didn't happen. A changed life is indeed a result of justification. After a person has exercised faith in Christ for eternal life, a radical positional shift is caused by regeneration (*Acts 10:43-45, Gal. 2:16, 3:2, Titus 3:5*). The term "regeneration" carries the idea of being "born-again." Just because we don't see the crucial positional changes between a man/woman and their Creator doesn't mean justification hasn't occurred. Reality is not limited by what we see. The biblical text allows us to know, understand, and appreciate the phenomenal shift in state and status which occurs when a person trusts in Christ for eternal life.

At a point in time, a person who trusts in Christ as their only hope of heaven passes out of death into life (*regeneration*). Jesus confirmed this dynamic, crucial positional change in John 5:24. Two people can stand directly in front of me and only one of them is a believer. I can't tell by looking at them which one is justified. Can you? And certainly visible conduct isn't a reliable consistent biblical standard to determine one's unseen eternal standing (*wolves, sheep, mere men*). But from a spiritual perspective, they're as different as night and day. Both are created in the image of God and are deeply loved by Him. But one is a spiritual corpse; the other is alive and kicking. The one who is born-again used to be spiritually dead but not anymore. Moving from death to life is an incredible change which is beyond my vision but is in fact a reality. What a relief to move beyond my subjective, self-righteous senses and standards and rely upon God's Word. Even though the fruits of the Spirit (*Gal. 5:22,23*) can be secondary "life-change" indicators which can escape our sight, the Bible confirms the reality of unseen spiritual change we can't or don't see.

In addition to passing out of death to life, as well as justification (*Rom. 4:25*), there are other unseen positional changes which take place in one's life the moment they trust in Jesus Christ for eternal life. In the section *The Goal is Eternal Life*, we briefly addressed these blessings and change in standing while considering eternal life as the objective of evangelism. The biblical text assures us of changes we can't see. Here are some of the invisible but real changes which are verified by the Bible.

- **Adoption** – Rom. 8:15, Gal. 4:5, Eph. 1:5. Movement from "a dead orphan" to "a living son/daughter" is a change in life. In the physical world, I can't tell with my eyes who lives under a court approved relationship of guardian and child. But it's real nonetheless. In God's Word there's documentation which assures us this permanent relationship is real.
- **Sealed** – 2 Cor. 1:22, 5:5, Eph. 1:13, 4:30. Movement from rejection by the Creator to approval is a radical transformation. To be "sealed" is be marked for possession, identification, and certification. In some contexts it means to mark as having been harvested. I can tell who a certified public accountant is by the certificate on his/her wall. Seeing believers don't walk around with framed documentation of approval, we can rely upon the Bible this change in a person's life has occurred.

- **Peace with God** – Rom. 5:1, 10, 11. Movement from war to peace is a huge shift in status. Just ask a prisoner of war. Undercover officers will engage in conduct and don an appearance which, by looking at them with our eyes, would lead us to believe they're criminals – enemies of the state. They look like the scum of the earth. In reality, they're peace officers pursuing the rule of law. Our eyes can't see everything, but when we look at the biblical text what we can see is God's assurance those who are believers have been reconciled to Him.
- **Body of Christ** – Rom. 12:5, 1 Cor. 12:27, Eph. 5:30. Movement from isolation to team member is what Paul might call "new creation—an entirely new situation (*2 Cor. 5:17*)!" We can't tell just by looking at a person what their role, gift, or function is in the Church. Still, God's Word gives us confidence even though we can't see this change, believers have crucial roles in serving the Body and will be held accountable for their usefulness to the Head – Christ.

In just a moment in time, things can change dramatically. As we've already seen, some godly Christian leaders demand to see changed lives as *the* primary proof a person is a Christian. They require discernible transformation of the person to prove conversion. Yet it seems their demand doesn't match His command. Jesus saw no problem in practicing low-visibility secret righteousness (*giving, prayer, fasting*) where no one could see (*Mt. 6:1-18*) humble obedience—in fact He encouraged it. Visibility doesn't determine reality. What we miss the Father sees – He sees so much in secret. Thankfully we can reject the subjective, limited standards of eyes, opinions, and rhetoric and rely upon what our Father observes. For those who have simply exercised faith alone in Christ alone for eternal life, their changed lives are readily confirmed in the Bible. Upon belief, God assures us of radical, positional, unseen paradigm shifts in a person's standing and status with their Creator, fellow believers, and the world. Don't look to works or a changed life for assurance, look to Christ. Remember that He is the giver of the free gift of eternal life.

CHAPTER 14

Failure Is an Option

Statistics may vary depending upon the source, but studies have consistently shown police officers are six times more likely to commit suicide than their civilian counterparts. A thirty year old police officer can be just as likely to take his/her own life as the seventy year old male citizen they protect. Police chaplains and counselors are very much aware of this problem of poor choices in the high stress world of law enforcement. The black-and-white thought processes found in alpha males can generate drastic and dangerous personal solutions to problems they perceive are insurmountable. And having easy access to weapons certainly doesn't help the problem. The Phoenix Police Department reeled in 2011 when the medical examiner's office ruled the on-duty death of highly successful, well liked sergeant was a suicide. The coroner's report presented the method of death as a self-inflicted shotgun wound to his head. Many believed the reason he took his own life was a pending criminal indictment for off-duty work allegations of fraud and theft. Sadly, over a year after his death, the indictment brought by the grand jury against this sergeant and other officers was thrown out by a judge who said the attorney general's office had presented a flawed, biased case which was untruthful and void of exonerating facts. When political agendas pollute police procedures, expect failure (*in this case suicide*) on the part of law enforcement.

An interesting historical account demonstrates the reality of suicide among police officers. In the Roman world the police force of the day was the army. And depending upon the unit one was assigned to, two rules were enforced. First, if you fell asleep on-duty, it would cost you your life. Second, if you let a prisoner escape, it would cost you your life—thus the birth of police unions! Luke shares the response of a Philippian law enforcement official who believed his prisoners had escaped.

> But about midnight Paul and Silas were praying and singing hymns of praise to God, and the prisoners were listening to them; and suddenly there came a great earthquake, so that the foundations of the prison house were shaken; and immediately all the doors were opened and everyone's chains were unfastened. When the jailer awoke and saw the prison doors opened, **he drew his sword and was about to kill himself, supposing that the prisoners had escaped**. But Paul cried out with a loud voice, saying, "**Do not harm yourself**, for we are all here!" And he called for lights and rushed in, and trembling with fear he fell down before Paul and Silas. (*Acts 16:25-29*)

Why let the boss terminate you when you can do it yourself. A biblical account shows us suicide (*failure*) is an option in the life of law enforcement personnel. Just as a police officer who "harms himself" makes a poor choice, a believer who disobeys God's Word also makes a poor choice. It's a choice which leads to failure. You see, failure is an option for Christians too. I believe Jesus presented an intriguing picture of the reality of failure in the Christian life as it relates to obeying God's Word. By means of a parable, Christ teaches us sadly, failure is easily accessible in the Christian life. Disobedience to the truth of His text is a choice readily available and commonly embraced. Luke documented the following historical account.

> When a large crowd was coming together, and those from the various cities were journeying to Him, He spoke by way of a parable: "The sower went out to sow his seed; and as he sowed, some fell beside the road, and it was trampled under foot and the birds of the air ate it up. Other seed fell on rocky soil, and as soon as it grew up, it withered away, because it had no moisture. Other seed fell among the thorns; and the thorns grew up with it and choked it out. Other seed fell into the good soil, and grew up, and produced

> a crop a hundred times as great." As He said these things, He would call out, "He who has ears to hear, let him hear." **His disciples** began questioning Him as to what this parable meant. And He said, "To **you** [*believers in the context*] it has been granted to know the mysteries of the kingdom of God, but to the rest it is in parables, so that seeing they may not see, and hearing they may not understand. Now the parable is this: **the seed is the word of God**. Those **beside the road** are those who have heard; then the **devil** comes and takes away the word from their heart, so that they **will not believe and be saved**. Those on **the rocky soil** are those who, when they hear, receive the word with joy; and these have no firm root; they believe for a while, and in **time of temptation fall away**. The seed which fell among **the thorns**, these are the ones who have heard, and as they go on their way they are choked with **worries and riches and pleasures of this life**, and bring **no fruit to maturity**. But the seed in **the good soil**, these are the ones who have heard the word in an honest and good heart, and hold it fast, and **bear fruit with perseverance**. Now no one after lighting a lamp covers it over with a container, or puts it under a bed; but he puts it on a lampstand, so that those who come in may see the light. For nothing is hidden that will not become evident, nor anything secret that will not be known and come to light. So **take care how you listen**; for whoever has, to him more shall be given; and whoever does not have, even what he thinks he has shall be taken away from him." And His mother and brothers came to Him, and they were unable to get to Him because of the crowd. And it was reported to Him, "Your mother and Your brothers are standing outside, wishing to see You." But He answered and said to them, "My mother and My brothers are these who **hear the word of God and do it**." (*Lk. 8:4-21*)

Christ defined the terms plainly. In Luke, the seed is the "word of God." In Matthew's version of this account he used the phrase "the word of the kingdom (*Mt. 13:19*)." Mark's version spoke of "the will of

God" (*Mk. 3:35*) just prior to utilizing the term "the word" (*Mk. 4:14*) in his version of Christ's parable.

The word of God can include the gospel message (*Rev. 6:9, 20:4*) but it's not limited to justification salvation issues (*Lk. 5:1, 11:28, Rom. 15:4, 1 Jn. 2:14*). The word of God is a supernatural source of truth and God's standard for Christian living (*Col. 1:25, Titus 2:5*). It includes how wives are to respond to their husbands (*1 Pt. 3:1-6*), how children are to financially care for their senior parents (*Ex. 20:12*), how fathers are to live with their children (*Eph. 6:4*), our obligation in paying taxes (*Lk. 10:25*), how the abuse of alcohol is unwise (*Prov. 20:1*), our attitude of thanksgiving (*Phil. 4:6*), understanding there is a time for everything under the sun (*Eccl. 3:1-8*), limitations on teachers in the church (*Jms. 3:1,2*), requirements for elders (*1 Tim. 3:1-7*), and the biblical ethic of hard work in the marketplace (*2 Ths. 3:10*).

Since Christ's audience consisted of born-again believers (*Mt. 13:11, Mk. 4:11*), maybe the four soils in Christ's fictional story are illustrations of Christian responses to the Bible. Or, seeing "the sower" is never identified in the story by Christ, it's not unreasonable to believe Jesus' disciples were being trained about the likely reactions they would encounter when it was their turn to cultivate people's hearts to receive God's Word. I believe the context of this parable does not mandate that justification salvation (*eternal life*) is the intended topic. Jesus' half-brother James plainly restated the parable's theme: Christians who are "doers of the Word" are fruitful and useful to the Master.

> This you know, my beloved **brethren** [*Christians in the context*]. But everyone must be quick to hear, slow to speak and slow to anger; for the anger of man does not achieve the righteousness of God. Therefore, putting aside all filthiness and all that remains of wickedness, in humility **receive the word implanted**, which is able to **save your souls** [*lives*]. But prove yourselves **doers of the word, and not merely hearers** who delude themselves. For if anyone is a hearer of the word and not a doer, he is like a man who looks at his natural face in a mirror; for once he has looked at himself and gone away, he has immediately forgotten what

> kind of person he was. But one who **looks intently at the perfect law**, the law of liberty, and **abides by it**, not having become a forgetful hearer but **an effectual doer**, this man will be blessed in what he does. If anyone thinks himself to be religious, and yet does not bridle his tongue but deceives his own heart, this man's religion is worthless. Pure and undefiled religion in the sight of our God and Father is this: to visit orphans and widows in their distress and to keep oneself unstained by the world. (*Jms. 1:19-27*)

As Christians, we can choose to listen to biblical truth. We can choose to believe this truth. We can choose to apply *("do it")* this truth. If we choose to "believe" what God tells us in the biblical text, it will "save" us from the spiritual and natural consequences connected to our disobedience. "Doing" God's Word "saves" us from spiritual immaturity, fruitlessness, and failure. Abiding in the "word implanted" saves our lives and has a life-saving impact on those in need around us. Or, as illustrated by Jesus, we can choose to disobey and embrace failure. Might I suggest the following perspective on the four soils.

1. The soil beside the road represents Christians who are on the "business end" of Satan and void of fruit. Satan can interfere with our understanding of the biblical text (*Mt. 13:19*). Scripture is clear through its warnings that Satan is a danger to believers and can negatively impact their lives, their fruitfulness, and their fellowship with the Father (*Mk. 1:13, Jn. 17:15-17, Acts 5:3, 1 Cor. 5:5, 2 Cor. 12:7, Eph. 4:27, 6:10-17, 1 Ths. 2:18, 1 Tim. 3:6,7, 2 Tim. 2:26, Jms. 4:7, 1 Pt. 5:8*).
2. The rocky soil represents believers who, because of temptation (*Lk. 11:4*), fail to obey God's Word (*Acts 17:11, 1 Ths. 1:6*) and "fall away" – not from salvation but from spiritual maturity and faithfulness (*Acts 11:23, Gal. 5:4, Heb. 3:12, 6:6, Jms. 1:12-18, 2 Pt. 3:17*). Doing the will of God can bring about "affliction and persecution" (*Mk. 4:17, 1 Pt. 2:18-22*). Failing to obey in pursuit of temporal worldly relief from these pressures causes believers to "stumble" (*Mt. 13:21, 1 Cor. 8:13, 2 Cor. 11:29*).
3. The thorny soil represents Christians who are distracted by the world (*Mt. 6:24-34, 1 Tim. 6:9-11,17-19, Jms. 4:4,*

1 Jn. 2:15-17). Biblical priorities and an eternal perspective are "choked" out of their lives. Because of this, they remain spiritually immature and fruitless.

4. The good soil represents a believer who "hears the word of God and does it" (*Lk. 8:21*). They take God at His word to acquire skill at living (*wisdom*). As a result (*Heb. 4:12,13, 1 Jn. 2:14*) they have a dynamic spiritual life (*2 Tim. 3:16,17*) and deep fellowship with their Father (*Psm. 1, Psm. 119*). They are faithful and fruitful.

It might be a stretch, but from this picture presented by Christ, it looks like He was providing His disciples (*as well as us*) a preview of the probable responses from Christians to biblical teaching—three out of four Christians are not "doers of the Word" and as a result they miss out on their potential as spiritual multipliers, obedient disciples, and men and women who are useful to the Master. Beyond this parable of Christ, there are other biblical examples which are stark reminders that failure is an option. Guess who the following describe:

- Sex outside of marriage with another man's wife. Tried to cover the affair up when the other man's wife was found to be carrying his child. Abused executive authority and conspired to have the husband murdered. Was outraged at similar conduct in the life of another. Failed to discipline unruly sons who were abusive of women and of governmental power. **Was a man after God's own heart** (*Acts 13:22*).
- Murdered a government official in a rage of anger. Became a fugitive from justice. Walked away in a rage of anger during key national peace talks. In a fit of rage damaged a unique judicial relic. Was reckless with his position of authority during a violent demonstration caused by a rage of anger. Forfeited a unique opportunity to lead during a time of national expansion. **Was looking forward to the reward of Christ** (*Heb. 11:26*).
- Selfishly took advantage of a good and senior family member in a land deal. Offered his daughters as targets of sexual assault to assuage the anger of a violent homosexual mob. Struggled to leave a lucrative business and a comfortable home even at the risk of losing the lives of his family. Abused alcohol and engaged

in an incestuous relationship by having sex with his daughters. **A righteous man with a righteous soul** (*2 Pt. 2:7,8*).
- Was inconsistent in completing tasks. Failed to recognize the eternal and spiritual implications of crucial events. Quickly resorted to violence and committed an aggravated assault against a law enforcement official. Proved to be disingenuous after making arrogant and grandiose claims. Publicly compromised his moral obligations as an apostolic leader by giving into the pressure of political correctness and social agendas. **Close confidant of Christ who set the standards for the early Christian church** (*Jn. 21:15-17*).

Men and women, who are heroes of the faith and played crucial roles in God's plan, are real and honest examples that failure is an option. David, Moses, Lot, and Peter failed. David died with Israel in political turmoil. Moses was not allowed to enter the Promised Land. Lot's conduct would have been questioned in San Francisco. And Peter had to be publicly challenged for complicating the simplicity of the gospel with works. The list of saints failing doesn't stop here.

- Not only was Peter not straightforward about the gospel, but Barnabas was carried away by this hypocrisy as well (*Gal. 2:13*).
- Demas, a fellow worker with Paul, deserted him because he "loved this present world" (*Col. 4:14, 2 Tim. 4:10*).
- Ananias and Sapphira thought lying to God was a good idea – they were wrong, dead wrong (*Acts. 5:1-11*).
- Simon thought he could buy spiritual success (*Acts. 8:13-24*).
- The Corinthian believers were a wreck in progress (*1 & 2 Cor.*).
- Euodia and Syntyche were quarreling with one another (*Phil 4:2*).
- Christians were dishonoring the poor through economic favoritism (*Jms. 2:6*).
- Onesimus failed to fulfill his labor obligations (*Philemon 1:10-11*).
- Hymenaeus and Alexander were engaged in blasphemy (*1 Tim. 1:20*).

- Christ had serious problems with five out of seven of the early churches (*Rev. 2-3*).

Take these human examples of failing believers and couple them with the various commands throughout the New Testament and it's not hard to see that failure is an option and obedience, far from being automatic, is a choice. But yet our failure and our faithlessness have no bearing on our eternal destiny.

CHAPTER 15

He Remains Faithful

Since faith and good works don't provide eternal life, we shouldn't look to them as the source of assurance. Take Christ at His word. Look to Christ for assurance. Assurance is confidence in the biblical fact of eternal security. Assurance comes from continued belief in Christ for His free gift of eternal life. If we doubt or stop believing, we'll lose assurance but the fact of security remains.

If I had to choose one biblical reference to address the fact of eternal security and assurance it would be Paul's final words to Timothy. It's likely in his instruction to Timothy that he quoted an ancient hymn of the early church. Paul wrote:

> It is a trustworthy statement: For if we died with Him, we will also live with Him; If we **endure**, we will also **reign with Him**; If we **deny** Him, He also will **deny us** [*the opportunity to reign*]; **If we are faithless, He remains faithful**, for He cannot deny Himself. (*2 Tim. 2:11-13*)

This hymn is laid out in a chiastic ("*X*") structure. By means of repetition and restatement, Paul used this literary device to impart truth. The form of the chiastic structure in this passage looks like this:

A – Verse 11b: "For if we died with Him, we will also live with Him."
B – Verse 12a: "If we endure, we will also reign with Him."
B' – Verse 12b: "If we deny Him, He also will deny us."
A' – Verse 13: "If we are faithless, he remains faithful, for He cannot deny Himself."

Paul used the term "trustworthy" with Timothy (*2 Tim. 2:2*)—entrust sound biblical teaching into "faithful" (*trustworthy*) men. He used the same term at the end of this passage to describe Christ—"He remains "faithful" (*trustworthy*). In describing the quality of the lyrics he was quoting we see the term again – "a trustworthy statement." Perhaps Paul was trying to cultivate confidence in the readers by emphasizing the reliability of the truth he's presenting by describing it as "trustworthy."

In verse 11b the phrase "For if we died with Him" indicates the concept of justification. This represents our position in Christ. In verse 12a he addresses the issue of endurance. He challenges his readers; "If we endure." Paul wasn't asking for anything he hadn't done. He said he "endured" all things to have an effective impact in his evangelistic efforts (*2 Tim. 2:10*). In this line, Paul compared his audience's position to their practice. This is the concept of sanctification. Those who endure shall receive a reward – they'll be compensated for their efforts. Endurance brings about the opportunity to "reign with Him (*Christ*)." Eternal significance is obtained by faithfulness.

Paul then contrasts the challenge of endurance with the negative reality of denial. In 12b he states, "If we deny Him, He also will deny us." Notice the plural personal pronoun "we" lumps Paul into the possibility of failure. He was "touchable." With this in mind, remember, Paul wrote "nothing" could separate these believers (*as well as us*) from the love of God. "Denying Him" is something. Only "nothing" can separate us. So what does Christ deny believers who deny Him? It can't be eternal life. And if it can't be eternal life, denial can't be an indication of justification and/or regeneration. The context tells us what is denied to those who deny Christ: The opportunity to reign with Him. Believers who deny Christ in the context of Paul's letter to Timothy will forfeit a unique and wonderful honor of ruling and reigning with Him as companions in the Millennial Kingdom. This echoes what Christ said in Matthew 10:32,33:

> Therefore everyone who confesses Me before men, I will also **confess** [*honor of public praise*] him before My Father who is in heaven. But whoever denies Me before men, I will

> also **deny** [*loss of public praise*] him before My Father who is in heaven. (*Mt. 10:32,33*)

We know **no one** and **nothing** can snatch us out of His hand. We know He will **never** desert or forsake us. So what is the believer denied? Believers who choose to deny (*and thus fail to confess*) Christ will be denied honor from Him before the Father. This is called accountability. In stark contrast, faithful Christians will receive a commendation and a promotion.

> **Well done**, good and **faithful slave**; you were faithful with a few things, I will **put you in charge** of many things, **enter into the joy of your master.** (*Mt. 25:21*)

Back to Paul's use of an ancient hymn in his last letter to Timothy. He concludes this short powerful passage with some of the most comforting and encouraging words in the Bible. He lays out the eternal safety net – the person of Christ. Even if Christians choose to be faithless (*faithlessness is "something," only "nothing" can separate us*), Christ has no choice. He remains "faithful" (*trustworthy*). Isn't every act of sin or disobedience in our lives faithlessness? What is the overall pattern of our lives? Are we "trustworthy" or faithless? Regardless of our response, Christ is the basis of a believer's eternal security.

We know trusting in Christ for eternal life brings about a dynamic positional life change. One of these changes is becoming part of the His body (*1 Cor. 12:12,27*). The reality of this positional life-change places Christ in a position where "He cannot deny Himself." As the head of the Body, Jesus is committed. Even if we fail, and we will, He must, and certainly does remain true. But even though security cultivates assurance it certainly doesn't eliminate accountability. What we see in the short hymn Paul shared in 2 Timothy is eternal security. Three words are the anchoring chorus of the hymn – "He remains faithful." The believer's spiritual destiny is unchanging – it's eternally secure. As long as we trust in Christ, we'll have assurance of this fact. Look to Christ for assurance.

CHAPTER 16

Why Does the Bible Command Obedience and Good Works?

Some police tools are optional. I don't have to use them. In Phoenix, a ballistic vest was one tool which was optional. It was only mandated when an officer chose to wear a utility uniform. Officers who wore non-utility type uniforms (*as well as officers assigned to undercover and plain clothes assignments*) had the choice not to wear a vest. In Arizona, the problem with a vest is heat. No, it's not a dry heat, it's a miserable one. This heat and an officer's exposure to danger influenced their decision whether they should wear body armor or not.

Another tool that was optional was a side-handle baton. This is a wooden dowel covered with spun aluminum that, when used properly, can produce a tip speed of around 60 miles an hours. Ouch! I, along with many other officers, chose not to use this tool. Even when an officer employed this tool within policy, it never looked good to beat someone with a stick (*remember Rodney King*). And it wasn't worth the pressure and pain of an administrative investigation for an allegation of excessive force. We referred to side-handle batons as "walking memos." It was easier just to leave it in the patrol car.

Ballistic vests and side-handle batons were not required for police work. They were an optional part of the package. Works, conduct, obedience, and fruit are like optional police tools. When it comes to becoming a Christian, they're not required either. In fact, they're not a part of the justification equation at all. So if works don't provide eternal life, and works don't reliably prove one has eternal life, then what's the point? It's seems like telling a police officer, "These tools aren't required and you don't have to use them but you'll be liable if you leave them at home." There's a reason police tools are provided—to improve effectiveness and increase safety. Moving from officer to believer: Why does the Bible command obedience and good works if they're not required for eternal life? Why am I held liable for the way I use the free gift of eternal life when eternal life came with no strings attached. I can live "like hell." So why obey? What's the point of obedience and good works for the Christian?

Here's why: Obedience and good works save a Christian from the power of sin (*and its consequences*). This theological concept is known as sanctification. Justification focuses on a person being saved from the penalty of sin – eternal separation from God. Faith in Christ is the means to justification/eternal life. Faithfulness by the Christian is the means to sanctification/eternal rewards. The Lord's commands protect and provide for us. I believe there are at least five biblical reasons to obey.

Obedience saves believers from God's discipline—If we obey our Father, we'll avoid (*be saved from*) His discipline. We saw this in our earthly homes, why wouldn't we expect it in our relationship as children of God? Sanctification is coupled to our faithfulness (*obedience*) and our obedience saves us from being disciplined by our Father. Scripture reminds us of the reality of God's discipline.

> But a certain man named Ananias, with his wife Sapphira [*Christians in the context*], sold a piece of property, and kept back some of the price for himself, with his wife's full knowledge, and bringing a portion of it, he laid it at the apostles' feet. But Peter said, "Ananias, why has Satan filled your heart to **lie to the Holy Spirit** [*implication – only believers can lie to the Spirit / 1 Ths. 5:19*] and to keep back some of the price of the land? While it remained unsold, did it not remain your own? And after it was sold, was it not under your control? Why is it that you have conceived this deed in your heart? You have **not lied to men, but to God**." And as he heard these words, **Ananias fell down**

and breathed his last; and great fear came upon all who heard of it. And the young men arose and covered him up, and after carrying him out, they buried him. And now there elapsed an interval of about three hours, and his wife came in, not knowing what had happened. And Peter responded to her, "Tell me whether you sold the land for such and such a price?" And she said, "Yes, that was the price." Then Peter said to her, "Why is it that you have agreed together to **put the Spirit of the Lord to the test** [*implication – only believers can test the Spirit / Eph. 4:30*]? Behold, the feet of those who have buried your husband are at the door, and they shall carry you out as well." **And she fell immediately at his feet, and breathed her last**; and the young men came in and found her dead, and they carried her out and buried her beside [*literally "face to face"*] her husband. And great fear came upon **the whole church** [*implication – this assembly of believers saw one of their own severely disciplined*] and upon all who heard of these things. (*Acts 5:1-11*)

I have decided to deliver such a **one** [*Christian in the context*] to Satan for the **destruction of his flesh**, that his spirit may be **saved** [*justification*] in the day of the Lord Jesus. (*1 Cor. 5:5*)

For this reason many among **you** [*Christians in the context*] are **weak and sick, and a number sleep** [*dead*]. But if we judge ourselves rightly, we should not be judged. But when we are judged, we are disciplined by the Lord in order that we may not be condemned along with the world. (*1 Cor. 11:30-32*)

and **you** [*Christians in the context*] have forgotten the exhortation which is addressed to you as sons, "My son, do not regard lightly the **discipline** of the Lord, nor faint when you are **reproved** by Him; for those whom the Lord loves He **disciplines**, and He **scourges** every son whom He receives." It is for **discipline** that you endure, God deals

> with you as with sons; for what son is there whom his father does not **discipline**? (*Heb. 12:5-7*)
>
> My **brethren** [*Christians in the context*], if any among **you** [*Christian in the context*] strays from the truth, and one turns him back, let him know that he who turns **a sinner** [*Christian in the context*] from the error of this way will **save his life from death**, and will cover a multitude of sins. (*Jms. 5:19,20*)
>
> If anyone sees **his brother** [*Christian in the context*] committing a sin not leading to death, he shall ask and God will for him give life to those who commit sin not leading to death. There is **a sin leading to death**; I do not say that he should make request for this. (*1 Jn. 5:16*)

Obedience saves us from foolish consequences. If a Christian wants to be saved from (*avoid*) a fine, drive the speed limit. If a believer wants to be saved from (*avoid*) having his/her wages garnished by the IRS, pay your taxes. If I want to be saved from (*avoid*) a prison term, I'll obey the law of the land.

> For rulers are not a cause of fear for good behavior, but for evil. Do **you** [*Christians in the context*] want to have no fear of authority? Do what is good, ...and you will have praise from the same; for it is a minster of God to you for good. But if you do what is evil, be afraid; for it does not bear the sword for nothing; for it is a minister of God, an avenger who brings **wrath upon the one who practices evil**. (*Rom. 13:3,4*)
>
> For what credit is there if, when **you** [*Christians in the context*] sin and are **harshly treated**, you endure it with patience? But if when you do what is right and suffer for it you patiently endure it, this finds favor with God. (*1 Pt. 2:20)*

> For it is better, if God should will it so, that **you** [*Christians in the context*] suffer for doing what is right rather than for **doing what is wrong**. (*1 Pt. 3:17*)

The wisdom of the Word and the common sense of the world, when embraced, save us from many foolish outcomes. Wisdom is simply skill at living. Wise people avoid many foolish consequences by means of obedience. God's Word commands me to enjoy the wife of my youth (*Prov. 5:18*). If I apply this wisdom it will save me from alimony payments, divorce attorneys, and sexually transmitted diseases. Common sense agrees with the biblical text – don't cosign for others on a debt (*Prov. 6:1-3*). Get out if you're in and "deliver yourself" from this financial burden. The Bible and our mother's advice match – you'll save yourself from unemployment if you keep your cool when the boss blows up (*Eccl. 10:4*). Unlike reality television, don't "get in a huff" and walk out in a moment of anger. We can save ourselves from looking foolish just by keeping our mouths shut (*Prov. 17:27,28*). But above all, the key to salvation from foolish consequences is found in the tenet which uniquely separates the Bible's wisdom literature from other Eastern wisdom writings:

> **The fear of the Lord** is the beginning of knowledge; Fools despise wisdom and instruction. (*Prov. 1:8*)

Obedience allows us to live up to our spiritual potential. God has provided us with the free gift of eternal life, every spiritual blessing (*Eph. 1:3*), a mandate which has eternal ramifications (*Mt. 28:19,20*), and a standard of holiness. Because we'll give account for how we utilized God's grace and mercy, Paul provides us an important admonishment.

> So then, my beloved, just as you have always, obeyed, not as in my presence only, but now much more in my absence, **work out** (*not "for"*) **your salvation** (*sanctification*) with fear and trembling, for it is God who is at work in you, both to will and to work for His good pleasure. (*Phil. 2:12,13*)

Both Paul and Peter focus on the importance of our behavior and choices as they relate to our positional standing. What are some ways we can "work out our salvation?" – Abstain, cleanse, and be holy.

> Nevertheless, the firm foundation of God stands, having this seal "The Lord knows **those who are His**, (*justification*)" and "Let everyone who names the name of the Lord **abstain from wickedness** (*sanctification*)." Now in a large house there are not only gold and silver vessels, but also vessels of wood and earthenware, and some to honor and some to dishonor. Therefore, if a man **cleanses himself from these things** (*vss. 14-18*), he will be a vessel for honor, sanctified, **useful to the master**, prepared for every good work. (*2 Tim. 2:19-21*)

> Therefore, gird your minds for action, keep sober in spirit, fix your hope completely on the grace to be brought to you at the revelation of Jesus Christ. **As obedient children**, do not be conformed to the former lusts which were yours in our ignorance, but like the Holy One who called you, **be holy yourselves** also in I all your behavior. (*1 Pt. 1:13-15*)

In addition to Peter and Paul, John provides us with a wonderful picture offered by Christ to His disciples. The upper room discourse (*Jn. 13-17*) provided a crucial and important occasion for Christ to invest His perspective, priorities, and values in His disciples. It should be noted Judas had left the group at this point in time (*Jn. 13:30*) which left a room full of believers (*Jn. 13:10,11*). As one studies chapters thirteen to seventeen in the Gospel of John, we see Christ changing topics and audiences—moving from evangelism (*justification*) to discipleship (*sanctification*) with His small group of believing disciples. John shifted his historical snapshots of how to become a Christian to a historical account of how to live the Christian life. In this portion of the historical account, Jesus addresses the call to prove discipleship (*Jn. 13*), the theology of discipleship (*Jn. 14*), the illustration of discipleship (*Jn. 15*), the provision for discipleship (*Jn. 16*), and the prayer for His disciples (*Jn. 17*). Since these men had already believed in Christ for eternal life (*some as early as the wedding at Cana Jn. 2:11*), evangelism and justification weren't the topic, sanctification was.

With this as the context, Christ makes a timeless illustration of what God expects from Christians who choose to be disciples and how the Father and the world interact with them if they fail. There's an expectation from God that believers produce fruit – obey and be faithful. The historical text says this:

> **I am the true vine**, and **My Father is the vinedresser**. Every branch in Me that does not bear fruit, He **takes away**; and every branch that bears fruit, He **prunes** [*only time used in New Testament*] it so that it may bear more fruit. You are **already clean** because of the word which I have spoken to you. **Abide** in Me, and I in you. As the branch cannot bear fruit of itself unless it abides in the vine, so neither can you unless you abide in Me. I am the vine, **you are the branches**; he who abides in Me and I in him, he bears much fruit, for apart from Me you can do nothing. If anyone does not abide in Me, he is **thrown away** as a branch and **dries up**; and **they** gather them, and cast them into the fire and they are burned. If you abide in Me, and My words abide in you, ask whatever you wish, and it will be done for you. My Father is glorified by this, that you bear much fruit, and so **prove to be My disciples.** (*Jn. 15:1-8*)

These words of Christ have the same tender tone and tenor as the song for the vinedresser in Isaiah 5:1-2:

> Let me sing now for my well-beloved. A song of my beloved concerning His vineyard. My well-beloved had a **vineyard** on a fertile hill. He **dug it all around**, **removed** its stones, and **planted** it with the choicest vine. And He **built a tower** in the middle of it and also **hewed out a wine vat** in it; Then He **expected it to produce good grapes**, but it produced only worthless ones. (*Isa 5:1,2*)

God the Father cares greatly for believers and wants them to honor Him by producing fruit. There are four parties involved in Christ's analogy: 1.) Christ is the vine. 2.) His Father is the vinedresser. 3.) Christians [*the disciples in the context*] are the branches. 4.) And lastly, the party of "they" as in "they gather" the branches and throw them into the fire.

The Vinedresser, our Father, shows divine care by assisting the branches, believers, in producing fruit. God's loving care assists spiritual growth through "pruning" (*cleaning*)—the removal of that which hinders growth and maturity (*Jms. 1:2-4*). In addition, if a branch didn't produce fruit, it was "taken away" (*airo*) from the ground. As long as the branches were on the ground, they were unable to produce edible grapes; the grapes would be hard and knotty if left on the dirt. There needed to be distance between the plant and the soil so the vinedresser would "lift up" the branches from the ground. The term "taken away" literally means "lifted up" and is used with this understanding in mind in John 5:12 (*"take up your bed and walk"*) and Matthew 24:38,39:

> For as in those days before the flood they were eating and drinking, marrying and giving in marriage, until the day that Noah entered the ark, and they did not understand until **the flood** came and **took them all away** [*lifted them up from the ground*]; so will the coming of the Son of Man be. (*Mt. 24:38,39*)

To understand this as a Christian who is disobedient and unfruitful and is subsequently taken away to hell is unwarranted and unreasonable. The context doesn't support this neither does the fact of eternal security. Christ understands His disciples had eternal life and were justified by claiming, with Judas absent, "you are already clean" (*Jn. 13:10,11*). The command to "abide" (*obey – Jn. 15:10*) indicates it's possible for a believer *not* to abide. Christians can (*and do*) choose to live fruitless lives of disobedience.

Branches which don't produce fruit are useless. Those believers who do "not abide in Me [*Christ*]" are pictured as useless (*not "worthless"*)

Christians. When a Christian's faith is void of good works, it's like a branch without fruit. Fruitlessness on our part causes the world *("they" not God the vinedresser or Christ the vine)* to miss out and fail to see the connection between the non-abiding (*disobedient*) believer and Christ. It appears God uses Christians as a source of spiritual truth for the world. This is a concept seen more than once in the biblical text.

> You are the salt of the earth; but if the salt has become tasteless, how can it be made salty again? It is no longer good for anything, except to be thrown out and **trampled under foot by men** [*useless*]. You are the light of the **world**. A city set on a hill cannot be hidden; nor does anyone light a lamp and put it under a basket, but on the lampstand, and it gives light to all who are in the house. Let your light shine **before men** in such a way that **they may see your good works**, and glorify your Father who is in heaven. (*Mt. 5:13-16*)

> By this **all men** will know that you are My disciples, if you have love for one another. (*Jn. 13:35*)

> And all those who had believed were together and had all things in common; and they began selling their property and possessions and were sharing them with all, as anyone might have need. Day by day continuing with one mind in the temple, and breaking bread from house to house, they were taking their meals together with gladness and sincerity of heart, praising God and **having favor with all the people**. And the Lord was adding to their number day by day those who were being saved. (*Acts 2:44-47*)

> You also became imitators of us and of the Lord, having received the word in much tribulation with the joy of the Holy Spirit, so that you became an example to all the believers in Macedonia and in Achaia. For the word of the Lord has sounded forth from you, not only in Macedonia and Achaia, but **also in every place** your faith toward God

> has gone forth, so that we have no need to say anything. (*1 Ths. 1:6-8*)

The world looks at our conduct. We're the only salt, light (*Mt. 5:13-16*) or chance they have at accessing special revelation. If the world struggles to see Christ in us as Christians, we become useless to them as Christ's ambassadors (*2 Cor. 5:20*). A spiritually dead world that's looking for answers has no use for fruitlessness – dried barren branches. Faithless, irrelevant believers get tossed aside into the fire. The analogy of the fruitful vine offers us a vivid picture of progressive sanctification. As we've seen previously, fruit (*obedience*) proves discipleship not justification.

Obedience allows us to avoid hindered prayer. When there's tension in a marriage, communication suffers. A normal and healthy relationship which freely exchanges ideas is based upon trust and respect. Friends talk. Add offense and this won't happen. Families talk. Add offense and this will come to an end. The same is true of our fellowship with God. In the following passages we can see disobedience has a negative impact on our prayer life (*communication*):

> If I regard wickedness in my heart, the Lord **will not hear**. (*Psm. 66:18*)

> The Lord is **far from the wicked**, but He hears the prayer of the righteous. (*Prov. 15:29*)

> You husbands likewise live with your wives in an understanding way, as with a weaker vessel, since she is a woman; and grant her honor as a fellow heir of the grace of life, so that **your prayers may not be hindered.** (*1 Pt. 3:7*)

Keeping in contact with police peers on the job was a great way to make it home alive at the end of the shift. But there would be times a police radio battery would go dead. If that happened, no one could hear you and you couldn't hear anyone else. To say the least, this makes it difficult to "holler for help" or to help others if trouble breaks out.

This was not a good place to be in. Cutting off communication never was and never is a good thing.

I don't know many important people in this world, but I'm friends with and have immediate access to the Ancient of Days. What advantage is there for me, or any of us, to impede or interfere with our communication with our heavenly Father? None.

Obedience allows us to gain eternal rewards. Who goes to work for free? I don't. In the labor arena, work that's done is work that's to be paid for (*Jms. 5:4*). This isn't rocket science and it certainly isn't unreasonable. Paul seemed like a good union guy; he saw the value in workers and used the term "fellow worker" (*sunergos*) twelve times in his writings. He wrote:

> For the Scripture says, "You shall not muzzle the ox while he is threshing," and "The **laborer** is worthy of his wages." (*1 Tim. 5:18*)

The concept of Yahweh paying us for our efforts is found in Hebrew wisdom literature and is one of the last issues Christ communicates to His bride.

> If you say, "See, we did not know this," Does He not consider it who weighs the hearts? And does He not know it who keeps your soul? And will He not **render to man according to his work**? (*Prov. 24:12*)

> Behold, I am coming quickly, and My reward is with Me, to render to every man according to **what he has done.** (*Rev. 22:12*)

The issue of compensation from Christ is extremely important as it relates to a believer's sanctification and usefulness to the Master. We'll be looking more at eternal rewards in section three.

CHAPTER 17

Ask the Question

The Bible is clear that a believer's eternal destiny is secure. **<u>Nothing</u>** can separate us. **<u>No one</u>** can snatch us. **<u>Never</u>** will He desert or forsake us. Assurance is confidence in this biblical fact. We've looked at the biblical text and have discovered that it's possible to fail in the Christian life.

- It's a biblical fact believers, based upon their actions, can look like "mere men."
- It's a Scriptural reality false non-Christian prophets look just like born-again sheep. We can't determine who has eternal life based upon conduct or works because externals are deceptive and besides, if works have nothing to do with justification, why should we look for them to determine one's eternal destiny.
- External evaluation for eternal life in the lives of others doesn't appear to be our job. Engaging in this conduct can cause damage (*Mt. 13:24-30*).
- Once we open the box of applying subjective fruit inspection standards in the pursuit of assurance, a litany of unanswerable questions begins to surface.
- The idea that disciples and Christians are two different things was demonstrated by Christ's own followers.
- We've seen the unseen through the lens of the biblical text – positional, spiritual changes which take place in a person's life once they trust in Christ for eternal life.
- Just because good works are useless in justification doesn't mean they're not vital for sanctification and an effective Christian life. There are numerous reasons why believers should engage in good works.

Since the faithfulness of Christ is the basis for our security, we should look to Him for assurance.

Challenge: Then how can we know if a person a Christian? Might I suggest asking them the following question: **In your opinion, how does a person get to heaven?** The answer to that simple yet powerful query can be a reliable indicator to let us know if a person has eternal life or not. "Well, they could lie about the answer!" Yes the "straw man" could be untruthful, but why? Unless they have a gun to their head, how would a deceptive answer to this question benefit anyone? Those who are relying upon works should have no shame in stating their position. In fact, an answer that good works are required to get to heaven is, in and of itself, a good work. Let's think the best of everybody and assume they're telling the truth. If they're not, that's an issue they'll have to deal with in front of their Maker at the Great White Throne Judgment (*Rev. 20:11-15*).

Years after I had finished my graduate work at Western Conservative Baptist Seminary, I took an evangelism class at another seminary. One thing I found odd about this class was the instructor didn't require anyone to share their faith. It was like taking a cooking class and not being required to bake anything. All students had to do was pray someone would trust in Christ. Heaven forbid we do the actual "work" of evangelism.

During one class the professor, who had been active in the mission field for years, expressed he had great concerns about his sister-in-law. Based upon the way she had lived her life, if he hypothetically had found himself at her deathbed, he wasn't certain he would have confidence she would go to heaven. He was truly worried about her and his own uncertainty about her eternal destiny was palpable. I raised my hand and simply said, "Why don't you just ask her, if at a point in time, she trusted in Jesus Christ for eternal life?" The class fell silent and there was no response. There was no response because the teacher had allowed no room for failure in the spiritual dimension of her life. There was no response because the rhetoric of expected works and a visibly changed life had sucked all the oxygen and grace out of the air. There was no response because his non-biblical theology left him without an answer. And they charged tuition for this class. I wonder if it's too late for me to get my money back. Hopefully you're not feeling the same way about this book!

Another challenge: How can I have confidence in the fact I'm going to heaven? Ask the following question: **Am I trusting in Christ right now for eternal life?** As a Christian, if the answer is "No" you'll lack assurance but you'll still be eternally secure. If the answer is "Yes" you'll have assurance and you'll still be eternally secure. I've said this before and I'll say it again—this is not rocket science. Look to Christ for assurance.

At this point, I'm hopeful this material has been beneficial at best, thought provoking in the least. So far we've dealt with issues of evangelism and principles of assurance. Biblically based spiritual multiplication and God's "safety net" can propel us down a path of purpose and perspective. We now know what's biblically required to obtain eternal life and how to communicate this good news in a manner that's consistent with the Bible. We know our eternal destiny is secure and regardless of our faithlessness, Christ, because of His character and commitment, has to remain faithful to us. Because God can't lie, He can't break His word.

In our moment in time, it's important for us to understand why to walk down the difficult path of discipleship. Paul looked at his Christian life as a race to be won and a fight to be fought. Why did he put so much effort into it? And here I thought we could just let go and let God. That sure doesn't sound like Paul. Let's discover what the biblical text teaches about eternal rewards, Christian accountability, and biblical motives for obedience.

Section 3: Issues of Rewards

Why Work Hard In The Christian life?

CHAPTER 18

Context & Rewards

In addressing the issue of eternal rewards, context is crucial. Paul admonished Timothy to handle the biblical text with accuracy (*2 Tim. 1:13,14, 2:2*), which implies respect and reverence. God chose to communicate with mankind by means of the written word using a known language (*in the Hebrew Scriptures, Aramaic and Hebrew, in the New Testament Koine Greek*). As with a newspaper, a term paper, a love letter, a recipe, or a police policy manual, utilizing context is how we understand the literal meaning in an author's work product. Even figures of speech and analogies convey a singular literal meaning. Unless the writer tells us, we can't determine the author's intent. We need to focus on what the author was trying to convey to us – the meaning. The audience, the culture, the theological framework, and the use of words in relation to one another are just some of the usual "clues" that all of us use to communicate in everyday life. Context is king. There's nothing tricky, difficult, or unusual about taking words in their context to determine the meaning. We do it all the time. For example, the word "pass." This is a simple four letter word which carries multiple meanings depending on the context. In one context it's a verb, in another context the same word is a noun. Once we hear the context, we can obtain a reasonable understanding of what it means by how it's used.

- "Pass" the salt means to give me a container with sodium in it.
- He made a "pass" at the girl means he was proactively flirtatious.
- This won't "pass" the headline test means the conduct is socially unacceptable.

- Cut them off at the "pass" means to stop them at a small opening in a mountain range.
- I need a hall "pass" means I need written permission to be move about in school.
- When offered another donut, he said "pass" meaning "no."
- She was able to "pass" the test meaning she was successful in an examination.
- The governor wanted to "pass" legislation meaning she wanted a new law approved.
- A good quarterback is able to "pass" a football meaning he can throw well.
- Too much alcohol will cause you to "pass" out meaning lose consciousness.

Who would have thought one simple word can have so many meanings? Each meaning is clearly determined by the grammatical context. None of this is unusual to us. In fact, we're able to handle the task of context to acquire meaning quite readily. If we can do it with our own language, we can do it with the language of the biblical text. If we're honest with the biblical text and let it speak for itself, the literal meaning being conveyed by the author can be obtained without any tricks or disingenuousness. There's no reason why our theology should be imposed on the biblical text any more than a square peg should be banged into a round hole. We need to do our best to leave the biblical text alone and let it speak for itself by means of context. When we do this, I believe we'll begin to see the issue of eternal rewards as a topic of routine discussion by the authors of the Bible. We'll begin to see the clear distinction between the free gift of eternal life and the earned wages of eternal rewards. Justification and sanctification will become distinctly complimentary to one another without conflict or contradiction. In just a few paragraphs we've been exposed to the art and science of biblical interpretation. Let's take it for a test drive and see where we get with it.

CHAPTER 19

Wages for Work

Law enforcement personnel have a unique relationship with the community. They're given a variety of privileges and tools. Young men and women, many of them in their mid or late twenties, are given guns, badges, cars, dogs, rifles, shotguns, computers, radios, Tasers, shields, batons, chemical spray, helicopters, airplanes, motorcycles, battering rams, armored cars, undercover funds and access to myriads of amounts of data. Public safety personnel are entrusted to use these tools to accomplish the vital task of enforcing the law. The community gives them power and expects them to use it properly. State law gives officers the discretionary ability to utilize deadly force, apply non-lethal force, pursue, search, interrogate, accuse, and detain. Because those hired to do police work come from the imperfect pool of humanity, the potential for both good and bad is linked to every badge.

I had the privilege of developing and teaching a career survival class to hundreds and hundreds of young new Phoenix Police Officers over the years. My favorite part of the class was asking a philosophical question: What makes something right and what makes something wrong? The question was designed to get a glimpse at the personal convictions and motivations in our officers' lives. These young employees knew what to do but did they know why they were doing it? Surely law enforcement officers grasp the moral foundation of the work they're entrusted with.

Frequently, "society" was the answer given in response to my question, "What makes something right or wrong?" I challenged this response by sharing that back in 1942 a German father and mother and the society they lived in were comfortable teaching their children the best Jew was a dead Jew. But yet judges at Nuremburg said this was wrong and people were hung. Maybe society isn't a good (*or safe*) gauge for morality. Sometimes the reply to the question would be "the law." But around one hundred years ago the law said women couldn't vote. Maybe right and wrong (*as well as a successful dating strategy for men*) aren't sourced in legislation. Another answer offered was "the court." Yet those in black robes said it was OK to own a black man. It must have been easy for a white Supreme Court Justice of the United States to rule against Dred Scott. In teaching this class I was always hoping someone would provide the answer I was looking for: "If it's consistent with the character of God it's right, if it's inconsistent with the character of God it's wrong." I never got what I was looking for.

Certainly a moral compass and conviction are crucial ingredients which move many men and women towards the thin blue line, but let's be honest, it's money that actually puts them on it. In the real non-Christian world, a moral compass without cash is like a Corvette without gas. Whether it's police work or a date on Saturday night, both a compass and a Corvette can inspire, but without funds and fuel, neither will get you far on the streets of Phoenix. "OK. I'm willing to risk my life. How much are you going to pay me for it?" That's a fair question. The dominating motivator which prompts many police officers to walk point and stand in the gap is a paycheck. Nobody does this work for free. Nobody should. A consistent income with merit steps, career enhancement money, sick leave conversion, longevity pay, a deferred compensation program, overtime, premium pay, vacation buyout, and a twenty year pension system pull numerous men and women out of a safe home and onto a dangerous street. Being able to take care of one's family pushes many to put up with the abuse, pressure, stress, risk, and discomfort the job generates. As I write these words, I was just informed a Phoenix Police Officer was shot at midnight responding to a trespassing call – he was shot in the leg and in the stomach through his ballistic vest. How he started his shift wasn't how he finished it. No one becomes a cop to get rich. But secure and consistent payment, protective contracts, and a reasonable pension sure help in getting officers to the precinct on time. A twenty year career of running to gunfights should be worth a unique and attractive wage and benefit package. A willingness to take risks for taxpayers warrants fair compensation. Reward is a major motivator for law enforcement personnel. That's life. Personal gain is not unreasonable and self-care is not selfish.

Getting an officer to work requires a fair wage – money is the answer to "Why should I go to work?" But once an officer is there, another question comes up. "How should I do the work?" That's where accountability comes in. Accountability prompts officers to work well. For rank and file officers and detectives, accountability and consequence are a way of life. Officers are held to high standards and they pay a price for missing the mark. Those who enforce the law should not be above the law. Accountability and high standards protectively minimize and filter out police abuse from reaching the public. Are police officers really accountable?

- A Phoenix Police Homicide Detective is in prison for child pornography on his home computer.
- A Phoenix Police Officer is in prison for "shaking down" a drug dealer for cash.
- A Phoenix Police Officer plead guilty for sexual misconduct with a 14 year old boy.
- A Phoenix Police Detective is an ex-convict for personally profiting from the release of stolen vehicles which belonged to insurance companies.
- A Phoenix Police Officer who pointed his gun at a detained juvenile to make a point lost his AZPOST (*Arizona Peace Officers Standards and Training*) certification—the certifying board made a point right back at him.
- Officers have been terminated for lying about the type of shoe polish they used.
- They've lost their jobs for being untruthful as to where they got a haircut.
- An officer in southern Arizona lost his certification for truthfully reporting that he took a small amount of cash he found in the middle of the road at an accident scene he had investigated ten years in the past.

Consequences for cops come in the form of suspensions, terminations, decertifications and prison. Gain and loss are at both ends of the motivation spectrum in police work. Lesson—with a great job comes great accountability.

Christians have a unique relationship with the Creator. They are given every spiritual blessing (*Eph. 1:3*) and entrusted with the incredible task (*Mt. 28:19,20*) of spiritually multiplying themselves. In an ancient universe, God has given believers a moment in time to impact the eternal. God's grace solved a humanly insurmountable problem. Jesus came down, went in, and stood up to pay for the sins of world and to freely provide eternal life. Faith alone in Christ alone for eternal life secures one's eternal destiny. It was only God's grace and love which prompted this free gift of eternal life. The key word is free. God asks nothing from us nor is anything we do acceptable or sufficient. At great cost to the Father a free gift was given to those with childlike faith. According to the Bible, eternal life comes with no expectations or requirements. And the free gift can't be lost. **Nothing**, **no one**, and **never** are the terms used to describe eternal life as eternally secure. A package like this is referred to in police labor circles as a "smokin' deal." Take it and run!

Since eternal life is free, and the gift is secure, why not just "live like hell," "eat drink and be merry" because, as Billy Joel said, "Only the good die young." Life is hard and then you die. It's obvious there's room for failure. Knowing God forgives, why not relax? What motivates me to obey? Why work hard at the Christian life? Sex is great, money is fun, and power is exhilarating. In contrast, carrying a cross doesn't look all that attractive. It didn't seem to work out too well for Paul. His life, in light of the physical, social, legal, and leadership abuse he went through, could be described as a nightmare. To say Jesus had it any better couldn't be further from the truth. The historical evidence doesn't link wealth, health and happiness with Jesus or His followers. And where were all His political solutions against an oppressive Roman empire? Maybe that's why so many rejected and deserted Christ. John, the Messiah's closest friend and confidant, died an old man—alone on an island in the middle of nowhere. Peter spoke of suffering for Christ. James let us know trials are guaranteed. The writer of Hebrews shared more possible outcomes as a result of faithfulness in the Christian life.

> Women received back their dead by resurrection; and others were **tortured**, not accepting their release, so that they might obtain a better resurrection; and others experienced **mockings** and **scourgings**, yes, also **chains** and **imprisonment**. They were **stoned**, they were **sawn in two**, they were **tempted**, they were **put to death** with the sword; they went about in **sheepskins**, in **goatskins**, being **destitute**, **afflicted**, **ill-treated** (men of whom the world was not worthy), **wandering in deserts** and **mountains** and **caves** and **holes in the ground.** (*Heb. 11:35-38*)

So what's the bad news? Wouldn't it be better to focus on the fun and the physical of the short-term since the long-term is locked in? If life is like a dot on a line, and the line of eternal life isn't going anywhere, why not avoid the burden of the dot? Why not live for the pleasure of the moment since the eternal is secure? Seeing that becoming a Christian is easy, why not steer clear of the difficulties of discipleship? What could possibly fuel and compel us to carry a cross?

Answer: The Bible assures and encourages believers that our faithfulness will be rewarded by Christ. In addition to eternal rewards, God's Word teaches with great grace comes great accountability.

Believers and police officers have multiple things in common. Both are legitimately motivated to do vital work for compensation (*wages or rewards*). Both are held accountable to high standards. The consequence for inappropriate conduct for both cops and Christians is loss; the loss of pay for officers, the loss of reward for Christians. But there's one remarkable difference between the two; while police officers forfeit their professional standing for serious flaws, Christians can **never** lose their positional standing for any failure. We can't be "fired" for our flaws and failures as believers. Labor calls this job protection, theologians call this eternal security.

To be precise, life is more like a dot on a ray. A line goes in two directions for eternity, a ray goes in one. The ray originates from one dot with an infinite amount of dots following in a straight line one after another. In a life analogy, one dot is worth about 70 years. What we do with the person of Jesus Christ on that first dot (*current life*) will determine where we spend the rest of the dots on the infinite ray. According to the Bible, what we do with God's gracious gift (*eternal life*) on that first dot of the ray impacts the direction of the ray (*eternal destiny*). If we choose to exercise faith alone in Christ alone for eternal life, our eternal destiny (*the ray*) in the presence of Lord is infinitely secure. But what we do with eternal life has eternal ramifications. Our faithfulness as believers during the dot determines the quality of the ray (*eternal significance*), the reward we'll receive from the Messiah, and the role we'll play in the Millennial Kingdom.

Just as there are a variety of tools, privileges and assignments in the Phoenix Police Department, there are multiple issues concerning eternal rewards in the text of Scripture. Eternal rewards can be found in both the Hebrew Scripture and the New Testament. In the upcoming pages we'll continue to discuss and briefly touch upon a medley of aspects concerning eternal rewards. It's not meant to be comprehensive but to provide a biblical framework and foundation for understanding and appreciating the compensation Christ has for us.

CHAPTER 20

The Christian and Sin

Sin is missing God's required standard or mark of perfection. The cost of sin is death. Christ's death paid for the spiritual death penalty attached to sin. In dealing with the sphere of justification, Christ's death allowed God to graciously provide eternal life to all who believe. Those who exercise faith alone in Christ alone for eternal life have their eternal destiny in the presence of the Lord secured. How did God respond to Christ's payment for our sin?

> **He** who was delivered over because of our transgressions, and **was raised because** [*not "for"*] **of our justification.** (*Rom. 4:25*)
>
> When **you were dead** in your transgressions and the uncircumcision of your flesh, He [*God*] made you alive together with Him [*Christ*], **having forgiven** [*literally "after giving grace"*] **us all our transgressions** having cancelled out the certificate of debt consisting of decrees against us, which was hostile to us; and He has **taken it out of the way**, having nailed it to the cross. (*Col. 2:13,14*)
>
> ...and He [*Christ*] Himself **is the propitiation** for our sins; and not for ours only, but also for those of the whole world. (*1 Jn. 2:2*)

Paul told us God has forgiven (*karidzomai*) us "all our transgressions." John taught Christ "is" the payment for our sins and the sins of the world. It appears the payment for the penalty of sin is a "done deal." If sin has been paid for, then why am I evaluated by Christ? If Jesus paid for the sins of the world, why am I, as a believer, held accountable for missing the mark? Why does John tell us to confess our sin when sin was dealt with on the cross?

> If we **<u>confess our sins</u>**, He is faithful and righteous to forgive us our sins and to cleanse us from all unrighteousness. (*1 Jn. 1:9*)

From a **<u>forensic</u>** (*legal*) perspective, the cost or consequence of imperfection (*sin*) is spiritual death (*separation from God*). Jesus, a perfect person who is also eternal, is the only one capable of paying for the sins of the world (*Rom. 5:12-21*) and the only one able to provide eternal life (*Jn. 14:6, Acts 4:12, 1 Cor. 15:22*). Christ's death paid that judicial penalty of sin (*1 Cor. 15:3, 54-57*). The penalty for all sinful conduct has been dealt with. Justification is the forensic aspect of salvation which focuses on God as our judge. In His court, God the Father has recognized and accepted His Son's payment for the sins of the world (*2 Cor. 5:15-19, 1 Jn. 2:2*). Because of Christ's payment, the only thing people lack is eternal life (*Rev. 20:12-15*).

I've spent my fair share of time in court. Trust me when I say court judgments only have an impact on the living. A declarative court action, from conviction to acquittal, has no bearing on a dead person. For God's acceptance of Christ's payment to be effective, a person who is spiritually dead (*Rom. 5:17a, 1 Cor. 15:22a—in Adam*) needs eternal life (*Rom. 5:17b, 1 Cor. 15:22b—in Christ*). Consequences or benefits can only impact the living. I can put a dollar in my dead grandmother's bank account and it won't do her any good. The dollar is real and has value but it can't benefit her because she's dead. She needs to be alive to benefit from the dollar I've given her. Only a born-again person can benefit from the cancelled "certificate of debt" provided by God (*Col. 2:13,14*). A person who refuses to believe in Christ for eternal life receives no eternal benefit from the payment which has been provided on his/her behalf (*Jn. 5:24,40, 8:21,24*). To reject the free gift of eternal life (*Acts 4:11,12*) is to choose eternal separation (*death*) from God (*Rev. 20:11-15, 21:27*). This is why people go to hell. Failing to believe in Christ, the giver of eternal life, as one's only hope of heaven, is to choose eternal death (*Jn. 3:36, 8:21,24, 2 Ths. 1:8-10*). A spiritually dead person who rejects eternal life (*Christ—1 Jn. 1:1,2, 5:20*) will be granted his/her request: spiritual death "in Adam" (*Rom. 5:17a, 1 Cor. 15:22b*) will become eternal death in hell (*Mt. 25:41, Jude 4,7,13*). Forensically, it appears Christ's gracious payment for the world's sin is real and available to all but God's acceptance of this payment spiritually impacts and benefits only those who are in Christ – those who have received the free gift of eternal life (*Rom. 5:12-21*). An alternative biblical view of Christ's propitiation which warrants consideration but differs from what is presented here is His payment for the world's sin is only "potential" in nature and does *not* become "actual" until a person trusts in Christ for eternal life.

From a **familial** perspective, God deals with our personal sin as our Father. Even though Christ's death makes both relationship and fellowship possible (*1 Jn. 1:7*), the removal of the judicial penalty (*spiritual death*) from Christ's payment does not remove the natural and/or familial consequences of sin in the life of a believer. Acquittal as seen in Colossians 2:13,14 (*justification principle*) is a forensic matter. Forgiveness as seen in 1 John 1:9 (*sanctification principle*) is a familial matter.

- Eternal life by faith brings the believer the benefit of a crucial singular act of justification (*Gal. 3:21-24*). Some of the ingredients, aspects, and components of justification are:

    - Forensic acquittal
    - Established by faith in Christ
    - Saves believers from the penalty of sin
    - One time past event
    - Establishes the believer's position
    - God is our Father
    - Relationship is the issue

- Eternal life with faithfulness (*"walk in the light" – 1 Jn. 1:7*) and confession (*1 Jn. 1:9*) brings the believer the benefit of ongoing forgiveness. Some of the ingredients, aspects, and components of sanctification are:

- o Familial forgiveness
- o Maintained by the believer's faithfulness
- o Saves believers from the power of sin
- o Continuous present event
- o Based upon the believer's practice
- o God is our Friend
- o Fellowship is the issue

Please allow an illustration which helps with a general point. OJ Simpson was acquitted in a criminal court of law for alleged lawlessness. Though forensically "not guilty," he was subsequently found responsible for the same conduct in a civil court of law. One action in two venues (*criminal/civil*) can have different outcomes. One sinful act from two perspectives (*forensic/familial*) can have different results. Forensically, my relationship with God was established (*Jn. 1:12*) and Jesus' payment for my sin became effective for me when I trusted in Christ for eternal life. From a familial perspective, my fellowship with God will continue as long as I obey Him and confess my personal sin which has already been judicially acquitted (*1 Jn. 1:9-2:1*).

It's certainly true that confessing personal sin restores fellowship with the Father. But let's not kid ourselves into thinking we can take advantage of God's faithfulness and righteousness. One would be hard-pressed to find in the biblical text where familial forgiveness eliminates the consequences of sin. Paul seemed to verify this in Galatians 6:7:

> Do not be deceived, **<u>God is not mocked</u>**; for whatever a man sows, this he will also reap. (*Gal. 6:7*)

Sadly, a man after God's own heart had to learn this lesson the hard way. It appears when God forgives us of our personal sin, He chooses not to bring the issue up anymore (*I don't think it's possible for God to forget anything*). "However" (*the same word Nathan used in bringing bittersweet news to King David*), God's forgiveness of our personal sin does *not* eliminate subsequent consequences.

> Then David said to Nathan, "I have sinned against the Lord." And Nathan said to David, "**<u>The Lord also has</u>**

> **taken away your sin**; you shall not die. **However**, because by this deed you have given occasion to the enemies of the Lord to blaspheme, **the child also that is born to you shall surely die**." (*2 Sam. 12:13,14*)

From eternity past, God saw I would become impatient with my children on a specific date in 2011. Over 2000 years ago, Christ paid the penalty for that sin (*Rom. 5:8*). We know God the Father accepted that payment because Christ rose from the dead (*Rom. 4:25*). In 1962 I was born spiritually dead in Adam (*Psm. 51:5, Rom. 5:17a, 1 Cor. 15:22a*). By 1968 I had freely chosen to engage in sinful conduct my mother didn't even have to teach me. Christ also paid for those sins 2000 years prior, but I was unable to benefit from that payment – dead people who lack eternal life in Christ miss out on a lot. Credit counts for nothing if you're dead. In the same year, as a six year old boy, I trusted in Christ to provide me the eternal life I was missing. I was regenerated in Christ (*born-again*) and moved from spiritual death to eternal life (*Jn. 5:24*). I was saved from the penalty of sin—the problem of spiritual death was eternally solved. Now that I was born-again (*spiritually alive*), His payment was credited to me (*Col. 2:14*). It was at that point that Christ's forensic payment benefitted me; I was declared righteous by God. Forty-two years later I'm at a specific date in 2011. I become impatient with my children – I sin (*Eph. 6:4*). The Spirit illumines the biblical text in my mind (*Eph. 1:18, 1 Cor. 2:9-13*) and subsequently God's Word convicts me (*Heb. 4:12,13*) of that sin. I recognize I missed His mark. I apologize to my children (*Jms. 5:16*). As family members, I offended them and did them wrong. But there's still one more family member involved. God my Father has been offended. Forensically, He's satisfied and I'm justified. My relationship with Him as my Father is secure – I've been declared righteous. From a familial perspective, I need to make it right. Even though my relationship is secure, this current personal sin has hampered my fellowship with God. I want my Father to remain my Friend. I need to be sanctified (*Rom. 6:19, 7:24,25, 1 Ths. 4:3*) – saved from the power of sin. I confess my impatience to God. He assures me in the biblical text that if I confess, He will forgive me of all my sin. I then move on. When I sin again, I need to confess again from a familial (*sanctification*) *not* a forensic (*justification*) aspect. I need to apologize to all offended parties (*Mt.*

5:23,24) and confess to my Father so as to be restored to Him again as His Friend (*Jn. 15:13-15*).

The Phoenix Police Department has rules and policies in a full size notebook which is four inches thick and ten pounds heavy. Out of the thousands of polices, my favorite was the "open mind" policy. In this policy, investigators are encouraged to keep an open mind a suspect did *not* commit the crime. Having been a defender of police officers, a policy that concurs with the law of the land (*innocent until proven guilty*) is a good policy. Open minds often have the ability to take various pieces of evidence and information, formulate "if and how" these pieces relate, and then put together a prosecutorial package that's consistent and coherent. A reasonable mindset is behind every fair and successful criminal case. Hopefully in this chapter we've seen several rules apply to both criminal investigations and theology: Use the easy to understand the complex, use clear statements to understand unclear ones, be mindful of context, and the simplest explanation is most likely the best one. An understanding of the distinction between justification and sanctification and of the difference between becoming a Christian and being a disciple can provide a complete, consistent, and coherent perspective of the Bible. When we allow the biblical text to speak, when we lay down the rhetoric, when we realize the role of grace and works and understand that failure, success, and accountability are realities in the Christian life, we'll be able to effectively and confidently use our platforms as dynamic spiritual multipliers and encouragers.

CHAPTER 21

The Christian and Accountability

Every three years Phoenix Police Officers have to provide a sample of urine to test for drugs. A urine analysis holds law enforcement accountable. Every year police personnel in Phoenix are evaluated for their performance by means of a Performance Management Guide (*PMG*). The ability to do the job, do it well, and do it consistently, as well as exceptional performance is related to pay steps and longevity benefits. Every year all sworn Department employees have to qualify with their primary (*and secondary if they have one*) weapons to maintain their AZPOST certification. If they fail three times on the range, there's the possibility they'll be removed from the street or their current enforcement assignment until the officer completes a refresher course and ultimately passes. Every month Special Assignment Unit (*SAU – our version of SWAT*) officers have to pass a physical fitness course. The rigorous physical fitness demands of their tactical job lends to their success of safely completing dangerous assignments. Just because a man or woman successfully completes the three month Phoenix Regional Police Academy, the three month Officer in Training (OIT) program, and then makes it off probation with one year under his/her belt doesn't mean expectations, standards, or performance are things of the past. Just because there is initial acceptance and a person moves from an unsworn to a sworn capacity in the City of Phoenix, this move doesn't remove the need for continued improvement and correction. Accountability is a fact of life that keeps us sharp, keeps us honest, and keeps us moving. If cops are held accountable, why not Christians?

Eternal security doesn't relieve believers from accountability. Eternal security doesn't guarantee Christians eternal significance. There are numerous verses in the Bible which touch upon reward and responsibility. Let me share with you what I feel are three key passages on eternal rewards and Christ's evaluation of Christians. In these passages, and in others, we'll see where there's great grace there's great accountability.

In the first passage, Paul spoke of his role in the Corinthian church as it related to Apollos. Both men were committed to the health of the Body. Both men had important roles and functions in partnership with God who caused spiritual growth. Both men were accountable and would be compensated by Christ for their work. Paul was certain each of them would receive a "reward according to their own labor" (*1 Cor. 3:8*). The term "reward" (*misthos*) means a payment for work or compensation for labor. It's an earned benefit or privilege. It should be noted, the antonym of a reward is a gift – like eternal life (*Eph. 2:8,9*). The term "reward" is used 29 times in the New Testament – 11 of the uses recorded in the Gospels were by Christ. It appears Paul wanted to impart to his audience that if he and Apollos were going to be held accountable and paid for their efforts, all believers could expect the same. He wrote:

> According to the grace of God which was given to me, like a wise master builder I laid a foundation, and another is building on it. But each man must **be careful** how he builds on it. For no man can lay a foundation other than the one which is laid, which is Jesus Christ. Now if any man builds on the foundation with gold, silver, precious stones, wood, hay, straw, **each man's work** will become evident; for the day will show it because it is to be revealed with **fire**, and the **fire** itself will test the quality of each man's work. If any man's work which he has built on it remains, **he will receive a reward**. If any man's work is burned up, **he will suffer loss**; but **he himself will be saved, yet so as through fire.** (*1 Cor. 3:11-15*)

Paul encouraged Christians to exercise caution ("*be careful*") in how they lived their lives. As believers, their Christian life and conduct ("*work*"), like his, was going to be severely tested. No believer was immune ("*each man*"). The value of a believer's work would be compensated accordingly. The "fire" in the context was in no way linked to eternal damnation. It seems Paul was using a picture of a process in which precious metals were refined and tested to acquire the best of the metal. The point of the picture – our works will be tested in a similar fashion. What affirms this disconnect between "fire" and hell is Paul's clarification, "but he himself shall be saved, yet so as through fire" (*vs. 15b*). For a Christian to produce nothing (*faithlessness*) of value with Christ's free gift of eternal life will cause him or her to "suffer loss." The loss is the loss of a reward not eternal life.

Paul lived his life with great courage but he was very much aware he too could suffer the loss of eternal rewards. This loss of rewards was a motivator (*2 Cor. 5:11, 7:1*). The man who taught that nothing could separate a believer from eternal life ("*the love of God*") also knew a believer, himself included, could be separated from eternal rewards. In the same letter to the Corinthian church he wrote:

> Do you not know that those who run in a race all run, but only one receives the prize? Run in such a way that you may win. Everyone who competes in the games exercises self-control in all things. They then do it to receive a perishable wreath, but we an imperishable. Therefore I run in such a way, as not without aim; I box in such a way, as not beating the air; but I discipline my body and make it my slave, so that, after I have preached to others, I myself will not **be disqualified.** (*1 Cor. 9:24-27*)

In the context of Corinthians and all of Paul's theology, disqualification is not the loss of eternal life but the loss of eternal reward. The apostle John, who couldn't have been clearer about receiving the free gift of eternal life by faith in Christ, also saw the reality of rewards and the potential of losing them by means of faithlessness.

> Watch yourselves, that you **do not lose** what we have accomplished, but that you may receive **a full reward.** (*2 Jn. 1:8*)

Peter was consistent with his apostolic peers in his concern about Christians being held accountable for their conduct by means of rewards or discipline.

> Therefore, prepare your minds for action, keep sober in spirit, fix your hope completely on the grace to be brought to you at the revelation of Jesus Christ. As obedient children, do not be conformed to the former lusts which were yours in your ignorance, but like the Holy One who called you, be holy yourselves also in all your behavior; because it is written, "You shall be holy, for I am holy." If you address as Father the One who **impartially judges according to each one's work**, conduct yourselves in fear during the time of your stay on earth; knowing that you were not redeemed with perishable things like silver or gold from your futile way of life inherited from your forefathers, but with precious blood, as of a lamb unblemished and spotless, the blood of Christ. (*1 Pt. 1:13-19*)

Peter, like Paul, spoke to those who were "born again" (*1 Pt. 1:3,23*) about fear in the Christian life. This fear was related to the discipline from God they would experience for faithless (*unholy*) living. In the last book of the New Testament, John records Christ's thoughts on the loss of rewards (*not "eternal life"*) as it relates to believers who respond poorly to persecution. Christ got the last word in about the reality of losing rewards:

> "I am coming quickly; hold fast what you have, so that no one will **take your crown.**" (*Rev. 3:11*)

The second passage in which Paul reveals impending accountability for all believers is in another letter to the church at Corinth. In 2 Corinthians 5:9,10 he writes:

> Therefore we also have as our ambition, whether at home or absent, to be pleasing to Him. For **we must all** appear **before the judgment seat of Christ**, so that each one may

> be **recompensed for his deeds in the body**, according to what he has done, whether **good or bad.** (*2 Cor. 5:9,10*)

The Greek term for "judgment seat" is "bematos." The bematos was a raised platform where athletic and judicial pronouncements were made. Both Christ and Paul (*Mt. 27:19, Acts 25:10*) stood before one of these as their conduct was evaluated by one whom God allowed to be in authority. Paul spells out plainly a biblical ambition to please Christ: We'll give account to Christ for what we did, what we thought, and what we said. The meaning of "we must all" is "we must all." Every Christian will be evaluated for the work they accomplished with the free gift of eternal life which was graciously given to them. The Bible sheds lights on the results of this evaluation in Revelation 21:3-5:

> And I heard a loud voice from the throne, saying, "Behold, the tabernacle of God is among men, and He will dwell among them, and they shall be His people, and God Himself will be among them, and **He will wipe away every tear from their eyes**; and there will no longer be any death; there will no longer be any mourning, or crying, or pain; the first things have passed away." And He who sits on the throne said, "Behold, I am making all things new." And He said, "Write, for these words are faithful and true." (*Rev. 21:3-5*)

Why would there be crying in the presence of the Lord in the New Jerusalem? I thought this was a good day and only good things happened. Doesn't the hymn say, "When we all get to heaven, what a day of rejoicing that will be?" But yet we see tears. Maybe hymns aren't the best source for theology. And the context certainly doesn't allow for them to be tears of joy (*death, mourning, crying, pain, first things have passed away*). Perhaps the tears in this future event are the result of failing in the Christian life or a poor showing in our commitment to Christ. Perhaps our evaluation by Christ will consist of a stinging rebuke. Perhaps the loss will be the disappointment of missing out on rewards, opportunities, and praise. John shares with us the possibility of shame before Christ is related to a believer's obedience.

> Now, little children, abide (*obey*) in Him, so that when He appears, we may have confidence and not shrink **away from Him in shame at His coming.** (*1 Jn. 2:28*)

Parables are stories which communicate general truth. It's improper to read too much into a parable and take each descriptor in the story to literal extremes. What the teller of a parable is trying to communicate is not a specific formula but an overall truth. A parable tells a fictional tale to get across a general principle in reality. Christ presented two parables about believers' conduct, His coming, and future accountability. In the two parables found in Matthew 25:1-30 Jesus provided insight as to the reality of His future assessment of believers. Christ's evaluation is a certainty for all Christians. It will come with criticism and commendation, loss and reward. The parable of the 10 virgins is as follows:

> **Then** the kingdom of heaven will be comparable to ten virgins, who took their lamps and went out to meet the bridegroom. Five of them were foolish, and five were prudent. For when the foolish took their lamps, they took no oil with them, but the prudent took oil in flasks along with their lamps. Now while the bridegroom was delaying, **they all got drowsy and began to sleep**. But at midnight there was a shout, '**Behold**, the bridegroom! Come out to meet him.' Then **all those virgins rose and trimmed their lamps**. The foolish said to the prudent, 'Give us some of your oil, for our lamps are going out.' But the prudent answered, 'No, there will not be enough for us and you too; **go instead to the dealers and buy some for yourselves.**' And while they were going away to make the purchase, the bridegroom came, and those who were ready **went in with him to the wedding feast**; and the door was shut. Later the other virgins also came, saying, 'Lord, lord, open up for us.' But he answered, 'Truly I say to you, **I do not know you**.' Be on the alert then, for you do not know the day nor the hour. (*Mt. 25:1-13*)

This is a picture of unprepared faithless believers who failed to live with eternity in mind. All the virgins *(believers)* were in the kingdom (*eternal life*). But only the faithful virgins were ready to participate in a unique kingdom event (*eternal reward*) – the wedding feast (*25:10*). A picture of loss is presented—the unprepared virgins were not allowed in – "the door was shut." It was too late. The response from the bridegroom (*Christ*) was, "I do not know you (*25:12*). The term "know" in this context appears to be used to describe trust and appreciation. It was used in this fashion to describe Potiphar's confidence in and friendship with Joseph (*LXX—Septuagint—Greek translation of the Hebrew Scriptures / Gen. 39:6*). It was used by Paul in 1 Thessalonians 5:12 where it can be translated as "appreciate." The lesson for all Christians is to "be on the alert then, for you do not know the day nor the hour (*25:13*)." Believers will be held accountable. If we're faithless and unprepared with the free gift of eternal life, if we live for the dot instead of the ray, we'll lose appreciation and honor from Christ which could have been ours. We see a similar principle taught in again Matthew 25 in the parable of the three servants.

> For **it** [*the kingdom of heaven*] is just like a man about to go on a journey, who called his own **slaves** and **entrusted his possessions** to them. To one he gave five talents, to another, two, and to another, one, each according to his own ability; and he went on his journey. Immediately the one who had received the five talents went and traded with them, and gained five more talents. In the same manner the one who had received the two talents gained two more. But he who received the one talent went away, and dug a hole in the ground and hid his master's money. Now after a long time the master of those slaves came and settled accounts with them. The one who had received the five talents came up and brought five more talents, saying, '**Master**, you entrusted five talents to me. See, I have gained five more talents.' His master said to him, '**Well done, good and faithful slave**. You were faithful with a few things, **I will put you in charge of many things**; **enter into the joy of your master**.' Also the one who had received the two talents came up and said, '**Master**, you entrusted two talents to me. See, I have gained two more talents.' His master said to him, '**Well done, good and faithful slave**. You were faithful with a few things, **I**

> **will put you in charge of many things**; **enter into the joy of your master**.' And the one also who had received the one talent came up and said, '**Master**, I knew you to be a hard man, reaping where you did not sow and gathering where you scattered no seed. And I was afraid and went away and hid your talent in the ground. See, you have what is yours.' But his master answered and said to him, '**You wicked, lazy slave**, you knew that I reap where I did not sow and gather where I scattered no seed. Then you ought to have put my money in the bank, and on my arrival I would have received my money back with interest. Therefore **take away the talent from him**, and give it to the one who has the ten talents.' For to everyone who has, more shall be given, and he will have abundance; but from the one who does not have, even what he does have shall be taken away. **Throw out the worthless slave into the outer darkness**; in that place there will be **weeping and gnashing of teeth.'** (*Mt. 25:14-30*)

Once again we see all believers are subject to accountability to Christ. The master (*Christ*) invested assets in his slaves (*believers – 1 Cor. 7:22*). There was wisdom and sensitivity on the master's part – no slave was given more or less than he could handle – "each according to his own ability" (*25:15*). We see that even though roles vary, accountability remains the same. Those servants (*believers*) who were found faithful upon his return (*2nd Advent*) were rewarded with responsibility, commendation, and satisfaction. "Well done, good and faithful slave . . . I will put you in charge of many things, enter into the joy of your master" (*25:21*). But the slave who was found faithless (*sounds like 2 Timothy 2:13*) will suffer loss.

- Faithless believers can expect sharp criticism – "You wicked, lazy slave" (*25:26*).
- Faithless believers can expect the loss of unique responsibility in the kingdom (*25:28*).
- Faithless believers can expect joy to be replaced with grief, sorrow, and shame (*25:30*) – "And cast out the worthless slave

> into the outer darkness; in that place there shall be weeping and gnashing of teeth."

The "outer darkness" sure sounds like hell but is it? This sure looks like a loss of eternal life. Really? Let's see if the context surrounding the phrase "outer darkness" leads us away from hell to a different understanding. The phrase "outer darkness" can literally be translated "the darkness outside." This phrase is used only three times in the biblical text of Scripture and all in Matthew's historical account of the life of Christ. It's found in Matthew 8:12, 22:13, and as we've seen in Matthew 25:30.

Remember, fictional parables are pointing out broad general principles found in reality. To take them too literally is to take them too far. Parables aren't designed for specifics. Additionally, cultural context can be very helpful in developing an accurate understanding of parables. First century social values (*honor codes*) were built around honor and shame and influenced the culture of the day. Absent of context, this honor code can seem extremely harsh and unusual when viewed from our cultural perspective.

In Matthew 8:11,12 Christ praised the wonderful faith shown by a Gentile Roman centurion. It seems Matthew recorded this historical event so as to teach his justified Hebrew audience that just because a person is a born-again Jew, he/she is not relieved or excused from accountability and consequence at Christ's evaluation. All believers will give account for all their works. Heritage makes no difference. Subsequent to His contact with the Gentile Roman centurion, Christ said:

> And I say to you, that many shall come from east and west [*outside of Israel – Gentiles*], and recline **at the table** with Abraham, and Isaac, and Jacob, **in the kingdom of heaven**; but the sons of the kingdom [*believing Israel*] shall be cast **out into the outer darkness**; in that place there shall be weeping and gnashing of teeth. (*Mt. 8:11,12*)

If Jewish believers are faithless, they'll be excluded from participating in unique fellowship found at the table with Abraham, Isaac, and Jacob. There is a unique opportunity for fellowship at a "table" in the kingdom. This statement by Christ tells us believers are already in the kingdom. The loss of reward for faithlessness (*just the opposite of what the centurion demonstrated*) is exclusion from reclining at the table (*"cast out into the outer darkness"*). Faithlessness is "something" and only "nothing" can separate a believer from the love of God and His kingdom. Eternal security teaches us that removal from the kingdom and the loss of eternal life are impossible. But eternal security does not ensure eternal rewards or a place at the table—only eternal life. In Matthew 22:1-14 we find another of Christ's parables which uses the phrase "outer darkness."

> Jesus spoke to them again in parables, saying, "The **kingdom of heaven** may be compared to king who gave a wedding feast for his son. And he sent out his slaves to call those who had been invited to the wedding feast, and they were unwilling to come. Again he sent out other slaves saying, 'Tell those who have been invited, "Behold, I have prepared my dinner; my oxen and my fattened livestock are all butchered and everything is ready; come to the wedding feast."' But they paid no attention and went their way, one to his own farm, another to his business, and the rest seized his slaves and mistreated them and killed them. But the king was enraged, and he sent his armies and destroyed those murderers and set their city on fire. Then he said to his slaves, 'The wedding is ready, but those who were invited were not worthy. Go therefore to the **main highways** [*in the kingdom*], and as many as you find there, invite to the **wedding feast**.' Those slaves went out into the streets and gathered together all they found, both evil and good; and the wedding hall was filled with dinner guests. But when the king came in to look over the dinner guests, he saw a man there who was **not dressed in wedding clothes**, and he said to him, 'Friend, how did you come in here without wedding clothes?' And the man was speechless. Then the king said to the servants, 'Bind him hand and foot, and throw him into

> **the outer darkness**; in that place there will be weeping and gnashing of teeth.' For many [*in the kingdom*] are called [*to the wedding feast*], but few [*in the kingdom*] are chosen [*to attend the wedding feast]."* (*Mt. 22:1-14*)

In this parable we see:

- A king:
  - ***God***
- His son:
  - ***Christ***
- A wedding feast/hall:
  - ***Unique Millennial event – Rev. 19:7***
- The king's slaves:
  - ***Prophets***
- A call to those:
  - ***Israel***
- Other slaves:
  - ***More prophets***
- Unwillingness to come, paid no attention:
  - ***Israel's rejection of God's invitation to fellowship***
- The seizure, mistreatment, and killing of the king's slaves:
  - ***Israel's treatment of the prophets***
- King's armies sent, destroyed murderers, burned cities:
  - ***God's discipline for violating Mosaic Covenant – Deut. 28:15-68***
- The main highways:
  - ***The location was <u>in</u> the kingdom***

- Good and evil dinner guest:
    - ***Believers at the feast in the kingdom***

- A man not dressed in wedding clothes:
    - ***Faithless believer—Psm. 96:9, 104:1,2, 1 Pt. 5:5, Rev. 19:8,9***

- Cast him into "the darkness outside":
    - ***Exclusion from a unique Millennial event***

- Weeping and gnashing of teeth:
    - ***Extreme disappointment***

The broad truth of the parable is that faithless believers will be held accountable and be excluded from a unique event in the Millennial Kingdom. If God held Israel responsible for their conduct, believers can expect the same. The most sobering statement by Christ is at the end of the parable. Many believers are invited (*"called" – Mt. 22:14*) to this unique event in the Millennial Kingdom, but few will be chosen to participate. It appears a seat at the table is not given out lightly. With great grace comes great accountability. Becoming a Christian is easy, being a disciple takes effort. Faith gets all believers into the kingdom. Faithfulness gets them into the banquet. What sharpens the picture of loss in this parable is that wedding feasts were normally a nighttime event. To be thrown out of the party was to be tossed from a lit banquet room to the "darkness outside." Thus "darkness outside" seems to consistently represent exclusion from unique events in the kingdom.

I should have practiced more at the shooting range. Even though I passed, there were times when my score at the range was low. The loss I suffered from faithlessness was being stuck with a poor annual score. "Do-overs" for a higher one weren't allowed. I missed the opportunity and it wasn't coming back. In school, we got a "C" when we could have gotten an "A." This is loss. We keep what we have but we could have had so much more – if just more effort. Our missed spiritual opportunities won't come back around forever. Each moment in time has eternal implications. A wonderfully true line from the movie *Gladiator* says it so well: "What we do in life echoes in eternity." Scripture reminds us there's no going back.

> And inasmuch as it is appointed for men to die once and after this comes **judgment.** (*Heb. 9:27*)

The third passage in which Paul reveals future Christian accountability is found in the book of Romans. Paul's letter to these Christians contains, what many believe, to be the richest theological meat on the bone in the New Testament. Paul was cognizant of the concept of justification. He utilized the term 27 times (*Rom. 3:4 is the exception*) in relationship to a believer's positional righteousness before God as a result of faith alone in Christ alone for eternal life. Paul made it clear works had nothing to do with justification (*Rom. 4:4,5, 2 Tim. 1:9*). Paul was adamant about eternal life being eternally secure (*Rom. 8:38,39*). He continued to present his belief that Christians, though justified and secure, would be held accountable for their actions. In Romans 14:10 he wrote:

> But you, why do you judge your brother? Or you again, why do you regard your brother with contempt? For **we will all stand before the judgment seat of God.** (*Rom. 14:10*)

Paul was addressing sensitivity (*or insensitivity*) among believers. To encourage Christ-like conduct and courtesy, he motivated them to correct living by means of a reminder – we'll give account for how we treat each other so be careful!

Combining God's Word and His Spirit with my obedience is the basis for Christian growth and sanctification. Paul taught us a combination of our effort and His power bring about spiritual maturity. Paul said:

> So then, my **beloved**, just as you have always obeyed, not as in my presence only, but now much more in my absence, **work out your salvation** with **fear and trembling**; for it is **God who is at work in you**, both to will and to work for His good pleasure. (*Phil. 2:12,13*)

Why would Peter (*1 Pt. 1:17*) and Paul command believers *("beloved")* to "work" and to engage in this effort with "fear and trembling?" Perhaps because both of them were trying to communicate with great grace comes great accountability. This is similar to the parables of Christ and in line with John's instructions.

The issue of works and obedience is like a road. Way on the right it seems we have godly leaders who tie justification to sanctification and struggle at seeing the distinction between a believer and a disciple; they add works to justification in an effort to address spiritual irresponsibility. Their theology appears to be a response to a perception which says free-grace advocates are indifferent to the biblical call for obedience and holiness and thus are "antinomian" ("*against law*"). But at the same time it appears there are some godly authors who seem comfortable in holding a view in which effort and accountability are of little or no consequence in our walk with God. Way on the left we have Christian leaders who want to minimize or eliminate all traces of responsibility and evaluation from the Christian life; they remove works from sanctification in the battle against legalism. Perhaps biblical reality can be found in the middle.

CHAPTER 22

Rest or Risk?

At the time I was writing this section, a federal scandal at the U.S. Attorney General's level was the focus of the media. The event in question was an investigation by the name of "Fast and Furious." In this federal criminal program, weapons from the United States were allowed to "walk" with known drug dealers in Mexico. U.S. federal authorities allowed known illegal Mexican national criminals to purchase guns from gun dealers in the United States. The goal was to track the guns back to major narcotic syndicates in Mexico. The thought process behind letting guns "walk" was, "Hey, we do it with drugs, why not guns?" Well, it sure sounds like a good idea until it collides with reality and with the life of a federal law enforcement employee. I'll tell you the reason why we "walk" drugs and do *not* "walk" guns: Border Patrol agents on the southern Arizona border are *not* gunned down by drugs, but with guns. And this is exactly what happened. One of the multitudes of "Fast and Furious" guns which weren't being tracked was used to murder a Border Patrol agent. I spoke to a Phoenix undercover agent attached to a federal task force who was involved in warning federal police managers that "Fast and Furious" was a bad idea. The response from federal law enforcement managers; "You have to crack a few eggs to make an omelet." The "eggs" they were talking about were the lives of law enforcement personnel; the "omelet" was their hair-brained policing strategy. Pure indifference embraces acceptable casualty rates. Shameful. There's a technical police labor term for an operation like "Fast and Furious"—it's "Stuck on stupid." Just because it sounds good to a bureaucratic manager and completes a political agenda doesn't make it safe for front line law enforcement, their families, and our communities. Perhaps police management's hunger for breakfast would tone down if the "eggs" that were broken consisted of their family members. To put this operation in motion, one had to go out of their way to ignore the obvious and turn a blind eye to the clear risks which were created.

Years ago there was something that sounded good in a Phoenix church I attended for two years. One adult enrichment class was just exploding with numbers and enthusiasm. The drawing card was a popular new book that seemed to energize everyone who read it. The author of this book was a godly man by the name of Steve McVey. His book Grace Walk promoted the idea that God's wonderful grace trumped Christian accountability and relieved believers from responsibility. This sure reminds me of a technical labor term and a botched federal gun investigation. Allow me to share some of the comments from his book which prompted me to express my great concern to the church's pastor.

- "The truth is that victory is not a reward but a gift. A person does not **experience** (*emphasis mine*) victory **in the Christian** (*emphasis mine*) life by trying hard to live for God. It just won't work . . ."[1]
- "We are to **use our will** (*emphasis mine*) to accept the gift of victory; we are **not to make an effort** (*emphasis mine*) to win the victory."[2]
- **God doesn't intend for us to struggle** (*emphasis mine*) for the victory."[3]

From the context of his comments, "victory" is not "walking by faith" (*Rom. 1:17, Gal. 2:20, 3:11, Heb. 10:38*) but an "experience . . . in the Christian life." According to McVey, an "experience" based upon "our will" brings victory to the life of a believer. "Not making an effort" is my definition of doing nothing. The text of the Bible seems to focus a great deal on what we do with our lives and our effort. Paul and

1 McVey, Steve. Grace Walk, (*Eugene OR, Harvest House Publishers, 1995*), pg. 16
2 Ibid, pg. 102
3 Ibid, pg. 103

Peter and James might agree to disagree with McVey's analysis of what victory is and what it takes to obtain it.

> Do you not know that those who run in a race all run, but only one receives the prize? **Run in such a way that you may win**. Everyone who competes in the games **exercises self-control** in all things. They then do it to receive a perishable wreath, but we an imperishable. Therefore I run in such a way, as not without aim; I box in such a way, as not beating the air; but **I discipline my body** and make it my slave, so that, after I have preached to others, I myself will not be disqualified. (*1 Cor. 9:24-27*)
>
> **Suffer hardship** with me, as a good soldier of Christ Jesus. No soldier in **active service** entangles himself in the affairs of everyday life, so that he may please the one who enlisted him as a soldier. Also if anyone **competes** as an athlete, he does not win the prize unless he **competes according to the rules**. The **hard-working farmer** ought to be the first to receive his share of the crops. (*2 Tim. 2:3-6*)
>
> I have **fought the good fight**, I have **finished the course**, I have **kept the faith**; in the future there is laid up for me the crown of righteousness, which the Lord, the righteous Judge, will award to me on that day; and not only to me, but also to all who have loved His appearing. (*2 Tim. 4:7,8*)
>
> Beloved, do not be surprised at the fiery ordeal among you, which comes upon you for your testing, as though some strange thing were happening to you; but to the degree that you **share the sufferings** of Christ, keep on rejoicing, so that also at the revelation of His glory you may rejoice with exultation. (*1 Pt. 4:12,13*)
>
> Consider it all joy, my brethren, when you encounter various **trials**, knowing that the **testing** of our faith produces **endurance**. And let endurance have its perfect result, so that

> you may be perfect and complete, lacking in nothing. (*Jms. 1:2-4*)

The Christian life, even though it begins at justification, doesn't end there. There's more to the Christian life than justification and the free gift of eternal life. Certainly Christ is our victory as far as the penalty of sin and justification is concerned (*1 Cor. 15:54-58*). But victory is not complete as far as the power of sin and sanctification is concerned. As we've already seen, loss and shame *(1 Jn. 2:28, 2 Jn. 1:8)* are realities in the lives of believers. One of the earned outcomes of effort and victory in the sanctification process is an eternal reward. In contrast, a gift is free. A reward is something merited. Paul seemed to communicate it takes "effort" and "hard work" in the Christian life to obtain victory and receive rewards. He understood victory in the Christian life was a combined effort of his work and Christ's power.

> For this purpose also **I labor, striving** according to **His power**, which mightily works **within me.** (*Col. 1:29*)

Paul encouraged others to "suffer hardship" with him. Similarly, Christ told us to pick up our cross and follow Him (*Lk. 14:27*). If we're not to make an effort to win the victory, then what was Paul doing? If victory was "in the bag" for Paul, why was he concerned about being disqualified? If victory is complete upon reception of eternal life, why did John share with Christians the reality of losing what they had obtained? Remember, the biblical fact of eternal security makes it clear the subject of loss or disqualification is never a believer's eternal destiny but their eternal reward. While some combine justification and sanctification to achieve their theological goal, it appears McVey has eliminated or minimized the biblical concept of sanctification to reach his goal.

McVey goes on to say:

- " . . . I discovered that **the key** (*emphasis mine*) to enjoying success is not strenuous work, but **spiritual rest** (*emphasis mine*)."[4]

It depends upon what "success" means. I believe success is utilizing spiritual expediency (*the best way to give God the most glory*) in fulfilling the Great Commission. More important than my definition, how does McVey's thinking line up with Paul's commands and the Psalmist's perspective of success as offered in the biblical text?

> O love the Lord, all you His godly ones!
> The Lord preserves the faithful
> And fully recompenses **the proud doer**.
> Be strong and let your heart take courage,
> All you who hope in the Lord. (*Psm. 31:23*)
>
> But I thought it necessary to send to you **Epaphroditus**, my brother and **fellow worker** and **fellow soldier**, who is also your messenger and minister to my need. (*Phil. 2:25*)
>
> But you, **be sober** in all things, **endure** hardship, **do the work** of an evangelist, **fulfill** your ministry. (*2 Tim. 4:5*)

Proud and fellow "resters" are not seen in the writings of the Hebrew poet or Paul. In fact, Paul sent a fellow "worker" to the brethren. He sent a fellow "soldier" to the church in Philippi. Workers make a difference and soldiers take a risk. In fact, Epaphroditus wasn't the only "fellow worker." There was also Pricilla and Aquila (*Rom. 16:3*), Urbanus (*Rom. 16:9*), Timothy (*Rom. 16:21*), Euodia, Syntyche and Clement (*Phil. 4:2,3*), Philemon (*Philemon 1*), Mark, Aristarchus, Demas, and Luke (*Philemon 24*).

McVey presents rest as a present cessation of effort and activity. Some might label this as "let go and let God." This can be an enticing plan

---

4 McVey, Steve. Grace Walk, (*Eugene OR, Harvest House Publishers, 1995*), pg. 23

of action (*or should I say inaction*) to those who aren't willing to make a difference and take a risk for Christ. McVey states:

- "**Resting** (*emphasis mine*) in Christ is the **sole responsibility** (*emphasis mine*) of the Christian. Everything else flows out of that."[5]

One could come to an understanding from reading the book of Hebrews that Christians aren't here in this moment in time to rest as described by McVey. Instead, we're training to reign (*Heb. 1:9*). The writer of Hebrews appears to present "rest" as an earned reward, subsequent to work, given to believers as a result of obedience—rest follows work. This is true in the police department, the mechanic's shop, the retailer's store, and every other real-world occupation. It's true in the Christian life too. In fact, in contrast to McVey, James and Peter might say life is a test, not a rest (*Jms. 1:1-4, 1 Pt. 4:12,13*).

The author of Hebrews assures us the reward of "rest" is patterned after the deep satisfaction of God at the end of creation (*"it was very good" – Gen. 1:31*). This "Sabbath type" of rest was seen at the conclusion of God's creation work when Adam (*Gen. 1:26*) was given rule over the earth. This "rest" still remains – satisfaction from one's work and the honor of ruling and reigning as a companion of Christ (*"metachos" – Heb. 1:9*) in the Millennial Kingdom – for believers who are diligently obedient.

> Therefore, since it remains for some to enter it [*promise of rest*], and those who formerly had good news preached to them **failed to enter because of disobedience**, He again fixes a certain day, "Today," saying through David after so long a time just as has been said before, "Today if you hear His voice, **do not harden your hearts**." For **if** [*2nd class condition – "and he did not"*] Joshua had given them **rest**, He would not have spoken of another day after that. So there remains a Sabbath **rest** for the people of God. For the one

[5] McVey, Steve, Grace Walk, *(Eugene OR, Harvest House Publisher, 1995)*, pg. 37

> who has entered His **rest** has himself also **rested from his works**, as God did from His. Therefore let **us** [*Christians in the context*] **be diligent** to enter that **rest**, so that no one will fall, through following the same example of **disobedience.** (*Heb. 4:6-11*)

The nation under Joshua had to fight and work in their conquest of Canaan. God gave Joshua and obedient Israel a temporal historical blessing of "rest" that provided possession and satisfaction.

> When you cross the Jordan and live in the land which the Lord your God is giving you to **inherit**, and He gives you **rest** from all your enemies around you so that you live in security. (*Dt. 12:10*)

> Remember the word which Moses the servant of the Lord commanded you, saying, 'The Lord your God gives you **rest** and will give you this **land.**' (*Josh 1:13*)

> So the Lord gave Israel all the **land** which He had sworn to give to their fathers, and they **possessed it** and lived in it. And the Lord gave them **rest** on every side, according to all that He had sworn to their fathers, and no one of all their enemies stood before them; the Lord gave all their enemies into their hand. Not one of the good promises which the Lord had made to the house of Israel failed; all came to pass. (*Josh. 21:43-45*)

But this rest, even though similar, was not equivalent to the future, eternal eschatological "Sabbath rest." In the coming Millennial Kingdom (*Ezek. 37:21,22*), satisfaction from hard labor as well as ruling and reigning with Christ (*possession*) also appear to be components of the "Sabbath rest." Like the nation under Joshua, Christians need to work hard in order to obtain this future "rest." "Hard hearts" and "disobedience" will result in the loss of this promised "rest."

All believers enter the Kingdom. But the book of Hebrews communicates the "promise" or "rest" for faithful believers (*Heb. 6:12*) is the future eschatological possession of (*Heb. 9:15, 10:34-36*) and authority in (*as companions of Christ—Heb. 1:9*) the Millennial Kingdom. "Rest" (*the inheritance*) is obtained by means of obediently "holding fast" and "drawing near" to God (*Heb. 3:6, 10:22,23*). Psalm 95:11 is quoted in Hebrews 4:3,5. It's likely this passage (*"they shall not enter my rest"*) was offered by the author as a sobering reminder to his wavering Jewish Christian audience about Israel; because of Israel's disobedience under Moses, the nation did not enter His rest. Historically we see the example of this forfeiture of "rest."

> For who provoked Him when they had heard? Indeed, did not all those who came out of Egypt led by Moses? And with whom was He angry for forty years? Was it not with those who sinned, whose bodies fell in the wilderness? And to whom did He swear that they would **not enter His rest**, but to those who were **disobedient**? So we see that they were not able to enter [*His rest*] because of **unbelief** [*faithlessness*]. (*Heb. 3:16-19*)

Out of two million people, only two, Joshua and Caleb, possessed the land (*Num. 14:6,24*). The remainder of the Exodus generation died along the way during the next forty years (*Num. 14:22,23*). It's interesting the nation complained by saying, "Oh that we would have died in the wilderness (*Num. 14:2*)." God gave them what they wanted. They lost the blessing of possessing the land. If loss happened to disobedient Israel (*Heb. 3:7-11*), it can happen to faithless Christians also – the forfeiture of "rest" (*not "eternal life"*).

In addition to Joshua and the nation, the writer of Hebrews gave us, as well as his Jewish audience, a glimpse into the priorities of the heroes of the Hebrew faith. With their moment in time, these men and women lived (*and worked*) for the ray and *not* the dot. By faith, with eternity and the reward of rest in mind, these men and women "tried hard," "made an effort," and "struggled" during their stay on earth.

> All these [*Abel, Noah, Abraham, Sarah*] died in faith, without receiving the promises, but having seen them and having welcomed them from a distance, and having confessed that

> **they were strangers and exiles on the earth**. For those who say such things make it clear that **they are seeking a country of their own**. And indeed if they had been thinking of that country from which they went out, they would have had opportunity to return. But as it is, they desire **a better country, that is, a heavenly one**. Therefore God is not ashamed to be called their God; for He has prepared a city for them. (*Heb. 11:13-16*)

"Rest" is based upon faithfulness (*Heb. 4:3*). There are only three times in the New Testament the term rest is used as a command.

- Mark 6:31 in which the disciples were told to take a lunch break.
- It's found in Luke 12:19 in which a fool in a parable used the term inappropriately.
- "Rest" can also be seen in Philemon 1:20; Paul asked another brother to give his heart "rest" by treating another brother appropriately.

In none of these verses, or anywhere else, do we find our "sole responsibility" is to rest. Biblical rest is the ends, not the means. McVey's concept appears unbiblical and contrary to the biblical pattern. Christ said He would give us rest after we "come" (*command*) and "take" (*command*). If our sole responsibility is to rest (*defined as not producing or performing*) why do we have numerous commands in the New Testament?

Believe it or not, in my moment in time as a police officer I had more than one conversation with more than one prostitute. Please don't let Julia Roberts and Richard Gere entice you through their movie *Pretty Woman* into believing prostitution is a clean, pretty and acceptable means to an end. It is nothing but dangerous, dirty, degrading and illegal. I talked to one young girl concerning her lawless conduct and the numerous problems attached to it; one of the problems was getting pregnant. She assured me pregnancy was no problem at all. As long as she didn't enjoy sexual interaction (*allow me to be respectfully blunt: have an orgasm*) she couldn't get pregnant. Her statement and the thought process behind it were shockingly comical. Her belief was sincere and a lucky test-drive up to that point bolstered this belief. It was clear in her mind the reason she hadn't gotten pregnant was because so far she hadn't enjoyed what she was doing. It was also clear she never took a health or sex education class in school. But the bottom line, she was wrong and because she was wrong there were serious consequences coming her way. McVey presents a shocking theological thought process which is just as sincere but even more dangerous than a dime store sex education. The problem of an unwanted pregnancy pales in comparison to the ramifications of McVey's beliefs. McVey writes:

- "God never proposed your lifestyle to be built around the principle of **right and wrong** (*emphasis mine*) . . ."[6]
- " . . . the believers shouldn't build their lifestyle around anything. They aren't involved in a **building project** (*emphasis mine*). Their goal is not to have a **moral lifestyle** (*emphasis mine*) but a **miraculous one** (*emphasis mine*). They are to rest in Christ and allow Him to express His life through them. As they abide in Christ, the divine virtues of Jesus will be revealed through their attitudes and actions."[7]
- It's a **feeble goal** (*emphasis mine*) for a Christian to only want **to live correctly** (*emphasis mine*)."[8]
- He [*God*] doesn't care about rules. **Right and wrong** (*emphasis mine*) are incidental to Him."[9]

How do these statements compare with Scripture, especially the Hebrew text?

> Then the Lord spoke to Moses, saying: "Speak to all the congregation of the sons of Israel and say to them, 'You shall **be holy, for I the Lord your God am holy.'** (*Lev. 19:1,2*)

---

6 McVey, Steve. Grace Walk, (*Eugene OR, Harvest House Publishers, 1995*), pg. 110

7 Ibid, pg. 113

8 Ibid, pg. 113

9 Ibid, pg. 117

> The conclusion, when all has been heard, is: fear God and keep His commandments, because this applies to every person. For God will bring every act to judgment, everything which is hidden, whether it is **good or evil.** (*Eccl. 12:13,14*)

> Thus says the Lord, "**Do justice and righteousness**, and deliver the one who has been robbed from the power of his oppressor. Also do not mistreat or do violence to the stranger, the orphan, or the widow; and do not shed innocent blood in this place. For if you men will indeed perform this thing, then kings will enter the gates of this house, sitting in David's place on his throne, riding in chariots and on horses, even the king himself and his servants and his people. **But if you will not obey these words**, I swear by Myself," declares the Lord, "that this house will become a desolation." (*Jer. 22:3-5*)

> Therefore the Lord Himself will give you a sign: Behold, a virgin will be with child and bear a son, and she will call His name Immanuel. He will eat curds and honey at the time **He knows enough to refuse evil and choose good**. For before the **boy will know enough to refuse evil and choose good**, the land whose two kings you dread will be forsaken. (*Isa. 7:14-16*)

Jesus appeared to care about right and wrong and taught obedience was crucial in maintaining fellowship with Him. Paul also communicated good deeds were vital for sanctification.

> If you **keep My commandments**, you will **abide** in My love; just as I have kept My Father's commandments and abide in His love. (*Jn. 15:10*)

> If you love Me, you will **keep My commandments.** (*Jn. 14:15*)

> This is a trustworthy statement; and concerning these things I want you to speak confidently, so that those who

> have believed God will **be careful to engage in good deeds**. These things are good and profitable for men. (*Titus 3:8*)

Jesus equates abiding with obedience. Since God is holy and perfect, how can one say right and wrong are unimportant to Him? The believer is evaluated on good and bad works (*2 Cor. 5:10*). Even the unbeliever who lacks eternal life is judged according to his/her works (*Rev. 20:12*). If we're to imitate our heavenly Father, and if He doesn't care about right and wrong, and if living a moral lifestyle isn't important, how are we to raise our children? How can a Christian police officer enforce the rule of law? One would be hard pressed to find anywhere in Scripture where we're to pursue a "miraculous" life over a "moral" one. Peter made it clear his miraculous "experience" with the transfigured Messiah didn't come close to the value of the "more sure prophetic word" (*2 Pt. 1:16-19*). Perhaps instead of pursuing McVey's "miraculous" lifestyle, the biblical pattern for our lives should be to look for God in the normal.

> So He said, "Go forth and stand on the mountain before the Lord." And behold, the Lord was passing by! And a great and strong wind was rending the mountains and breaking in pieces the rocks before the Lord; but the Lord was not in the wind. And after the wind an earthquake, but the Lord was not in the earthquake. After the earthquake a fire, but the Lord was not in the fire; and after the fire a **sound of a gentle blowing** [*literally – "the sound of a thin silence"*]. When Elijah heard it, he wrapped his face in his mantle and went out and stood in the entrance of the cave. And behold, a voice came to him and said, "What are you doing here, Elijah?" (*1 Kgs. 19:11-13*)

Maybe, like Elijah and Peter, we ought to give up chasing experiences and seek for God's guidance and counsel in His Word. If right and wrong are minor, secondary issues, why does Paul provide encouragement to "not lose heart in doing good?" Quick answer – "in due time we shall reap [*a reward*]."

> Let us not lose heart in **doing good**, for in due time we will reap if we do not grow weary. So then, while we have opportunity, let us do good to all people, and especially to those who are of the household of the faith. (*Gal. 6:9,10*)

Contrasting McVey, Paul presented a picture of the Christian life as a "building project" (*1 Cor. 3:10*). If it's a feeble goal to want to live correctly and if we're not involved in a "building project" then what was Paul talking about? A godly author who disregards the doctrine of Christian accountability is like the Department of Justice allowing known and dangerous criminals to walk away with weapons. A godly author who minimizes the biblical concept of effort in the believer's life is like the young girl who missed the sex education class. The consequences created by these dangerous moments in time can be life altering. "Let go and let God" appears to have the same principle embedded in it as "Fast and Furious." One has to go out of their way to ignore the clear text of Scripture and turn a blind eye to the obvious costs of disobedience which can impact all believers. "Let go and let God" seems to conflict with the Bible as much as the prostitute's understanding contradicted biology. As tragic as the lost lives behind a politically driven police agenda or the dangerous life of prostitution, the tragedy of lost eternal rewards created by theologies that go beyond or fall short of the biblical text is just as alarming.

CHAPTER 23

Companions of Christ

Partners can accomplish many things. Companions make all the difference. Good friends are of great value. Famous partners include Batman and Robin (*superheroes*), Holmes and Watson (*detectives*), Hope and Crosby (*movies*), Bush and Cheney (*politics*), Ben and Jerry (*ice cream*) and Butch Cassidy and the Sundance Kid (*outlaws*). Some pairs come quickly to mind. In 1989 another pair unfamiliar to most except those who lived in the Duppa Villa Public Housing Projects in Phoenix was "Mark and Danny."

It was a wonderful privilege and unique experience to have had my brother-in-law (*and my good friend*) Danny Boyd as my partner when we were assigned to the Walking Beat in the public housing projects. We worked so long and so well together, our names were always presented as a pair. People in the projects wouldn't ask, "Where's Mark?" They would ask, "Where's Mark and Danny?"

One time Danny and I were working in the Henson Projects in South Phoenix. We were out on foot patrol and ran across a small group of guys drinking beer outside of their apartment. This was a City Code as well as a tenant rule violation. In the course of our contact with the group, I found myself on the wrong end of a fight. Losing a fight is a surreal experience. Time seems to stand still when you find yourself on your back on the ground with the bad guy on top of you in a clearly advantageous position. You think to yourself, "Hold it – this isn't the way this is supposed to be." Before I lost the fight even further, Danny knocked the guy off and we finished our business with one bad guy in handcuffs.

What made this fight memorable (*by the way, everyone should lose at least one fight in their life just to know what it feels like*) is there were two other officers with us who stood by and did absolutely nothing to help. I approached one of them later on in the shift and asked him why he didn't jump in and help out. His response; "I didn't want to get my uniform dirty." To say I was upset is an understatement. Two officers, same employer, same badge, same location, same task, same event – one officer jumps in and one stands by. There is a Greek term for partners like Danny who choose to jump in. The term is "metachos." A "metachos" is a partner in an enterprise, a companion.

The term is used six times in the New Testament; five of them In the book of Hebrews. The other New Testament passage where it's used is Luke 5:7. In the LXX (*Septuagint—Greek translation of the Hebrew Scriptures*) it can be found in several verses including 1 Samuel 20:30, 1 Kings 12:8 and Ecclesiastes 4:10.

> Then Saul's anger burned against Jonathan and he said to him, "You son of a perverse, rebellious woman! Do I not know that you are **choosing** [*literally "a metachos of"*] the son of Jesse to your own shame and to the shame of your mother's nakedness?" (*1 Sam. 20:30*)

> King Rehoboam consulted with the elders who had served his father Solomon while he was still alive, saying, "How do you counsel me to answer this people?" Then they spoke to him, saying, "If you will be a servant to this people today, and will serve them and grant them their petition, and speak good words to them, then they will be your servants forever." But he forsook the counsel of the elders which they had given him, and consulted with **the young men** who grew up with him and served him. (*1 Kgs. 12:6-8*)

> For if either of them falls, the one will lift up his **companion**. But woe to the one who falls when there is not another to lift him up. (*Eccl. 4:10*)

> Simon answered and said, "Master, we worked hard all night and caught nothing, but I will do as You say and let down the nets." When they had done this, they enclosed a great quantity of fish, and their nets began to break; so they signaled to their **partners** in the other boat for them to come and help them. And they came and filled both of the boats, so that they began to sink. (*Lk. 5:5-7*)

The context of each passage clearly helps confirm a "metachos" is a long-time trusted partner in an important venture whose council is of great value. To put it simply, a "metachos" is a wise and trusted friend who has input on important decisions. The passage from 1 Samuel quickly calls to mind the partnership of Jonathan and David.

In reading the book of Hebrews it's not hard to see it was written to Jewish believers who were under intense persecution and who were contemplating going back to an archaic, outdated Hebrew sacrificial religious system. These Christians were contemplating abandoning their faith in order to find less persecution and more comfort in the status quo of the day. The persecution was real and painful and the encouragement and admonishment from the author were heartfelt and passionate. "Don't go back. If you do there are consequences. If you endure you'll be rewarded. Look at the history of faithful believers and stay the course! Christ is superior." Not a bad summary from a poor beat cop. With this in mind, let's look at how the term "metachos" is used in this inspired biblical text.

> You have loved righteousness and hated lawlessness; Therefore God, Your God, has anointed You with the oil of gladness above Your **companions** [*metachos*]. (*Heb. 1:9 quoting Psm. 44:8*)

> Therefore, holy brethren, **partakers** [*metachos*] of a heavenly calling, consider Jesus, the Apostle and High Priest of our confession. (*Heb. 3:1*)

> For in the case of those who have once been enlightened and have tasted of the heavenly gift and have been made **partakers** [*metachos*] of the Holy Spirit. (*Heb. 6:4*)
>
> For we have become **partakers** [*metachos*] of Christ, **if we hold fast** the beginning of our assurance firm until the end. (*Heb. 3:14*)
>
> But if you are without discipline, of which all have become **partakers** [*metachos*], then you are illegitimate children and not sons. (*Heb. 12:8*)

One isn't born a companion or partner or partaker, one chooses to become a metachos. In the context of Hebrews chapter 3, where the term is used twice, it seems the choice of becoming a "metachos" involves adhering to several clear commands:

- 3:1 – pay attention to Jesus
- 3:8, 15, (*also 4:7*) – don't harden your hearts
- 3:12 – take care (*from stepping from the believers' priestly function*)
- 3:13 – encourage one another day after day

I believe the key concept to the book of Hebrews is being a partner of Christ (*Heb. 1:9*). "If we hold fast" then we become a "metachos." If we live faithfully and our mindset is on fulfilling the Great Commission and engaging in spiritual multiplication during our brief moment in time, we become a trusted and loyal friend of the Messiah. Am I sharing my faith as a way of life? If so, then I'm a metachos. Am I interested in the spiritual success of others? If I am, then I'm a metachos. Do my priorities revolve around the eternal? I'm a metachos if I can answer yes. It's important to know what a metachos looks like, but it's also important to know what a metachos gets for his/her faithfulness.

In looking at disobedient Israel (*1 Cor. 10:11, Heb. 4:11*), we can learn believers who are not partners of Christ will not enter His "rest." Faithless Christians, like the disobedient nation of Israel under Moses, are not good partners and as such they will forfeit "rest."

> As I swore in My wrath, "**They** [*disobedient Israel*] shall not enter My **rest.**" (*Heb. 3:11*)

> And to whom did He swear that **they** [*disobedient Israel*] would **not enter His rest**, but to those who were **disobedient**? (*Heb. 3:18*)

> Therefore, let **us** [*Christians in the context*] fear if, while a promise remains of **entering His rest**, any one of you may seem to have **come short of it**. For indeed we have had good news preached to us, just as they also; but the word they heard did not profit them, because it was not united by faith in those who heard. For **we** [*Christians in the context*] who have believed enter that **rest**, just as He has said, "As I swore in My wrath, they shall **not enter My rest**," although His works were finished from the foundation of the world. For He has said somewhere concerning the seventh day: "And God rested on the seventh day from all His works"; and again in this passage, "They shall **not enter My rest.**" (*Heb. 4:1-5*)

In a lesson of grace, what believers can learn from disobedient Israel is, even though faithlessness caused a forfeiture of Israel's rest under Moses, the nation was still forgiven by Yahweh. The reality of consequence doesn't negate the stability of our relationship with God.

> So the Lord said, "**I have pardoned them** according to your word; but indeed, as I live, all the earth will be filled with the glory of the Lord. Surely all the men who have seen My glory and My signs which I performed in Egypt and in the wilderness, yet have put Me to the test these ten times and have not listened to My voice, **shall by no means see the land** which I swore to their fathers, nor shall any of those who spurned Me see it. (*Num. 14:20-23*)

In contrast to faithless believers, those Christians who live a lifestyle consistent with that of an obedient and useful companion of Christ – their reward is rest.

> So there remains a Sabbath **rest** for the people of God. For the one who has entered His rest has himself also rested **from his works**, as God did from His. Therefore let **us** [*Christians in the context*] **be diligent** [*by working hard*] to **enter that rest**, so that **no one** [*of the "holy brethren" – Heb. 3:1*] will fall, through following the same example of disobedience. (*Heb. 4:9-11*)

Once again we're reminded rest comes after work – the work of a companion, the effort of a metachos. Rest is satisfaction from work. Rest is *not* entering into the Millennial Kingdom. Rest is possessing and inheriting this future kingdom. Rest implies a future of ruling and reigning with Christ in His kingdom. "Diligence" is required to "enter that rest." This is consistent with the function of a metachos, a partner, or a companion.

As a citizen of the United States, I voted for George Bush. I pay taxes. I obey the law. I contribute to the country. With all this said, when George Bush won the presidential election, I wasn't given a cabinet position. How can this be? I wasn't shocked at all. I spent no money for his campaign. I volunteered a limited amount of time in his bid for election. I hadn't done any work for him nor did I make any investments of time or effort in the past on his behalf. So, with all this said, why in the world should I have expected to be given any authority at all in his cabinet? I didn't work for it. He didn't know me. I'm not a trusted friend – a metachos. Just because I'm a citizen of the greatest country in the world doesn't mean I'm a reliable partner of the most powerful man on earth. We really shouldn't think it's any different with the most powerful person in the universe. Our involvement in the Cause as a metachos, a partner of Christ, during our moment in time now will directly determine our role in His future Millennial Kingdom.

Danny and I were partners who functioned well together and as a result we had a phenomenal impact on the community we served and the beat we walked. We generated a proposal, the first of its kind in the City of Phoenix, to utilize bicycles in a patrol capacity in the projects. It turned out to be a wonderful success which subsequently spread throughout the Department to the patrol precincts.

The bike was a fantastic tool for proactive police work. It was faster than being on foot but offered more exposure to the environment than just sitting in a patrol car. One of the great joys of police work was getting in a foot pursuit on a bike with a guy who was merely running. There would be times I would purposely keep a lengthy distance from a bad guy we were contacting in order to encourage him to run so that I could chase him on my bike. At night on a bike, we would black out by wearing dark police uniforms (*even covering up our bike helmets with a dark cloth cap*). The halogen headlamps on our handlebars were like the sun. More than one person got caught with their pants down (*and sometimes that was literally*). We got to the point on our bikes where we could swoop down on people without warning, like a bat in the night, and take dope right out of their hands. It was great fun and highly effective.

Later on during my time working the projects I had a different partner. We patrolled the projects in south Phoenix on our bikes. There was an apartment complex down the street where the drug dealers were almost throwing dope at people in the area. It was out of control. On one evening I offered up to my partner we should swoop down into the parking of this complex on our bikes, light the dealers up with our halogens, and see what happened. Just moments before, we had seen about five of them standing around in the complex parking lot after we had driven by in our car. Now was the time to pull out the bikes – that's why God made them. My partner was very uneasy about the plan. I reassured him I would do all the paperwork. He still didn't seem excited about the adventure. I reassured him I would do all the impounding. He still had cold feet. I reassured him I would do all the booking. Surely this was a deal he couldn't refuse. I then took off down the street to the complex.

As I pulled into the complex, I lit up the group of males standing in front of me in the parking lot. They were clearly "hanky" and bothered after having been warned too late by the whistles from the lookouts. As I was getting off my bike to make contact with the five, I could see through the front window of an apartment. My position and timing were truly unique – one in a million. From where I was at I could see through the living room of the apartment and into the kitchen. Inside the kitchen I could see a bag of drugs on the kitchen table. I then saw a female run into the kitchen, grab a bag of drugs off the table, and throw the bag out the back door. I should have bought a lottery ticket at the start of the shift.

As I was preparing to grab the dope and the girl, I turned around to see I was all alone in the complex with the five guys in front of me. My partner was stopped on the street at the entrance. He hadn't followed me in. I had to beg and coax him to come to me (*like calling my dog . . . come on boy, come here*) as he just sat there. Once I got him to come to my location and watch the pack of dealers, I was able to run to the rear of the complex, grab the drugs and arrest the girl who had thrown them.

Minutes later a marked patrol car came to our location to transport the girl back to our car where we would meet them and subsequently book her into jail. On the bike ride back to our car my partner said something to me I will never forget. "Don't you ever do that to me again. I don't get paid to get killed for drugs. I have a wife and kid at home." I was shocked. Let me share with you, as I did with him, some information about police work.

First, police work is a full contact sport. If you're not willing to run into bar to break up a fight, go be a firefighter. Having said that, if you're foolish enough to go to the bar fight by yourself, expect to lose. Hard work and smart cops shun foolishness. Second, we're always going to be outnumbered by the bad guys. That's why they give us guns and vests – for our protection and the protection of the community. Third, speaking of the community, what they pay us for is to embrace the inherent risks of police work to enforce the law so as to provide them with safe communities. Fourth, for forty hours a week the most important person in a police officer's life should be his partner. His wife and his kids are safe at home not walking point on the street in the middle of the night in a drug infested neighborhood. The most important person in my world was the guy I was riding with. Needless to say, our partnership soon ended. Years later, he became a commander. He was a good test-taker!

Partners and partnerships have come to mean a great deal to me. They seem important to Christ also. When your life depends upon a partner, a partner becomes a priority. The Great Commission is a serious task with inherent risks. Eternal destinies are on the line.

> For our **struggle** is not against flesh and blood, but against the rulers, against the powers, against the world forces of this **darkness**, against the spiritual forces of **wickedness** in the heavenly places. (*Eph. 6:12*)

We all know the value of a good partner and a trusted friend. In the struggle and fight against crime, a metachos makes all the difference in the world. The same seems to hold true for the spiritual battles in life. What type of companion, partner, or metachos are we? When Christ turns around, where will He find us? Do we jump in or stand by? According the book of Hebrews, faithful friends will be rewarded with the privilege and opportunity to rule and reign with Christ. The reward of rest waits for the metachos.

CHAPTER 24

I'm No Mercenary

No one goes to work for free. At the PLEA office, the pictures of over 36 slain police officers who died in the line of duty are sobering reminders to anyone who thinks first responders make too much money. It prompts one to re-evaluate their accounting methods. Frontline Phoenix Police Officers consistently carry the ultimate risk of death due to the reality of violence fostered in the 6th largest city in the country. Certainly, the flow of illegal aliens, narcotics and violence from the southern Arizona border aggravate the danger for rank-and-file officers. When it comes to police protection for a community, there's an economic truth which rings true – you get what you pay for.

In Nairobi Kenya, the citizens live under the rule of the third. A third of the people hire another third of the people to protect them from the remaining third of the people. This has to be done because the police are unreliable. Corruption is rampant in law enforcement. Why? They don't pay their law enforcement personnel a fair wage. If paying police officers a decent salary isn't a priority, one shouldn't be surprised if the authority given to officers is utilized illegally to provide for their families. You get what you pay for. It's wise to make the job of police work financially attractive. When pay and benefits are reasonable, incentive is created to engage in lawful and moral behavior among police employees. The job becomes more than just a disposable paper cup. If you want to get rich, don't become a police officer. But if you want a fair wage and a secure pension for risking your life for twenty years, police work begins to look attractive. Sure the job is exciting. It's an occupation that can have a life-changing impact. But I'm telling you, no one would do it for free. As noble as the job is, if you don't pay me what's it's worth, it's safer and more lucrative being a plumber. Our community partners understood this and were consistently protective of our wages and benefits. They appreciated our commitment and knew money motivates; wages impact quality – you get what you pay for.

Surely a Christian life which has an eternal impact is just as noble, if not more, than the work of a police officer. Notice I equated the Christian life to work. What holds true for police officers holds true for believers – no one works for free. I've spoken to Christians who have been immediately offended when I explain a biblical motive for Christians to obey is payment – eternal rewards from Christ. This is perceived as living like a mercenary. "I don't obey to get a reward; I obey because I love Jesus." The pursuit of eternal rewards is cast as shameful or inferior or inappropriate. The believer's expectation of payment for faithfulness is a valid motive in the Christian life only if it's in line with the text of God's Word and with the words of Christ. What did Jesus say about eternal rewards and the priority they should play in our lives?

One of the most important recorded teaching events in the life of Christ is found in the historical account by Matthew. It's referred to as the Sermon on the Mount (*Mt. 5-7*). I believe Matthew wrote his gospel between AD 50-70 and his audience consisted of Jewish believers. The theme of his written product was to present the Messiah's redemptive ministry and kingdom offer to Israel. His goal was to demonstrate Jesus was the Messiah of the Hebrew Scriptures and to explain God's offer of His kingdom, its rejection, and its present outworking.

Matthew's gospel is not the best place to go to learn how to obtain the free gift of eternal life. But if one wants a practical, insightful, inspired blueprint on how to live the Christian life, the Sermon on the Mount is worth looking at. In the Sermon on the Mount, Christ doesn't focus on justification because His disciples, who were already justified (*except Judas*), were His primary audience. Matthew identifies Christ's disciples as His primary audience at the beginning of His discourse and then, at the end, makes another distinction between these disciples and the great multitude which was also present and listened to His instruction.

> And when He saw the multitudes, He went up on the mountain; and after He sat down, His **disciples** came to Him. And opening His mouth He began to **teach them** . . . (*Mt. 5:1,2*)

> The result was that when Jesus had finished these words, **the multitudes** were amazed at His teaching; for He was **teaching them** as one having authority, and not as their scribes. (*Mt. 7:28,29*)

Jesus took the opportunity to teach His disciples not only how to live a life that is pleasing to the Father and impacting on the world, but also taught them why. Christ provided His disciples a motive for engaging in the eternal. And considering Christ knew the task of the Great Commission was going to cost them their lives, motivation makes a lot of sense. When we look at Christ's teaching, a formula emerges; faithfulness from Christians results in compensation from Christ. Jesus shares the priorities of God and the resulting payment to obedient Christians for their effort. Jesus specifically commands the pursuit of eternal rewards and then shares as to why this pursuit is important. The biblical text that primes the pump in regards to eternal rewards is found in the section known as the Beatitudes.

> Blessed are the poor in spirit, for theirs is the kingdom of heaven.
> Blessed are those who mourn, for they shall be comforted.
> Blessed are the gentle, for they shall inherit the earth.
> Blessed are those who hunger and thirst for righteousness, for they shall be satisfied.
> Blessed are the merciful, for they shall receive mercy.
> Blessed are the pure in heart, for they shall see God.
> Blessed are the peacemakers, for they shall be called sons of God.
> Blessed are those who have been persecuted for the sake of righteousness, for theirs is the kingdom of heaven.
> Blessed are you when people insult you and persecute you, and falsely say all kinds of evil against you because of Me. Rejoice and be glad, for your reward in heaven is great; for

> in the same way they persecuted the prophets who were before you. (*Mt. 5:3-12*)

Jesus encouraged faithful conduct by means of rewards – we'll be paid for patterning our life after the character of God. The Beatitudes provide a summary of the payments a Christian receives for different acts of faithfulness.

- Believers who have an attitude which is dependent upon God will be rewarded with current possession of the future Millennial Kingdom. (*Mt. 5:3*)
- Believers who are saddened by sin shall be encouraged. (*Mt. 5:4*)
- Christians who have a cool spirit (*Prov. 17:27*) will be rewarded with future ownership of the New Earth. (*Mt. 5:5*)
- Christians who desire the will of God will be rewarded with contentment. (*Mt. 5:6*)
- Believers who are merciful will be rewarded with mercy at the Bema Seat. (*Mt. 5:7*)
- Believers who are obedient will have intimate fellowship with God. (*Mt. 5:8*)
- Christians who cultivate peace will be rewarded with unique fellowship with God. (*Mt. 5:9*)
- Christians who suffer for doing what God requires will be greatly rewarded with current possession of the future Millennial Kingdom. (*Mt. 5:10-12*)

In addition to the Beatitudes, Christ connected conduct with compensation (*reward*) six times in the Sermon on the Mount and two additional times in Mt. 10:41. Perhaps rewards were important to Christ. In Matthew 6 Christ used the term "reward" no less than four times (*6:1, 2,5,16*). He spoke of "treasure" three times (*6:19,20,21*) in His sermon and one additional time in Mt. 19:21. Like rewards, Christ encouraged obedience by means of payment. In the NASB translation of the Sermon on the Mount, the Greek term "apodidomi" is translated as "repay" or "reward." The word is used 18 times in Matthew (*5:26,33, 6:4,6,18, 12:36, 16:27, 18:25 x 2, 18:26,28,29,30,34, 20:8, 21:41, 22:21, 27:58*). Work done will be paid for. Depending upon the context the term "repay" can mean pay off a debt, provide a wage, pay a tax, fulfill an oath, give account, or as seen in Mt. 16:27:

> "For the Son of Man is going to come in the glory of His Father with His angels, and will then **repay** every man **according to his deeds.**" (*Mt. 16:27*)

In Chapter 6 of the Sermon on the Mount, the principle of pay for performance is seen again and again. Christ restates a repeated theme and an important concept in the Christian life; God will repay Christians for engaging in "quiet righteousness."

> But when you give to the poor, do not let your left hand know what your right hand is doing, so that your giving will be in secret; and your Father who sees what is **done in secret** will **reward** you. (*Mt. 6:3,4*)

> But you, when you pray, go into your inner room, close your door and pray to your Father who is in secret, and your Father who sees what is **done in secret** will **reward** you. (*Mt. 6:6*)

> But you, when you fast, anoint your head and wash your face so that your fasting will not be noticed by men, but by your Father who is in secret; and your Father who sees what is **done in secret** will **reward** you [*"**openly**" – Majority Text*]. (*Mt. 6:17,18*)

"Quiet righteousness" must cause "fruit inspectors" to pull their hair out. This style of obedience, which is clearly well-pleasing to and rewarded by our "Father who sees in secret," completely runs against the grain of Reformed theology and the demand to see evidence (*good works like giving, praying and fasting*) as the primary proof a person has eternal life. Seeing that eternal life is a free gift (*Rom. 3:24, 5:15 Eph. 2:8,9*), these works and rewards can't have any connection to justification salvation. The pattern of pay for performance in the teaching of Christ in the Sermon on the Mount is summarized with a command: "Treasure up treasures."

> Do not store up for yourselves treasures on earth, where moth and rust destroy, and where thieves break in and steal. But **store up for yourselves treasures in heaven**, where neither moth nor rust destroys, and where thieves do not break in or steal; **for** [*reason*] where your treasure is, there your heart will be also. (*Mt. 6:19-21*)

Christ gave two clear commands in this short section. First, stop living for earthly assets. Christ isn't against planning but materialism. We don't have to have money to be materialistic. Materialism is a fruitless and futile mindset.

> And this also is a grievous evil – exactly as a man is born, thus will he die. So, what is the advantage to him who **toils for the wind?** (*Eccl. 5:16*)

To pursue wealth on earth during our brief moment in time is to pursue a vapor – a vapor that can't satisfy and ultimately has no staying power. In contrast to Christ's prohibitive first command is His second proactive command. Christ literally says, "Treasure up treasures." Treasure, treasure, treasure – I wonder what was on Christ's mind? Running to win those things that have eternal value and meaning in the kingdom impacts our priorities. Why pursue eternal rewards? Jesus tells us. "For where your treasure is, there will your heart be also (*Mt. 6:21*)." What we value impacts how we live. Hugh Hephner's treasure impacts how he lives. A cocaine addict's treasure impacts how he lives. A believer's treasure will impact how they live. If we live to acquire eternal rewards, we are adopting a biblical mindset, motive, and strategy for the Christian life; a strategy approved by Christ. It's never wrong for us to desire what God wants us to have.

We see Jesus' theology of eternal rewards again when He challenged a young man who was distracted from eternal life and eternal rewards by his wealth. Jesus said to him;

> If you wish to be complete, go and sell your possessions and give to the poor, and you shall have **treasure in heaven**; and come, follow Me. (*Mt. 19:21*)

Unlike childlike faith (*Mt. 19:13-15,23,24, Mk. 10:15, Lk. 18:17*), Jesus didn't say the man's efforts and obedience would bring about eternal life (*"enter into the kingdom"*). Christ said compliance with kingdom priorities would result in compensation – treasure in heaven.

Shortly following this historical event, Peter questioned Jesus. He and his peers had "left everything and followed" Him. And then the question: "What then will there be for us?" Peter wanted to know what he was going to get for his investment. He was working hard and was making great sacrifices for Christ. What was he going to get for it? Jesus could have been indignant with His reply. "You're lucky I even let you hang out with Me. Who do you think you are? I can't believe you're asking for compensation. Love for Me should be enough!" But that's not what we read. Jesus replied according to His formula: pay for performance, reward for work, compensation for commitment. Here's what Christ told Peter and the disciples the eternal reward was for their efforts:

> And Jesus said to them, "Truly I say to you, that **you who have followed Me**, in the regeneration when the Son of Man **will sit on His glorious throne, you also shall sit upon twelve thrones, judging the twelve tribes of Israel.**" (*Mt. 19:28*)

This specific group of men who made a specific investment in eternity would receive a specific reward in the Millennial Kingdom. Eternal rewards can motivate us to do great, risky, and uncomfortable things for God. It certainly did with these men. Christ consistently encouraged conduct motivated upon compensation. He seemed glad to pay for work done. Remember, Matthew was presenting Jesus as the Messiah. And it shouldn't be surprising the Messiah would promote a concept that was common in the Hebrew Scriptures (*Psm. 18:20, 19:11, 58:11, Prov. 11:18,31, 25:22*): Yahweh pays wages for work.

> The Lord has **rewarded** me according to my righteousness;
> According to the cleanness of my hands He has recompensed me. (*2 Sam. 22:21*)

> O love the Lord, all you His godly ones! The Lord preserves the faithful and fully **recompenses** the proud doer. (*Psm. 31:23*)

> And lovingkindness is Yours, O Lord, for You **recompense** a man according to his work. (*Psm. 62:12*)

> If you say, "See, we did not know this," does He not consider it who weighs the hearts? And does He not know it who keeps your soul? And will He not **render** to man **according to his work**? (*Prov. 24:12*)

> Behold, the Lord God will come with might, with His arm ruling for Him. Behold, His **reward** is with Him, and His **recompense** before Him. (*Is. 40:10*)

> I, the Lord, search the heart, I test the mind, even to **give** to each man according to his ways, **according to the results of his deeds.** (*Jer. 17:10*)

We see compensation for conduct in the Hebrew Scriptures. Certainly a New Testament book with a Jewish audience in mind is the book of Hebrews (*you think the title might be a clue*). With the ability to view the Hebrew Scriptures from a New Testament perspective, the author tells us about Moses' motives:

> By faith Moses, when he had grown up, refused to be called the son of Pharaoh's daughter, choosing rather to endure ill-treatment with the people of God than to enjoy the passing pleasures of sin considering the reproach of Christ greater riches than the treasures of Egypt; for he was looking to the **reward.** (*Heb. 11:24-26*)

The same writer teaches us rewards are linked with the character of God.

> And without faith it is impossible to please Him, for he who comes to God must believe that He is and that He is a **rewarder** of those who seek Him. (*Heb. 11:6*)

The term "rewarder" (*misthapodotes*) simply means "one who pays wages." This is the only time in the entire biblical text this term is used. God loves to give gifts – eternal life. God loves to pay wages – eternal rewards. Faith in Christ results in eternal life. Faithfulness to Christ results in eternal rewards.

I've had no less than four people die right in front of me; a suicide by shotgun, a suicide by cop, a drug deal gone bad, and a domestic violence homicide. I've literally heard some take their last breath. Interesting and sobering. In the courts there's a concept known as a dying declaration. The last words spoken by a person who is dying are given great weight. We see this (*"For I am being poured out as a drink offering, and the time of my departure has come."/ 2 Tim. 4:6*) in Paul's final words to Timothy. They are worth paying attention to – he wasn't going to say anything else after that. Even though death isn't part of the context, the importance of last words still holds validity. It's been more than two thousad years since the last words of Christ were recorded by John. His final words to the church as found in the book of Revelation are also interesting and sobering. He had many things to say, but one of the last statements He holds off making to Christians until the very end is about eternal rewards. Jesus said:

> Behold, I am coming quickly, and My **reward** is with Me, to render to every man according to what he has done. (*Rev. 22:12*)

Believers are going to be held accountable for how they lived. Life can be hard work. No one works for free and no one is expected to. It appears Christ thought the motivation of eternal rewards contained practical wisdom which would impact priorities and subsequently change lives. I'm confident Jesus is smarter than me, so I take Him at His word when it comes to rewards. So, one of the ways I biblically motivate my kids to excel and to be Christ-like is through a parting phrase prior to any event they're involved in; "Remember, it pays to serve Jesus." It's never wrong to pursue, chase, strive for, and desire what the Creator of the universe wants us to have. If eternal rewards are critical to Christ but offensive to me, I wonder where the problem lies. Remember, it pays to serve Jesus!

CHAPTER 25

Psssst. I've Got a Secret

Based only upon information received from an informant, a search warrant can be drawn and doors can be kicked down. Informants are valuable tools in accomplishing effective police work. Managing and utilizing informants ("*snitches*") is both an art and a science. They frequently can go places many officers can't and they know people and things most in law enforcement have extremely limited access to. Thus, as a source of information, I found "snitches" could be extremely helpful. But to reach the point in which their information could be used, the informant had to be "reliable." In Arizona, the courts and the Phoenix Police Department continue to have reasonably high standards informants must achieve in order to be considered reliable. When it came to narcotic enforcement, some of the criteria used to determine informant reliability consisted of the following:

- Did they use narcotic drugs?
- Did they buy narcotic drugs?
- Did they know the terminology in the use and sale of narcotic drugs?
- Could they provide verifiable names of people who had been arrested for narcotic drug violations?
- Did they know how narcotics were manufactured, packaged, priced, and hidden?
- Did they know active locations where narcotic drugs were sold?
- Did they know how to ingest narcotic drugs?
- Did they know the affects various narcotic drugs produced in a person?

- Were they on probation or parole (*if they were, we couldn't work with them*)?
- Could they successfully call, contact, and meet officers in a timely manner?
- Lastly, could they successfully make a controlled buy for an officer with undercover funds?

If the informant could get through these hoops, they were good to go. Any activity they saw with their own eyes within a specified period could be the basis of a search warrant. I used informants successfully for years. The best informants were females—males were notoriously unreliable (*code talk for "stupid and cocky"*). A person normally became an informant to work off a criminal charge. Some stayed on beyond their work-off obligations to make money. There were times when we were able to provide a free apartment in the public housing projects to facilitate the success of productive informants. Money from Silent Witness would be awarded to informants based upon the results of their information – the number of arrests, the amount of drugs, and the quantity of weapons. One could make a decent living. At one point in time, undercover money was extremely limited so we had to spend it carefully. I only had a $20 bill and asked an informant to do her best to buy as much crack cocaine as she could with the small amount of money I had. She came back with not only several rocks of crack, but she had also gotten change. She gave me a $10 bill back. She could have pocketed it and I would never have known. She was a great C.I. (*confidential informant*) who had a phenomenal impact on the drug activity in our area. The information I received from the same informant resulted in hundreds of arrests. One of her search warrants led to thirty arrests in less than two hours. Just as a side note, one of the drug addicts we arrested on the Friday we served the C.I.'s warrant showed up in an adult enrichment church class I taught on Sunday two days later. Maybe failure is an option in the Christian life!

With all this said, another key element for a reliable informant was confidentiality. For the most part, informants demonstrated incredible courage. The world they operated in (*drugs*) didn't mix well with the company they kept (*police*). On search warrants, the source of information on which probable cause was based upon came from a "reliable, ***confidential*** informant." Confidentiality protected the informant from having their name released in court or any other legal proceeding. If it came down to it, and the judge demanded the name, we would drop the case. Even though this didn't happen to my information sources, the reality was an informant who was "burned" was usually an informant who was dead. This was an unacceptable risk in the pursuit of a criminal drug case. For an informant to be useful they needed to remain secret and silent. No one could know who they were or what they were doing. To go public with an informant's identity was a great way to get them seriously hurt or killed and a sure way to render them useless.

When it comes to Christians, it's just the opposite. Secret Christians who fail to publicly confess Christ are never victorious in their spiritual life. For a believer to have a dynamic eternal impact for the cause of Christ, public identity with Him is crucial. Failing to confess Christ causes us to miss out on the joy He provides in our moment in time. If we're not courageous with our role in the Great Commission, we're missing out. If we're not public with our faith, we've got a problem—we need to be "saved." Let me explain.

Surely a life-long blind child receiving his sight back from the Messiah would be a cause for great celebration and joy. But without courage, the fear of men can quickly dominate life and dissipate joy. We see the power of fear in a historical account involving two Jewish parents.

> The Jews then did not believe it of him, that he had been blind and had received sight, until they called the **parents** of the very one who had received his sight, and questioned them, saying, "Is this your son, who you say was born blind? Then how does he now see?" His parents answered them and said, "We know that this is our son, and that he was born blind; but how he now sees, we do not know; or who opened his eyes, we do not know. Ask him; he is of age, he will speak for himself." His parents said this because **they were afraid of the Jews**; for the Jews had already agreed that if **anyone confessed Him to be Christ**, he was to be **put**

> **out of the synagogue**. For this reason his parents said, "He is of age; ask him." (*Jn. 9:18-23*)

In another example from John, we see believers failing to publicly identify themselves (*confess*) with Jesus due to fear. Failing to confess Christ results in a useless and limited Christian impact.

> Nevertheless many even of the rulers **believed in Him** [*Christians*], but because of the Pharisees **they** [*believers*] were **not confessing Him**, for **fear** that they would be **put out of the synagogue**; for [*reason they were afraid*] **they** [*believers*] loved the approval of men rather than the approval of God. (*Jn. 12:42,43*)

When sanctification and justification, two distinct theological issues, are contextually kept separate in the biblical text, a passage from Paul's pen, which is sometimes misused in evangelistic efforts, can be utilized more appropriately in addressing a Christian's spiritual effectiveness. It appears Paul understood the connection between confessing Christ and a dynamic usefulness to the Master. He instructed believers, who were already justified, that their public confession of Christ would result in their "salvation." Confessing Christ and calling upon the Lord are clearly righteous acts – good works. And the Bible (*including Paul's inspired writings*) is very clear good works have nothing (*Rom. 4:4,5, Gal. 2:16*) to do with justification (*eternal life*). But yet Paul writes if believers "confess Jesus as Lord" and "call on the name of the Lord" they will be "saved." Saved from what? Hell or something else? In a passage worthy of a dissertation please allow me a few pages. Paul wrote in Romans 10:9-14:

> that if **you** [*believers in the context – Rom. 10:1*] **confess** with your mouth Jesus as Lord, and **believe** in your heart that God raised Him from the dead, **you will be saved**; for with the heart a person **believes, resulting in righteousness** [*justification*] and with the mouth he **confesses, resulting in salvation** [*sanctification*]. For the Scripture says, "Whoever **believes** [*not "confesses" or "calls"*] **in Him** will not be disappointed." For there is no distinction between Jew and

> Greek; for the same Lord is Lord of all, abounding in riches for all who **call on Him**; for "Whoever will **call on the name of the Lord** will be **saved** [*sanctification*]." How then will they **call** on Him in whom they have not **believed**? How will they **believe** in Him whom they have not **heard**? And how will they **hear** without a **preacher**? (*Rom. 10:9-14*)

In the book of Romans, the term "call" is only used three times (*Rom. 10:12,13,14*) and "confess" is only used twice (*Rom. 10:9,10*). Thus the context of these terms in Romans is limited to this passage. And prior to this passage, Paul restated once again the sole requirement for justification:

> For Christ is the end of the law for righteousness to everyone who **believes** [*not "confesses" or "calls"*]. (*Rom. 10:4*)

A person first has to hear how to obtain eternal life (*justification salvation*) before they can believe. Men and women who share the gospel with them (*"preacher"—kerusso / participle: those who speak with the goal to persuade*) provide "hearers" a moment in time to trust in Christ for eternal life. Subsequent to belief in Christ as their only hope of heaven, Christians can choose to receive a new power to be "saved" from the power of sin (*sanctification salvation*) if/when they go public (*confess*) with their faith. Christians have the option to receive a new power to be "saved" from faithlessness when they exhibit dynamic and courageous faith (*call upon the Lord*) in crucial moments for the cause of Christ. Nicodemus and Joseph of Arimathea showed great resolution in the face of a dangerous and volatile situation.

> After these things **Joseph of Arimathea**, being **a disciple** of Jesus, but **a secret one** for **fear of the Jews**, asked Pilate that he might take away the body of Jesus; and Pilate granted permission. So he came and took away His body. **Nicodemus**, who had first come to Him by night, also came, bringing a mixture of myrrh and aloes, about a hundred pounds weight. So **they took the body of Jesus** and bound it in linen wrappings with the spices, as is the burial custom of the Jews. (*Jn. 19:38-40*)

This is what I call "raw courage." When the right person (*Christ*) and the right principles (*His Word*) drive people, great and memorable things can happen. There are other historical events which demonstrate the sanctifying and supernatural power of courage, confessing, and calling.

> But being full of the Holy Spirit, **he** [*Stephen*] gazed intently into heaven and saw the glory of God, and Jesus standing at the right hand of God; and he said, "Behold, I see the heavens opened up and the Son of Man standing at the right hand of God." But they cried out with a loud voice, and covered their ears and rushed at him with one impulse. When they had driven **him** [*Stephen*] out of the city, they began stoning him; and the witnesses laid aside their robes at the feet of a young man named **Saul** [*later called Paul*]. They went on stoning Stephen as he **called on the Lord** and said, "Lord Jesus, receive my spirit!" Then falling on his knees, **he** [*Stephen*] cried out with a loud voice, "Lord, do not hold this sin against them!" Having said this, he fell asleep [*died*]. (*Acts 7:55-60*)

If anyone knew about the power brought to the Christian life by means of confessing and calling, it was Paul. As an eyewitness, Paul saw what raw courage and great faith were in the life of Stephen as he was murdered. The sanctification salvation brought about by confessing and calling wasn't isolated to only Stephen's life. Other Christians chose to be courageous in the face of persecution as well.

> But Ananias answered, "Lord, I have heard from many about **this man** [*Paul*], how much harm he did to Your **saints** at Jerusalem; and here he has authority from the chief priests to bind all who **call on Your name**." But the Lord said to him, "Go, for he is a **chosen instrument** of Mine, to bear My name before the Gentiles and kings and the sons of Israel; for I will show him how much he must suffer for My name's sake." So Ananias departed and entered the house, and after laying his hands on him said, "Brother Saul, the Lord Jesus, who appeared to you on the road by which you

> were coming, has sent me so that you may regain your sight and be filled with the Holy Spirit." And immediately there fell from his eyes something like scales, and he regained his sight, and he got up and was baptized; and he took food and was strengthened. Now for several days he was with the disciples who were at Damascus, and immediately **he** [*Paul*] **began to proclaim Jesus in the synagogues** [*confessing Christ*], saying, "He is the Son of God." All those **hearing him** continued to be amazed, and were saying, "Is this not he who in Jerusalem **destroyed those who called on this name**, and who had come here for the purpose of bringing them bound before the chief priests?" (*Acts 9:13-21*)

According to Ananias, those who had "called upon Your name" in Jerusalem were "saints." And they did so in crucial moments (*"much harm" and "bind"*) while fulfilling the Great Commission. We see in the biblical text it's only people who are born-again (*"saints"—1 Cor. 1:2*) who "call upon the Lord." "Calling on the Lord" appears to be a requirement for sanctification *not* justification. The spiritual courage of Stephen coupled with the grace of God looks like it had a life-altering impact on Paul. He went from killing Christians to confessing Christ. In the book of Romans, Paul seems to have been convinced that believers, in the same fashion as Stephen, who "call on the Lord" (*courageous act of faith*) and "confess Christ" (*publicly identify with Jesus*) will be "saved" – saved from the power of sin. Courage, confessing, and calling were key ingredients in Paul becoming a "chosen instrument." It's likely they're essential for us in becoming useful to the Master. Paul referred to mature believers who were "useful to the Master" as "those who call upon the Lord."

> Therefore, if anyone cleanses himself from these things, he will be a vessel for honor, **sanctified**, **useful to the Master**, prepared for every good work. Now flee from youthful lusts and pursue righteousness, faith, love and peace, with **those who call on the Lord** from a pure heart. (*2 Tim. 2:21,22*)

A wedding ring is how many publicly identify a private commitment with a spouse. Through a round piece of metal on their hand, men and women "confess" to the world they're married. One elected labor official I knew would remove his wedding band while out of town on his association's business. Apparently a "public confession" (*a gold band on his finger*) hindered his extracurricular (*some might say "extramarital"*) activities. Here was a married Christian man that didn't look or act like he was a husband (*or a disciple*); He failed to confess. Did his failure to identify himself as the spouse of another negate the fact that he was indeed a husband? No. But did his faithlessness have a negative impact on the success and health of his marriage? Yes.

Like bad husbands who don't look married, there are bad believers who don't look like they're born-again. Their failure to confess has absolutely no impact on their justification (*standing as a child of God*) but their faithlessness certainly impedes their sanctification (*standing as God's friend*). The eternal destiny of a believer does *not* depend upon their public courage but entirely on the person of Christ. If we choose to deny Him, we'll forfeit present joy, a dynamic Christian impact, and future commendation but *not* our eternal life. Courage is the ability to carry on in spite of fear. From a negative aspect, the greater fear casts out the lesser fear. One certainty from our moment in time is giving account to God (*not "the world"*) for our silence. Thus a fear of God is a biblical motivator in overcoming the fear of men. From a positive perspective, we can recall during a raging storm while walking on water, Jesus told His fearful crew, "I AM. Stop being afraid (*Jn. 6:20*)!" God's care for us today is as real as it was for His disciples over 2000 years ago. Because of this, stop being afraid and remember courage by means of confessing and calling brings compensation.

CHAPTER 26

Sons & Children, Heirs & Co-heirs

Christians are described as children of God. We take on this new relationship with the Creator of the Universe the moment we trust in Christ for eternal life. Some verses which shed light on this wonderful biblical fact are:

> But as many as received Him, to them He gave the right to become **children of God**, even to those who **believe** in His name, who were born, not of blood nor of the will of the flesh nor of the will of man, but of God. (*Jn. 1:12,13*)

> See how great a love the Father has bestowed on us, that we would be called **children of God**; and such we are. For this reason the world does not know us, because it did not know Him. Beloved, now we are **children of God**, and it has not appeared as yet what we will be. We know that when He appears, we will be like Him, because we will see Him just as He is. (*1 Jn. 3:1,2*)

The moment a person exercises faith alone in Jesus Christ alone for eternal life, the Creator becomes their Father and the believer becomes His child. A new and permanent relationship is established based upon God's grace. No conduct or works are relevant or necessary for this positional change to take place between someone who was spiritually dead but who now has been born-again. But in the Sermon on the Mount, Christ takes the conduct of loving one's enemies and seems to link it with a special relationship beyond the status of a child. We see the faithfulness of a believer who is a child of God is rewarded with the unique privileged identifier and status as a "son."

> But I say to you, love your enemies, and pray for those who persecute you in order that you **<u>may be sons of your Father</u>** who is in heaven; for He causes His sun to rise on the evil and the good, and sends rain on the righteous and the unrighteous. (*Mt. 5:44,45*)

The choice of a Christian patterning his/her life after the character of their Father will be rewarded with a unique relationship with God – "sons of your Father." Whenever works or conduct are injected or coupled to the Christian life, we know it deals with sanctification (*eternal rewards*) and not justification (*eternal life—Rom. 4:4,5*). God cares for those who are hostile to Him and we should too. Those who do will be rewarded. As we've previously seen in dealing with the subjunctive mood, the context and the grammatical use in the English translation of "may be" demonstrates the issue is one of possibility *not* certainty. This special designation of "sons" is dependent upon conduct and choice. The conduct required to be a "son of your Father" is to "love your enemies, and pray for those who persecute you." Maybe we will, maybe we won't.

Depending upon the context, the term "son" can indicate a special privilege of friendship. Christ referred to "sons" in Matthew 5:9 in connection with being a "peacemaker." God is a peacemaker (*Rom. 5:1*) and we should be too. Those who are peacemakers will be rewarded. "Son" is also seen in Mt. 9:15 when Jesus pictures his faithful band of disciples as "sons (*attendants – NASB*) of the bridegroom." There are times in the Scripture where the term "sons of God" in fact does refer to the positional relationship consistent with justification, certainly when it is solely related to faith apart from works.

> For you are all **<u>sons of God</u>** through faith in Christ Jesus. (*Gal. 3:26*)

Just as the term "pass" can mean "no" in one context and "yes" in another, so the context of the phrase "sons of God" determines whether the subject of discussion is a relational position based upon faith or an earned honor based upon faithfulness.

In the context of Romans 8, like Christ, Paul utilizes the term "son" as a term of earned honor. It appears Paul makes a distinction between "sons of God" and "children of God" in the same way he communicates a distinction between "heirs of God" and "fellow heirs with Christ." Children and heirs are positional as a result of faith in Christ for eternal life (*justification*). Sons and co-heirs are linked with faithfulness by the believer in the Christian life (*sanctification*).

> For all who are being **led by the Spirit of God, these are sons of God**. For you have not received a spirit of slavery leading to fear again, but you have received a spirit of adoption as sons by which we cry out, "Abba! Father!" The Spirit Himself testifies **with** [*not "to"*] our spirit that **we are children of God**, and if **children, heirs also, heirs of God** and **fellow heirs with Christ, if indeed** (*emphatic marker of condition*) **we suffer with Him** so that we may also be glorified with Him. (*Rom. 8:14-17*)

Believers who are "led by the Spirit" are equated as "sons of God." Specific conduct brings about this unique privilege of friendship with God. Paul reminded his audience they were not adopted to be fearful but to be friends – "adoption as sons." Paul continues in the Romans passage by stating the Spirit testifies "with" *not* "to" our spirit we are "children of God." God's Spirit is continually vouching for and vouching with us before the Father "since" we are His children. This is not a subjective personal experience of assurance but a positional declaration to God by the Spirit of our justification. The eternal destiny and relationship of all believers as "children of God" is secure.

But Paul and Christ weren't the only ones who saw that being a "son" was a merited privilege. John links faithful Christian conduct with the special relationship as a "son" in Revelation 21:7. John records the words of God in his prophetic written product:

> He who overcomes shall inherit these things, and I will be his God and he will be My **son**. (*Rev. 21:7*)

Once again, the distinction of a special earned honor as a "son" is implied. To add further clarification, it's interesting to note Jesus is referred to and designated as a "Son" and not a child; Jesus is the Son of God. And as such, He enjoys a special relationship with the Father because He is pleasing to Him (*Mt. 3:17*). Just as Paul made a distinction between "son" and "children" he now makes another distinction between "heirs" and "co-heirs."

Justification relates to being a child, sanctification relates to being a son. In the same way, "since" all believers are "children of God" they are also "heirs of God." Faith in Christ made this possible. But only believers who are faithful, those who "suffer with Him" enjoy a special designation and the honor that comes with it; faithful Christians become "fellow" or "co-heirs" with Christ "if indeed we suffer with Him." A co-heir appears to designate a unique, intimate (*Heb. 11:9*), inclusive (*Eph. 3:6*) role of honor (*1 Pt. 3:7*) in the Millennial Kingdom. Justification was made possible by Christ's suffering and as a result we enjoy the positional right as children and heirs. Sanctification is made possible by our suffering and as a result we'll enjoy the earned reward of being designated as sons and fellow heirs. In this chapter we've briefly seen that faithful Christians are rewarded with the special, earned designations of "sons" and "co-heirs." In the next chapter, another earned designator is available for faithful and obedient believers—overcomers.

CHAPTER 27

Overcomers

Everyone in the Phoenix Police Department goes through an intensive hiring process which includes a written test, a criminal background check, a physical examination, a polygraph, a psychological evaluation, and an oral board interview. Out of 1000 applicants, only around 200 make it through these filters. Each officer then goes through a fifteen week police academy, a fifteen week field training program, and a one year probationary period. During the one year probationary period management can fire you for just looking funny – we call this "at will." In the end, out of all these stages of the hiring process, less than one out of ten makes it to the street. In addition to this, it takes the average new officer eighteen months to become fully functional in the job. The rule of thumb is, if an officer can make it to the seventh year, they'll make it to their twentieth. Every sworn officer on the Phoenix Police Department gets a badge, gets a gun, and gets a paycheck. Each sworn employee is provided the opportunity to serve the same boss, the citizens of Phoenix. With all of these commonalities impacting all officers, only a few receive earned citations of honor or medals of recognition.

The Phoenix Police Department recognizes officers at awards ceremonies by means of five distinct and separate awards. The requirements to win these unique and visible honors are clearly spelled out in the Department's Operations Orders.

- The Medal of Valor – Awarded to an employee for a conspicuous act of valor during the actual performance of police service that involves risk of life and knowledge of that risk. This act must clearly delineate valor from other forms of courage and is clearly above and beyond the call of duty.

- The Medal of Merit – Awarded to an employee for an act of courage and dedication to duty during the actual performance of a police service involving significant risk or danger to personal safety.
- The Medal of Lifesaving – Awarded to an employee for an act that results in the saving or preservation of a human life or lives that otherwise would have immediately expired without the employee's direct involvement in providing first aid, medical, or physical intervention.
- The Distinguished Service Award – Presented to any member of the Department who has made a significantly noteworthy and exceptional contribution to the Department.
- The Community Based Policing Award – Presented to an employee for outstanding performance or conduct exemplifying dedication to duty involving either a single act or continuing excellence that fosters or furthers the Department's community-based policing philosophy.

It's not uncommon for an officer to put in decades of work and not receive any of the aforementioned awards or medals. These are unique honors to recognize stellar accomplishments and to motivate officers to engage in a high level of service to the community. Biblical writers, certainly John, might have been comfortable in referring to officers whose conduct merits the compensation of an award as an overcomer.

It's quite common to see people wearing shoes with a "swish" symbol on the side. The logo is linked to the brand name "Nike." The word "Nike" comes from the Greek word "nikao" and means to carry the day, to win, to overcome. Positionally, faith in Christ for eternal life makes all believers permanent and secure "overcomers."

> For whatever is born of God **overcomes** the world; and this is the victory that has overcome the world—our faith. Who is the one who **overcomes** the world, but **he who believes** that Jesus is the Son of God? (*1 Jn. 5:4,5*)

Out of the 28 times the word "overcome" or "overcomer" is used in the New Testament, John used the term 23 times. In the context above, when a person exercises faith alone in Christ alone for eternal life, positionally they "overcome" or are saved from the penalty of sin. This justification salvation, as it relates to being saved from an eternal death penalty, is based upon God's grace and is in no way connected or tied to works or conduct. With this said, let's go back to the word "pass." Depending on the context, it can mean to make flirtatious advances or to throw an oblong leather ball in a game. Context provides two completely different yet singular literal meanings behind the same word. Paul used "overcome" to warn his Christian audience they were susceptible to real and practical defeat in their spiritual journey. They could be "overcome" by evil.

> Do not be **overcome** by evil, but **overcome** evil with good. (*Rom. 12:21*)

Context allows us to understand "overcoming" can go beyond the issue of justification (*eternal life*) and be clearly related to sanctification (*eternal rewards*) depending upon the context. When "overcoming" is linked to works, it's connected to sanctification. A believer is saved from the power of sin (*sanctification*) by overcoming it with good. Once again, this isn't rocket science. And in the same way Paul used the term "overcome" in relation to sanctification and obedience, John also used the word to recognize the recipients of various eternal rewards for faithfulness.

In the book of Revelation, John recorded Christ's thoughts on "overcomers." Christ described faithfulness in specific ways and then linked this specific faithful conduct to specific eternal rewards and honors. Christians who prevail or are victorious in their moment of time (*"overcome evil with good"*) will be compensated for their conduct. Practically, obedience to Christ makes faithful Christians "overcomers" *not* from the penalty of sin, but from power of sin. "Overcoming" saves a believer from the power of sin and results in reward. Just like in the Police Department, it appears that, even though available to all, not every believer is an overcomer (*Mt. 20:16, 22:14, Rev. 3:4*).

Similar to the honors section of the Operations Orders in the Phoenix Police Department, Christ's commendations to the seven churches in John's prophetic work provide us with specific conduct required for specific compensation in our Christian walk. It's worth the effort to take a brief look at Christ's appraisal of the believers in these seven historical churches. The consistent pattern of each communique involves various combinations of commendations, criticisms, commands, warnings, encouragement, and motivational rewards.

Church of Ephesus

Jesus said to believers in the church of Ephesus:

> To the angel of the church in Ephesus write: The One who holds the seven stars in His right hand, the One who walks among the seven golden lampstands, says this: "I know your deeds and your toil and perseverance, and that you cannot tolerate evil men, and you put to the test those who call themselves apostles, and they are not, and you found them to be false; and you have perseverance and have endured for My name's sake, and have not grown weary. But I have this against you, that you have left your first love. Therefore remember from where you have fallen, and repent and do the deeds you did at first; or else I am coming to you and will remove your lampstand out of its place—unless you repent. Yet this you do have, that you hate the deeds of the Nicolaitans, which I also hate. He who has an ear, let him hear what the Spirit says to the churches. **To him who overcomes, I will grant to eat of the tree of life which is in the Paradise of God.**" (*Rev. 2:1-7*)

Christ's commendation to these believers seemed to focus on their commitment to doctrinal purity in the face of the false teaching of the Nicolaitans (*1 Kgs. 11:1-13, Acts 20:28-31, 1 Tim 6:20,21*). It can be easy, when focusing on principles, to forget the value of people.

> For this reason I too, having heard of the faith in the Lord Jesus which exists among you and **<u>your love for all the saints.</u>** (*Eph. 1:15*)

Perhaps Christ's criticism of these Christians (*"You have left your first love"*) was their forgetfulness to love people. People are a priority for God and they should be for us as well. There should be no acceptable casualty rate in the Christian assembly. Thus, Christ's commands for this church are consistent with what God values: people. It's been said, "It is the doom of men that they forget." Remembering to love people is crucial in the Christian life. Jesus also provides a warning to the Ephesians. He tells them about the possibility of loss for leaving people behind. Since we know nothing can separate us from the love of God (*Rom. 8:35-39*) and faithlessness on our part does not impact our eternal security (*2 Tim. 2:13*), this can't be about the loss of eternal life but the loss of honor in the kingdom. Like Israel's glory (*Zech. 4:2, Is. 49:6, Mt. 23:37-39*), He addressed they might have their lampstand removed. **We learn overcomers are Christians who are faithful in doctrinal purity and in loving others**. They'll receive a reward; the privilege of eating of the tree of life. With vague caution on my part, it appears from other references to the tree of life in Revelation this reward is a recognizable honor or an intimate experience of fellowship (*dining / Psm. 23:5,6*) which is an earned right based upon righteous living.

> Then he showed me a river of the water of life, clear as crystal, coming from the throne of God and of the Lamb, in the middle of its street. On either side of the river was **<u>the tree of life</u>**, bearing twelve kinds of fruit, yielding its fruit every month; and the leaves of the tree were for the healing of the nations. (*Rev. 22:1,2*)

> Blessed are those who wash their robes, so that they may have **<u>the right to the tree of life</u>**, and may enter by the gates into the city. (*Rev. 22:14*)

Out of hope, faith, and love, Paul told us the greatest was love (*1 Cor. 13:13*). When our moment in time is dominated by love, certainly love for others in the Body, faithful believers can expect special honor and recognition—access to the tree of life.

Church of Smyrna

Jesus said to believers in the church of Smyrna:

> And to the angel of the church in Smyrna write: The first and the last, who was dead, and has come to life, says this: "I know your tribulation and your poverty (but you are rich), and the blasphemy by those who say they are Jews and are not, but are a synagogue of Satan. Do not fear what you are about to suffer. Behold, the devil is about to cast some of you into prison, so that you will be tested, and you will have tribulation for ten days. **Be faithful until death, and I will give you the crown of life.** He who has an ear, let him hear what the Spirit says to the churches. **He who overcomes will not be hurt by the second death.**" (*Rev. 2:8-11*)

Christ's commendation to these believers focused on their suffering as a result of obedience. This is a pattern provided by Jesus (*Phil. 2:5-8*) and followed by this assembly of Christians. What stands out in this communique is Christ did not have a single criticism for the Christians in this church. His silence is loud praise. Christ continues by providing two commands: First, they were told not to fear upcoming suffering and second, they were commanded to be faithful until death. Beside an indication their faithfulness might cause them to forfeit their lives, Jesus provides a warning which contains more specificity. He shared three upcoming difficulties with them: the Devil was about to cast some of them into prison, they would be tested, and they would have tribulation for 10 days. This sounds similar to political pressures experience by Daniel, Hananiah, Mishael, and Azariah in Daniel 1:11-14. By the way, why do we always refer to these three men by their foreign pagan names – Shadrach, Meshak, and Abed-nego?

> But Daniel said to the overseer whom the commander of the officials had appointed over Daniel, Hananiah, Mishael and Azariah, "Please **test your servants for ten days**, and

> let us be given some vegetables to eat and water to drink. Then let our appearance be observed in your presence and the appearance of the youths who are eating the king's **choice food** (*this food was sacrificed to idols*); and deal with your servants according to what you see." So he listened to them in this matter and **tested them for ten days.** (*Dan. 1:11-14*)

Subsequently, Christ offered a word of encouragement to these Christians who valued their spiritual convictions. **From this passage we see overcomers are those believers who faithfully pay a price for their commitment to Christ.** He told them if they remain faithful, He'll give them the crown of life. This seems to be a unique and visible honor (*1 Cor. 9:25*) in the kingdom for a committed lifestyle of obedience under pressure. In addition to this eternal reward, by means of a litotes (*lie-tow-tees*), He assures them of further honor.

A litotes is a literary device which uses a deliberate form of understatement with the purpose of overemphasizing an idea. In Acts 21:39 Paul described Tarsus as "no ordinary city." His literal meaning: a very impressive city. Luke described a great storm by using a litotes in Acts 27:20 when he wrote "and no small storm was assailing us." We use this form of expression frequently in our conversations.

- "That's not bad." – IT'S GOOD
- "What you did is no small accomplishment." – IT'S GREAT
- "What you've asked is not an unreasonable question." – IT'S VERY REASONABLE
- "He's no dummy!" – HE'S SMART

Christ uses a double negative in the Greek to engage in the same type of emphatic language. In this passage we see the phrase "ou me" which can carry the meaning "absolutely in no way" or "most certainly will not." In the context of a litotes, this double negative can also carry a hyper-positive connotation. Christ assures the believers at Smyrna of a literal truth by means of figurative speech; "There is no possible way ever you'll even come close to the second death. Our relationship is more than secure. Life is most certainly yours." There's no reason to read into this word of encouragement the possibility of a believer being subjected to the second death. This simple understatement shows high marks and sincere praise.

Church of Pergamum

Jesus said to Christians in the church of Pergamum:

> And to the angel of the church in Pergamum write: The One who has the sharp two-edged sword says this: "I know where you dwell, where Satan's throne is; and you hold fast My name, and did not deny My faith even in the days of Antipas, My witness, My faithful one, who was killed among you, where Satan dwells. But I have a few things against you, because you have there some who hold the teaching of Balaam, who kept teaching Balak to put a stumbling block before the sons of Israel, to eat things sacrificed to idols and to commit acts of immorality. So you also have some who in the same way hold the teaching of the Nicolaitans. Therefore repent; or else I am coming to you quickly, and I will make war against them with the sword of My mouth. He who has an ear, let him hear what the Spirit says to the churches. **To him who overcomes, to him I will give some of the hidden manna, and I will give him a white stone, and a new name written on the stone which no one knows but he who receives it.**" (*Rev. 2:12-17*)

Christ commended these Christians for courage. It took great courage for Christ to come down to earth, to go into Jerusalem, and to stand up and take a beating I clearly deserved. If it was me and it came to the sins of the world, I would have stayed put, ran away, and cowered down. Christ showed great courage and we should too. But Jesus still had "a few things against them." He described some believers in the assembly as engaging in moral compromise. They are described as "some who hold the teaching of Balaam" (*1 Kgs. 11:1-13*) and more specifically as "Nicolaitans" (*Acts 20:28-31, 1 Tim 6:20,21*). Christians who were justified, born-again, and possessed eternal life were engaged in conduct which was highly offensive to Christ – spiritual insensitivity and immorality. And to aggravate the situation, it appears this conduct was having a negative impact on the body and was not being addressed by church leadership according to the mandate of the biblical text (*Mt. 18:15-20*). Christ provided a command to correct the situation. These Christians needed to repent – change their mind and, like Christ, courageously come down, go in, and stand up. If they didn't there was a consequence. Remember, where there's great grace there's great accountability. Disobedient believers will experience God's wrath. Christ brought to their attention that, in light of eternity and their brief moment in time, He was coming quickly – not with the open hand of fellowship but an aggressive and painful word of truth. Christians who were engaging in this sinful conduct would be held liable. **In contrast to the Nicolaitans and in the context of this communique, overcomers are Christians who are faithful in moral purity and courage.** Believers who are overcomers will be given two eternal rewards. The first reward is "hidden manna." It's possible this reward is descriptive of a unique privilege similar to what Israel's priest had access to.

> Moses said to Aaron, "Take a jar and put an omerful of manna in it, and place it before the Lord to be **kept throughout your generations.**" (*Ex. 16:33*)

The second reward for faithfulness in moral purity and courage is described by Christ as "a white stone, and a new name written on the stone which no one knows but he who receives it." This appears to be another special honor. A person's name says a lot about his/her character.

> Thus says the Lord, "Preserve justice and do righteousness, for My salvation is about to come and My righteousness to be revealed. How blessed is the man who does this, and the son of man who takes hold of it; who keeps from profaning the sabbath, and keeps his hand from doing any evil. Let not the foreigner who has joined himself to the Lord say, 'The Lord will surely separate me from His people.' Nor let the eunuch say, 'Behold, I am a dry tree.'" For thus says the Lord, "To the eunuchs who keep My sabbaths, and choose

> what pleases Me, and hold fast My covenant, to them I will give in My house and within My walls a memorial, and **a name better than that of sons and daughters; I will give them an everlasting name which will not be cut off**." (*Is. 56:1-5*)

Conduct brings about compensation. The Hebrew Scriptures demonstrate God honors those who pursue justice and do the right thing. The fuel that makes this positive movement possible is courage. In the same way, Christ will reward and repay those overcomers who are morally sound and bold with special compensation.

Church of Thyatira

Jesus said to believers in the church of Thyatira:

> And to the angel of the church in Thyatira write: The Son of God, who has eyes like a flame of fire, and His feet are like burnished bronze, says this: "I know [*you*], [*the*] deeds, and [*the*] love and [*the*] faith and [*the*] service and [*the*] perseverance, and that your deeds of late are greater than at first. But I have this against you, that you tolerate the woman Jezebel, who calls herself a prophetess, and she teaches and leads My bond-servants astray so that they commit acts of immorality and eat things sacrificed to idols. I gave her time to repent, and she does not want to repent of her immorality. Behold, I will throw her on a bed of sickness, and those who commit adultery with her into great tribulation, unless they repent of her deeds. And I will kill her children with pestilence, and all the churches will know that I am He who searches the minds and hearts; and I will give to each one of you according to your deeds. But I say to you, the rest who are in Thyatira, who do not hold this teaching, who have not known the deep things of Satan, as they call them—I place no other burden on you. Nevertheless what you have, hold fast until I come. **He who overcomes, and he who keeps My deeds until the end, to him I will give authority over the nations; and he shall rule them with a rod of iron,**

> **as the vessels of the potter are broken to pieces, as I also have received authority from My Father; and I will give him the morning star.** He who has an ear, let him hear what the Spirit says to the churches." (*Rev. 2:18-29*)

One concept repeated throughout Christ's words to these historical churches is the reality that actions have consequences – cause and effect. And it appears Christians are not immune from this fact of life (*and of Scripture*).

> Do not be deceived, God is not mocked; for whatever a man **sows**, this he will also **reap.** (*Gal. 6:7*)

Christ commends those in Thyatira for their consistent good works and spiritual growth. What He has against them is moral compromise and a failure to address what appears to be a Satanic mindset (*"the deep things of Satan"*) in the lives of Christians (*Acts 5:3, 2 Pt. 2:18-22*). False teaching can be found in churches today (*1 Cor. 11:18,19*) as much as in the past. We see this in Christ's criticism; "You tolerate the woman Jezebel who leads **my bondservants** [*believers in context*] astray so that **they** [*believers in context*] commit immorality (*"pornea"—we get our English word "pornography" from this Greek term*) and eat things sacrificed to idols." This is the only time John used this Greek word for "adultery" in the book of Revelation. It's the same term John used in John 8:4 – the woman "caught in adultery." Sexual sin in the church is harmful and inappropriate (*1 Cor. 6:15-20*). Christ warned these believers He literally would "kill her **children** [*mislead believers*] with 'death.'" Perhaps a holy God is not willing to tolerate sin (*1 Jn. 5:16*). Thus, His harsh and justified discipline of born-again believers is clear – "I will give each one of **you** [*believers in context*] according to **your** [*believers in context*] deeds." In contrast to faithless Christians who were "holding fast" to an ungodly and unbiblical world-view, Christ commands the faithful remainder to "hold fast" to what they have – biblical teaching. **In the context of this section, we see overcomers are Christians who faithfully maintain sexual purity – they "keep My deeds until the end."** Only those believers who are overcomers will obtain the rewards of authority over the nations and the morning star.

John and Jeremiah provide insight about the future setting in which believers will exercise authority over the nations in the Millennial Kingdom.

> Then I saw an angel coming down from heaven, holding the key of the abyss and a great chain in his hand. And he laid hold of the dragon, the serpent of old, who is the devil and Satan, and bound him for **a thousand years**; and he threw him into the abyss, and shut it and sealed it over him, so that he would not deceive the nations any longer, until **the thousand years** were completed; after these things he must be released for a short time. Then **I saw thrones, and they sat on them**, and judgment was given to them. And I saw the souls of those who had been beheaded because of their testimony of Jesus and because of the word of God, and those who had not worshiped the beast or his image, and had not received the mark on their forehead and on their hand; and they came to life and **reigned with Christ for a thousand years.** (*Rev. 20:1-4*)

> 'For I know the plans that **I have for you** [*Israel in the context*],' declares the Lord, 'plans for welfare and not for calamity to give you a future and a hope. Then you will call upon Me and come and pray to Me, and I will listen to you. You will seek Me and find Me when you search for Me with all your heart. I will be found by you,' declares the Lord, 'and I will restore your fortunes and will gather you from **all the nations** and from all the places where I have driven you,' declares the Lord, 'and **I will bring you back to the place** from where I sent you into exile.' (*Jer. 29:11-14*)

It's important for us to maintain a distinction between the Millennial Kingdom and heaven. They are not the same. In an example of how to pray, Jesus instructed us with these words; "Thy **kingdom** come (*Mt. 6:10*)." He did not equate the kingdom with heaven. It's in this physical and literal kingdom on earth where faithful Christians will rule and reign with Christ, where the nation of Israel (*"I have plans for you" – Israel not the church or Christians*) will be restored, and where the disciples will rule over the twelve Hebrew tribes with Christ from Jerusalem (*Mt. 19:27,28*).

To be given "the morning star" is possibly a descriptive phrase of another unique honor given by Christ to overcomers. On many mornings, Venus and Mercury are "lights" easily seen in the sky when others have faded away. These stars remain distinct and visible while others have dimmed. This idea and concept is addressed in the Hebrew Scriptures and in the writings of Paul.

> When the **morning stars** sang together and all the sons of God shouted for joy? (*Job 38:7*)
>
> Now at that time Michael, the great prince who stands guard over the sons of your people, will arise. And there will be a time of distress such as never occurred since there was a nation until that time; and at that time your people, everyone who is found written in the book, will be rescued. Many of those who sleep in the dust of the ground will awake, these to everlasting life, but the others to disgrace and everlasting contempt. **Those who have insight will shine brightly** like the brightness of the expanse of heaven, and those who lead the many to righteousness, **like the stars forever and ever.** (*Dan. 12:1-3*)
>
> All flesh is not the same flesh, but there is one flesh of men, and another flesh of beasts, and another flesh of birds, and another of fish. There are also heavenly bodies and earthly bodies, but the glory of the heavenly is one, and the glory of the earthly is another. There is one glory of the sun, and another glory of the moon, and another glory of the stars; **for star differs from star in glory**. So also is the resurrection of the dead. It is sown a perishable body, it is raised an imperishable body; it is sown in dishonor, it is raised in glory; it is sown in weakness, it is raised in power; it is sown a natural body, it is raised a spiritual body. If there is a natural body, there is also a spiritual body. (*1 Cor. 15:39-44*)

It seems the ability to reflect the glory of God in a manner consistent with the faithfulness of the believer will be a great and wonderful reward earned by overcomers.

Church of Sardis

Jesus said to Christians in the church of Sardis:

> To the angel of the church in Sardis write: He who has the seven Spirits of God and the seven stars, says this: "I know your deeds, that you have a name that you are alive, but you are dead. Wake up, and strengthen the things that remain, which were about to die; for I have not found your deeds completed in the sight of My God. So remember what you have received and heard; and keep it, and repent. Therefore if you do not wake up, I will come like a thief, and you will not know at what hour I will come to you. But you have a few people in Sardis who have not soiled their garments; and they will walk with Me in white, for they are worthy. **He who overcomes will thus be clothed in white garments; and I will not erase his name from the book of life, and I will confess his name before My Father and before His angels.** He who has an ear, let him hear what the Spirit says to the churches." (*Rev. 3:1-6*)

This group of believers received the barest of commendations – at least you have eternal life. Christ clearly presented that the faith of a born-again person can be dead. Thus He tells them, "**You** [*believers in the context*] are alive but **you** [*believers in the context*] are dead." To be "dead" in this context is to be useless (*not "worthless"*). They were asleep and not paying attention. We see this same line of thinking from Paul and James.

> For this reason it says, "**Awake, sleeper** (*pay attention*), and **arise from the dead** (*be effective*), and **Christ will shine on you** (*rewards are coming*)." Therefore be careful how you walk, not as unwise men but as wise. (*Eph. 5:14,15*)

> But you, **brethren**, are not in darkness, that the day would overtake you like a thief; for you are all sons of light and sons of day. We are not of night nor of darkness; so then **let us not sleep** (*Greek—katheudō*) as others do, but let us **be alert and sober**. For those who sleep do their sleeping at night, and those who get drunk get drunk at night. But since we are of the day, **let us be sober**, having put on the breastplate of faith and love, and as a helmet, the hope of salvation. For God has not destined us for wrath but for obtaining salvation through our Lord Jesus Christ, who died for us, so that **whether we are awake or asleep, we will live together with Him.** (*1 Ths. 5:4-10*)

Paul tells these believers [*"brethren . . . us . . . we"*] to pay attention to the spiritual dimension of life because Christ could return at any moment. Don't get caught short and be found in a disobedient (*unruly – 1 Ths. 5:14*) lifestyle—live by faith, love people, and hope for the rapture. The term for "asleep" in1 Thessalonians 4:13 is "koimaomai."

> But we do not want you to be uninformed, brethren, about those who are **asleep** (*Greek – koimaomai*), so that you will not grieve as do the rest who have no hope. (*1 Ths. 4:13*)

In 1 Thessalonians 5:10 the Greek term is "katheudō." The different figurative terms for "sleep/asleep," just a chapter apart, seem to indicate a distinction between "being dead" (*1 Ths. 4:13*) and "being disobedient or unaware" (*1 Ths. 5:10*). It's interesting to note the conduct of Christians, "awake [o*bedient*] or asleep [*disobedient*]," has no impact on their rapture or their glorification. James' familiar passage is also a reminder that justified men and women can live lives which are useless to the Master (*2 Tim. 2:19-21*). James defines "dead" faith as "useless" faith.

> Even so faith, if **it** [*faith*] has no works, is **dead**, being by itself . . . But are you willing to recognize, you foolish fellow, that faith without works is **useless**? . . . For just as the body without the spirit is dead, so also faith without works is **dead.** (*Jms. 2:17,20,26*)

The problem these believers in Sardis seemed to have was a lack of an eternal perspective. It appears they weren't paying attention in accomplishing biblical tasks and had priorities inconsistent with Christ's priorities. This problem is addressed by means of five commands given by Christ to these believers:

1. Wake up!
2. Strengthen the things that remain!
3. Remember what you received and heard!
4. Keep [*what you have received and heard*]!
5. Repent (*change your mind*)!

If these believers didn't wake up, He would come unexpectedly like a thief. This picture implies loss. Not a loss of eternal life, but of eternal rewards. Any unprepared victim of a burglary understands the concept of loss portrayed by this word picture. Christ offered words of encouragement for the few Christians who were awake, obedient, useful, and faithful. He described their righteous living as not having soiled their garments. **Overcomers are faithful believers who live with the end in mind.** As a result of this conduct, they were compensated. These overcomers were assured they would be provided a unique and special honor – they would walk with Him in white because they earned it (*"they are worthy"*). Walking with Christ appears to paint an image of intimate fellowship with Christ. This fellowship, while wearing white clothing, seems to be a reward of recognizable honor due to God's grace and a believer's obedient lifestyle. We see the concept of clothing linked with conduct and honor in the Hebrew text and again near the end of John's work.

> Let your **clothes be white** all the time, and let not oil be lacking on your head. (*Eccl. 9:8*)
>
> "Let us rejoice and be glad and give the glory to Him, for the marriage of the Lamb has come and His bride has made herself ready." It was given to her to **clothe herself in fine linen, bright and clean; for the fine linen is the righteous acts of the saints.** (*Rev. 9:7,8*)

Remember, Jesus also used this picture of clothing and conduct in His parable describing a disobedient believer who was excluded (*a loss of reward not eternal life*) from the marriage feast of the Lamb as described in Revelation 9:7,8.

> But when the king came in to look over the dinner guests, he saw a man there who was **<u>not dressed in wedding clothes</u>**, and he said to him, 'Friend, how did you come in here **<u>without wedding clothes</u>**?' And the man was speechless. Then the king said to the servants, 'Bind him hand and foot, and throw him into the outer darkness; in that place there will be weeping and gnashing of teeth. For many are called, but few are chosen.' (*Mt. 22:11-14*)

It's interesting to note at the time of John's writing, half of the residents in Rome weren't citizens. Disobedient citizens could lose privileges but not their residency. They could be "removed from the book of citizens." In stark contrast, Christ compensates and commends faithful conduct by means of greatly assuring believers with "over the top language" in addressing the presence of their name in the book of life. Another eternal reward given to overcomers is again expressed by means of a litotes. As you may recall, a litotes is a literary device which uses a deliberate form of understatement with the purpose of emphasizing an idea.

As in Revelation 2:11 with the church of Smyrna, Christ uses a double negative in the Greek to engage in this emphatic language. In this passage we see a phrase which literally carries the meaning "absolutely no way will I erase." Imagine a room with five people. Christ comes up to the first and tells them, "I won't erase your name from the book of life." He comes up to the second person and says, "I won't erase your name from the book of life." He comes up to the third person and says, "I won't erase your name from the book of life." He comes up to the fourth person and says, "I won't erase your name from the book of life." Then He comes up to the last person and says, "There is absolutely no way possible that I'd even consider erasing your name from the book of life. Your name is in there, **bolded** and <u>underlined</u>!" All of them are equally secure, but it's the last person who receives a unique honor in the way Christ addressed them. This is the reward overcomers will obtain – a word of confident commendation.

Another reward earned by overcomers as presented in this passage is the honor of having Christ confess the faithful Christian's name before His Father and all of the angels. Christ spoke of this special honor to His disciples in Matthew 10:32,33.

> Therefore everyone who **confesses** Me before men, I will also **confess** him before My Father who is in heaven. But whoever denies Me before men, I will also deny him before My Father who is in heaven. (*Mt. 10:32,33*)

Faithfulness brings reward, faithlessness bring loss. Not a loss of eternal life but the loss of forfeiting a wonderful personal introduction with the Creator of the universe by the most important person who ever walked the face of the earth. Christian conduct is connected with compensation and this special recognition is a relevant biblical motivator in our moment in time to be useful to the Master.

Church of Philadelphia

Jesus said to believers in the church of Philadelphia:

> And to the angel of the church in Philadelphia write: He who is holy, who is true, who has the key of David, who opens and no one will shut, and who shuts and no one opens, says this: "I know your deeds. Behold, I have put before you an open door which no one can shut, because you have a little power, and have kept My word, and have not denied My name. Behold, I will cause those of the synagogue of Satan, who say that they are Jews and are not, but lie—I will make them come and bow down at your feet, and make them know that I have loved you. Because you have kept the word of My perseverance, I also will keep you from the hour of testing, that hour which is about to come upon the whole world, to test those who dwell on the earth. I am coming quickly; hold fast what you have, so that no one will take

> your crown. **He who overcomes, I will make him a pillar in the temple of My God, and he will not go out from it anymore; and I will write on him the name of My God, and the name of the city of My God, the new Jerusalem, which comes down out of heaven from My God, and My new name.** He who has an ear, let him hear what the Spirit says to the churches." (*Rev. 3:7-13*)

Christ did not have a single critical word for these believers. He commended these Christians in Philadelphia for their humble obedience to the Word. Christ's encouragement to these believers translates well for us today. We see the phrase "I will" several times in this passage which indicates a future event. One future event in particular is; "I will keep you from [*not through*] the hour of testing, that hour which is about to come upon the whole world, to test those who dwell upon the earth [*literally "earth—dwellers"*].

In prophetic biblical literature, predictive comments can be presented from a "near view" and a "far view." The "near view" speaks of events (*i.e. Is. 7:14*) that will happen within the lifetime of the hearers (*Is. 7:18-25*) while the "far view" of the same prophecy points to events beyond the lifetime of the author's audience (*Mt. 1:22,23*). Each view is useful for both audiences in authenticating the authority of the prophet. From a "near view," the "hour of testing" likely refers to the current time period and struggles of these believers. But from a "far view" it's interesting to consider this word of encouragement appears consistent with a pre-tribulation eschatology as presented in the following New Testament passages.

> For they themselves report about us what kind of a reception we had with you, and how you turned to God from idols to serve a living and true God, and to wait for His Son from heaven, whom He raised from the dead, that is Jesus, **who rescues us** [*believers*] **from the wrath to come.** (*1 Ths. 1:9,10*)

> But we do not want you to be uninformed, brethren, about those who are asleep, so that you will not grieve as do the

> rest who have no hope. For if we believe that Jesus died and rose again, even so God will bring with Him those who have fallen asleep in Jesus. For this we say to you by the word of the Lord, that we who are alive and remain until the coming of the Lord, will not precede those who have fallen asleep. For the Lord Himself will descend from heaven with a shout, with the voice of the archangel and with the trumpet of God, and the dead in Christ will rise first. **Then we who are alive and remain will be caught up together with them in the clouds to meet the Lord in the air, and so we shall always be with the Lord.** Therefore comfort one another with these words. (*1 Ths. 4:13-18*)

> Now as to the times and the epochs, brethren, you have no need of anything to be written to you. For you yourselves know full well that the day of the Lord will come just like a thief in the night. While they are saying, "Peace and safety!" then **destruction will come upon them [*earth-dwellers*]** suddenly like labor pains upon a woman with child, and **they [*earth-dwellers*] will not escape**. **But you, brethren, are not in darkness, that the day would overtake you like a thief**. (*1 Ths. 5:1-4*)

> Then the kings of the earth and the great men and the commanders and the rich and the strong and every slave and free man hid themselves in the caves and among the rocks of the mountains; and **they [*earth-dwellers*]** said to the mountains and to the rocks, "Fall on us and hide us from the presence of Him who sits on the throne, and from the wrath of the Lamb; **for the great day of their wrath has come, and who is able to stand**?" (*Rev. 6:15-17*)

Like a good police investigator armed with Occam's Razor (*the simplest explanation is normally the best*) as a guide, putting the previous passages together might lead a reasonable person to believe:

1. Christ will keep all believers from "the hour of testing."
2. "The hour of testing" is for earth-dwellers not believers.

3. Christ rescues all believers from this wrath to come.
4. He rescues living believers from this wrath by catching them up in the air with Him (*rapture*).
5. Destruction will come on the earth-dwellers and they won't escape.
6. That day of destruction won't overtake believers.
7. Earth-dwellers will not be able to stand in the great day of His coming wrath.

Following this future word of encouragement to those in Philadelphia is a command. Christ's imperative to these Christians, in light of His imminent return, is consistent with the understanding that failure is an option and loss a possibility in their spiritual lives. Thus Christ directs them to "Hold fast to what you have in order that **no one takes your crown**." This warning of a loss of reward (*2 Jn. 1:8*) may be connected to a poor response from these Christians to those who would persecute them.

Overcomers in this context are believers who faithfully lay aside their pride. They stay low. Humility is a consistent part of their character. Meek does not mean weak. The meek, those who have the strength and ability to bend, are patterning themselves after Moses (*Num. 12:3*) and the person of Christ (*Phil. 2:5-8*). Christians who are overcomers will receive rewards for this flexible strength. One of the rewards is becoming a "pillar." I believe to be made a pillar in the temple of "My God" is another form or aspect of earned and recognizable honor. Boaz, the great great grandfather of King David (*Ruth 4:21,22*) was a "man of capacity" – a gracious and courageous servant-leader during a time in Israel's history when "everyone did what was right in his own eyes (*Jgs. 21:25*)." To honor him, it appears Solomon may have named one of the pillars in the Jerusalem temple (*1 Kgs. 7:21*) "Boaz"—a great and recognizable honor. This same type honor is available for overcomers who faithfully live in our world of moral relativism.

One more reward is found by means of overstated assurance in the form of another litotes. Once again, Christ uses a double negative to overwhelmingly assure the impossibility that overcomers will in no way ever "go out from it [*temple*] anymore – you're in there for good!" This special honor and fellowship with God is permanent and consistent with what Peter said – God exalts believers who humble themselves before Him (*1 Pt. 5:6,7*).

Lastly, overcomers will be rewarded with one more unique honor; "I will write upon him: (1.) The name of My God, and (2.) The name of the city of my God, the new Jerusalem, which comes down out of heaven from My God, and (3.) My new name."

Only men and women who meet the rigorous standards of the Phoenix Police Department are allowed to wear a uniform which has a patch and a badge with the words (1.) Police, (2.) Phoenix and, (3.) Arizona. Police officers aren't of any more value to society than other taxpayers. But yet, not every citizen gets the honor of wearing this patch. In fact, non-sworn civilians who don a police uniform are committing a crime – impersonating a police officer. These uniform identifiers are worn in public and are easy to ascertain as a symbol of recognizable authority and honor. Perhaps the names Christ gives to overcomers carry the same identifiable praise. All Christians are loved and are of great value to God, but only faithful overcomers will obtain these special names.

Church of Laodicea

Jesus said to Christians in the church of Laodicea:

> To the angel of the church in Laodicea write: The Amen, the faithful and true Witness, the Beginning of the creation of God, says this: "I know your deeds, that you are neither **cold** nor **hot**; I wish that you were **cold** or **hot**. So because you are **lukewarm**, and neither hot nor cold, will I spit you out of My mouth. Because you say, "I am rich, and have become wealthy, and have need of nothing," and you do not know that you are wretched and miserable and poor and blind and naked, I advise you to buy from Me **gold** refined by fire so that you may become rich, and **white garments** so that you may clothe yourself, and that the shame of your nakedness will not be revealed; and **eye salve** to anoint your eyes so that you may see. Those whom I love, I reprove and discipline; therefore be zealous and repent. Behold, I stand

> at **the door** and knock; if anyone hears My voice and opens the door, I will come in to him and will **dine with him**, and he with Me. **He who overcomes, I will grant to him to sit down with Me on My throne, as I also overcame and sat down with My Father on His throne.** He who has an ear, let him hear what the Spirit says to the churches." (*Rev. 3:14-22*)

Whereas the Christians in Philadelphia received no criticism from Christ, the believers in the church of Laodicea didn't garner a single commendation. The basic message behind the criticism of Christ highlighted a useless spiritual walk and an arrogant spiritual mindset. Christ relayed their spiritual condition wasn't hot and it wasn't cold. Their "deeds" were lukewarm. Seeing the context in this communique has a reference to dining (*"I will come in and dine with him"*), Christ's statement about temperature can be reasonably related to usefulness. As a general rule of thumb, hot and cold drinks and dishes are considered to be in an optimal useful state when it comes to consumption by diners. "Hot" and "cold" are descriptors of usefulness. Because Christ categorized the conduct of these Christians as "lukewarm," His response was to spit them out of His mouth. Thus, being tepid is to be useless. This picture should *not* be taken to imply a loss of eternal life but as conduct that's inadequate and halfhearted and not worthy of compensation. Being useless is "something" and only "nothing" can separate us from the love of Christ. In addition to uselessness, they were brash. In the spiritual dimension of life, self-reliance is the cousin of ignorance. These believers didn't have a clue (*"you do not know"*) of the predicament they were in. Paul's words to believers at Corinth reflected a concern consistent with Christ's evaluation of Laodicea.

> Therefore let him who thinks he **stands** [*picture of arrogance*] take heed that he does not **fall** [*picture of failure*]. (*1 Cor. 10:1-12.*

These arrogant Christians were met with harsh descriptions by Christ. Their uselessness, ignorance and pride generated descriptive terms such as wretched (*Rom. 7:24*), miserable (*1 Cor. 15:19 – pitiful*), poor (*Gal. 4:9 – relatively worthless*), blind (*Mt. 15:14*), and naked

(*Rev. 16:15 – implied shame*). It's too bad their spiritual health didn't match their worldly wealth. Wealth isn't bad. The attitude in which we handle money is the issue. Sadly, arrogance and wealth are frequently companions. Arrogance can cause us to cling to the temporal and ignore the eternal. Paul told Timothy:

> But **those** [*Christians in the context*] who **want to get rich** fall into temptation and a snare and many foolish and harmful desires which plunge men into ruin and destruction. For **the love** [*not money itself*] **of money** is **a** [*not "the"*] root of all sorts of evil, and **some** [*Christians in the context*] by longing for it have wandered away from the faith and pierced themselves with many griefs. But flee from these things, you man of God, and pursue righteous, godliness, faith, love, perseverance and gentleness. (*1 Tim. 6:9-11*)

To correct this problem in Laodicea, believers are commanded by Christ to change their mind (*repent*) and replace half-hearted effort with whole-hearted action (*be zealous*). The cultural context of the day is helpful in understanding the comments of Christ. They were to aggressively make three corrective investments.

- First, pursue eternal rewards – "gold." With the same imagery used by Paul of the refining process for precious metals (*1 Cor. 3:10-15*) and competitive athletic games (*1 Cor. 9:24-27*), Christ tells them to prioritize the eternal over the temporal. Correct living is connected to "treasuring up treasures in heaven (*Mt. 6:20*)."
- Second, invest in correct living – "white clothing" (*a righteous and faithful lifestyle—Eccl. 9:8, Rev. 3:4,5, 19:7,8*). This investment is a crucial remedy for uselessness. Faithfulness and obedience forego any shame which can meet us at His coming and evaluation (*Gen. 3:7-11, 1 Jn. 2:28*).
- Third, acquire a proper perspective – "eye salve." Perhaps this term was used with the backdrop of a well-known medical school in their town. God's Word affects how we live and how we view life, most certainly when we apply it. We can see this in James 1:22-25.

> But prove yourselves doers of the word, and not merely hearers who delude themselves. For if anyone is a hearer of the word and not a doer, he is like a man who looks at his natural face in a mirror; for once he has looked at himself and gone away, he has immediately forgotten what kind of person he was. But one who **looks intently at the perfect law**, the law of liberty, and **abides by it**, not having become a forgetful hearer but an effectual doer, this man will be blessed in what he does. (*Jms. 1:22-25*)

It almost seems as if the three investments are linked to and dependent upon one another. The Word (*eye salve*) produces righteous living (*white garments*) which in turn results in eternal rewards (*gold*). Like these believers, we have a choice if we're going to pursue, invest, and acquire those things which are important to God. Disinterested (*disobedient*) Christians shouldn't be surprised if they experience God's loving but corrective discipline. It's how He adjusts our "investment strategies." We see this "adjustment" in the book of Hebrews:

> You have not yet resisted to the point of shedding blood in your striving against sin; and you have forgotten the exhortation which is addressed to you as sons, "My son, do not regard lightly the discipline of the Lord, nor faint when you are **reproved** by Him; For those whom the Lord loves He **disciplines**, and He **scourges** every son whom He receives." It is for discipline that you endure; God deals with you as with sons; for what son is there whom his father does not discipline? But if you are without discipline, of which all have become partakers, then you are illegitimate children and not sons. Furthermore, we had earthly fathers to discipline us, and we respected them; shall we not much rather be subject to the Father of spirits, and live? For they disciplined us for a short time as seemed best to them, but He disciplines us for our good, so that we may share His holiness. All discipline for the moment seems not to be joyful, but sorrowful; **yet to those who have been trained by it, afterwards it yields the peaceful fruit of righteousness.** (*Heb. 12:4-11*)

Death is reserved for some Christians (*Acts 5:1-11, 1 Cor. 11:30, 1 Jn. 5:16*); discipline is reserved for all Christians. This passage indicates there are various and increasing levels of "training:" a. He reproves. b. He disciplines. c. He scourges. The reason God disciplines us is "for our good." The result of His "training" is a life patterned after the holiness of God. God wants our character to match His.

In a word of encouragement, Christ's desire for this historical church (*and our church now*) is presented – intimate fellowship with Christians. God wants to be our friend. The picture of Christ standing outside of the door of this church in the hope of having a "sit-down" dinner with them provides us with a wonderful portrait of His gracious and kind heart. In our brief moment in time, there's still time for fellowship, reward, and honor. **With this background in place, we can see overcomers are believers who are faithfully useful to the Master.** And for this effort, Christ's reward for faithfulness is a great honor: to sit down with Christ on His throne. Co-ruling and co-reigning with Christ is a marvelous reward given to faithful Christians. This is not an uncommon (*Look—a litotes!*) theme in the biblical text.

> But the saints of the Highest One will **receive the kingdom and possess the kingdom** forever, for all ages to come. (*Dan. 7:18*)

> And he said to him, 'Well done, good slave, because you have been faithful in a very little thing, you are to be in **authority over ten cities**.' The second came, saying, 'Your mina,master, has made five minas.' And he said to him also, 'And you are to be **over five cities.**' (*Lk. 19:17-19*)

> and if children, heirs also, heirs of God and **fellow heirs with Christ**, if indeed we suffer with Him so that we may also be glorified with Him. (*Rom. 8:17*)

> You have made them to be a kingdom and priests to our God; and **they will reign upon the earth.** (*Rev. 5:10*)

In conclusion, a description of overcomers as presented in Christ's communiques to these seven historical churches can be summarized as believers who:

1. Are faithful in doctrinal purity and in loving others.
2. Faithfully pay a price for their commitment to Christ.
3. Are faithful in moral purity and courage.
4. Faithfully maintain sexual purity.
5. Live with the end in mind.
6. Faithfully lay aside their pride.
7. Are faithfully useful to the Master.

The eternal rewards for those who are overcomers include special and exclusive privileges, unique and visible honor, co-ruling and co-reigning with Christ, and distinct fellowship with the Jesus. In the law enforcement world we know all police officers in Phoenix have a badge and gun but not all police officers have or will receive earned honors, awards and recognition. We have discovered all Christians have eternal life and will enter into the kingdom but not all believers will obtain unique and special privileges and honors which are earned only by those who are overcomers. Christ-like motivation for faithful living can be found in the pattern provided to us today by the historical overcomers in the churches of the past. Overcoming in our moment in time will result in a future reward.

CHAPTER 28

Eternal Life – Gift, Reward, or Both

Early in my career and in our marriage, Shannon and I would routinely watch the real-life television show *Cops*. When the producers came to Phoenix with their cameras, my squad took them out on a narcotic search warrant I had written and my squad had served. Even though the warrant came up dry, my claim to fame was a brief shot of my butt going through the front door of the apartment in the opening credits of the show. Yes, I made national television. Who wouldn't feel proud of that moment?

It was interesting as we watched the numerous episodes of the show, even though Shannon and I were watching the same program on the same screen, our response to it was vastly different. I would see things she didn't. I would notice the type of gun the officer had, the interview method, the vehicles and radio codes utilized by various departments, and would get thoroughly excited whenever a foot pursuit broke out. I was fascinated by the use-of-force applications and the validity of any search and seizure issues which were presented. All Shannon saw for 30 minutes was a tribe of alpha males with guns and badges chasing and beating up bad guys. Our appreciation of the show was immensely different. The reason our appreciation and awareness levels didn't match was simple – I put more time into police work than she did thus I got more out of the show. Same show, different investment level, different outcome.

Eternal rewards are similar to watching the show *Cops*. The more one puts into the Christian life, the richer and more meaningful the Christian life becomes. Christians who faithfully pursue the priorities of Christ and who invest great effort into fulfilling the Great Commission will be rewarded with eternal life – a deeper appreciation of the free gift.

Remember our discussion about the word "pass." A single, simple word, depending upon the context, has multiple meanings. No word games or deception have to be employed. Language is broad and flexible as well as specific and focused in conveying meaning. It's a dynamic form of communication that relies upon context. Just as context determines the meaning of the word "pass," so context determines the meaning of the biblical term "eternal life." Depending upon the context, most of the time eternal life is presented in the biblical text as a justification issue but occasionally it can be presented as an earned reward. Frequently the word "pass" is utilized as a verb: "Pass the salt." Similarly, eternal life is consistently presented as a free gift by the inspired authors of the Bible.

> For God so loved the world, that He gave His only begotten Son, that whoever **believes** in Him shall not perish, but have **eternal life.** (*Jn. 3:16*)

> Truly, truly, I say to you, he who hears My word, and **believes** Him who sent Me, **has eternal life**, and does not come into judgment, but has passed out of death into life. (*Jn. 3:36*)

> Truly, truly, I say to you, he who **believes** [*"in Me" – Majority Text*] **has eternal life.** (*Jn. 6:47*)

> Jesus said to her, "I am the resurrection and the life; he who **believes in Me will live** even if he dies, and everyone who lives and **believes in Me will never die**. Do you believe this?" (*Jn. 11:25,26*)

> But the **free gift** is not like the transgression. For if by the transgression of the one the many died, much more did the **grace** of God and **the gift** by the **grace** of the one Man, Jesus Christ, abound to the many. The **gift** is not like that which came through the one who sinned; for on the one

> hand the judgment arose from one transgression resulting in condemnation, but on the other hand the **free gift** arose from many transgressions resulting in **justification**. For if by the transgression of the one, death reigned through the one, much more **those who receive** the abundance of grace and of the **gift of righteousness** will reign in life through the One, Jesus Christ. So then as through one transgression there resulted condemnation to all men, even so through one act of righteousness there resulted **justification of life** to all men. (*Rom. 5:15-18*)

> Yet for this reason I found mercy, so that in me as the foremost, Jesus Christ might demonstrate His perfect patience as an example for those who would **believe in Him for eternal life.** (*1 Tim. 1:16*)

> For by grace you **have been saved** through **faith**; and that not of yourselves, it is the **gift** of God; not as a result of works, so that no one may boast. (*Eph. 2:8,9*)

As is clearly seen, eternal life within the context of the aforementioned Scripture is obtained by faith alone in Christ alone. It is presented as a present possession. Justification and one's eternal destiny are the core issues. Back to our analogy of the word "pass." Most of the time eternal life is presented as a free gift just as frequently "pass" is presented as a verb. But depending upon the context, "pass" can move from being a verb to a noun, as in "hall pass." Thus in the same sentence, without any confusion, the word "pass" could be used as both a verb and a noun. "Pass me the hall pass." Context makes the difference. When it comes to eternal life, there are several times in the biblical text where eternal life appears to be presented as a reward based upon works *not* as a free gift received through faith. Eternal life can take on the dimension of a sanctification issue completely apart from justification. Infrequently it appears to be presented as a form of compensation. Context makes the difference. Remember, language allows for words to be flexible things and it's context which narrows and pinpoints the specific meaning of flexible, multi-faceted, broad words and terms. John used the term eternal life numerous times in his gospel as a free gift. But he also presented it as an earned form of compensation.

> He who loves his life loses it, and he who hates his life in this world will keep it to **life eternal**. If anyone serves Me, he must follow Me; and where I am, there My servant will be also; if anyone serves Me, the Father will **honor** him. (*Jn. 12:25*)

In this passage, John records the historical words of Christ. There is no confusion in this passage that Christ connects eternal life with the choice of sacrificial living (*"hates his life" and "serves"*). But in the context of this passage, we see Christ defines eternal life in the next verse as future honor from the Father (*"the Father will honor him"*). Thus, believers who choose to serve Christ in their moment of time will receive the reward of eternal life – eternal life in this context being future honor from the Creator of the universe. Remember, "pass" can mean "yes" in one context (*"it's important to pass this legislation"*) and "no" in another (*"he said 'pass' when it came to more pork rinds"*). Context makes the difference in understanding eternal life also. In the following passage by Paul (*one of the most challenging in all of Romans*) we see eternal life presented as a reward.

> But because of **your** [*Christian in the context*] stubbornness and unrepentant heart you are storing up wrath [*not hell*] for yourself in the day of wrath and revelation of the righteous judgment of God, who will render to each person according to his deeds: to **those** [*Christian in the context*] who by perseverance in doing good seek for glory and honor and immortality, **eternal life**; but to **those** [*Christian in the context*] who are selfishly ambitious and do not obey the truth, but obey unrighteousness, **wrath and indignation**. There will be tribulation and distress for every soul of man who does evil, of the Jew first and also of the Greek, but glory and honor and peace to **everyone** [*Christian in the context*] who does good, to the Jew first and also to the Greek. (*Rom. 2:5-10*)

In the chapter *He Remains Faithful* we were introduced to a "chiastic" structure: a literary device which was often used by authors of the Bible. We see it again in this passage. By means of a "chiastic" structure, an author would lay his issue out in the form of an "X" (*Greek letter "chi"*) and utilize repetitive structure and restatement to make his meaning clear. This structure is crucial in providing context. In the book of Romans, it appears Paul is writing to believers. He identifies his audience with plain language; "to all who are **beloved of God** in Rome, called as **saints**: Grace to **you** and peace from **God our Father** and the Lord Jesus Christ *(Rom. 1:7).*" In Romans 2 we can see the following chiastic structure Paul used to communicate to these Christians about cause and effect, conduct and compensation.

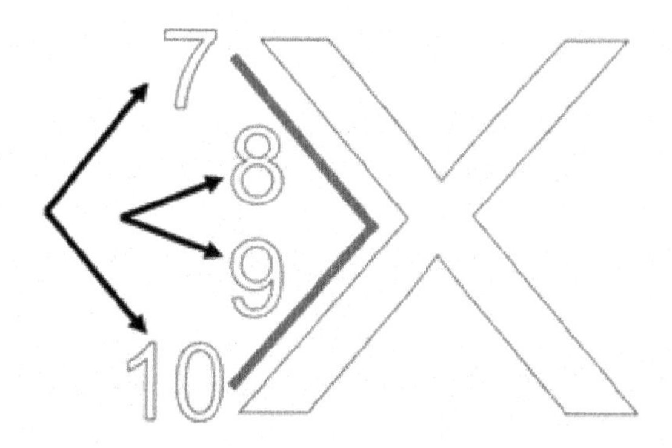

A—Verse 7 to those [*Christians*] who by perseverance in doing good seek for **glory and honor and immortality, eternal life**;

B—Verse 8 but to those [*Christians*] who are selfishly ambitious and do not obey the truth, but obey unrighteousness, **wrath and indignation**.

B'—Verse 9 There will be **tribulation and distress** for every soul of man who does evil, of the Jew first and also of the Greek,

A'—Verse 10 but **glory and honor and peace** to everyone [*Christian*] who does good, to the Jew first and also to the Greek.

In the context of this structure, it appears eternal life is presented as a reward based upon work *not* a gift based upon faith. Eternal life in verse seven is the result of "perseverance in doing good." This conduct of "perseverance in doing good" is restated in verse ten as "do[*ing*] good." Eternal life is further equated in the same verse as "glory and honor and peace." Not only does a chiastic structure restate and define, it also contrasts and compares. Those Christians who "are selfishly ambitious and do not obey the truth, but obey unrighteousness" will experience the consequence of "wrath and indignation." This "wrath and indignation" is further defined in verse nine as "tribulation and distress." There doesn't seem to be a good reason to equate "wrath" in this passage (*or any other passage in the New Testament*) with eternal separation from God—hell. Here's why.

In Romans chapter 1 and chapter 13 Paul shares with his Christian audience what wrath is. He states:

> For the **wrath of God is revealed** [*present tense*] from heaven against all ungodliness and unrighteousness of men who suppress the truth in unrighteousness because that which is known about God is evident within them; for God made it evident to them. For since the creation of the world His invisible attributes, His eternal power and divine nature, have been clearly seen, being understood through what has been made, so that they are without excuse. For even though they knew God, they did not honor Him as God or give thanks, but they became futile in their speculations, and their foolish heart was darkened. Professing to be wise, they became fools, and exchanged the glory of the incorruptible God for an image in the form of corruptible man and of birds and four-footed animals and crawling creatures. Therefore **God gave them over** in the lusts of their hearts to impurity, so that their bodies would be dishonored among them. For they exchanged the truth of God for the lie, and worshiped and served the creature rather than the Creator, who is blessed forever. Amen. For this reason **God gave them over** to degrading passions; for their women exchanged the natural function for that which is unnatural, and in the same way also the men abandoned the natural function of the woman and burned in their desire toward one another, men with

> men committing indecent acts and receiving in their own persons the due penalty of their error. And just as they did not see fit to acknowledge God any longer, **<u>God gave them over</u>** to a depraved mind, to do those things which are not proper, being filled with all unrighteousness, wickedness, greed, evil; full of envy, murder, strife, deceit, malice; they are gossips, slanderers, haters of God, insolent, arrogant, boastful, inventors of evil, disobedient to parents, without understanding, untrustworthy, unloving, unmerciful; and although they know the ordinance of God, that those who practice such things are worthy of death, they not only do the same, but also give hearty approval to those who practice them. (*Rom. 1:18-31*)

> Therefore it is necessary to be in subjection [*to the government*], not only because of **<u>wrath</u>** [*consequence of governmental punishment for breaking the law*] but also for conscience' sake. (*Rom. 13:5*)

From these passages, wrath is *not* eternal separation from the goodness of God. Wrath is presented as the current and on-going consequences suffered by men and women whom God has given over to their sinful desires – the flesh. Wrath is being turned over to the tyranny of sin. People choose to disobey the law of the land. People choose to suppress truth by ignoring the evidence of God in their conscience and in His creation. Sinful people have become futile in their thought process and the spiritual dimension of their life is impeded. They choose to worship and receive direction from the creation rather than the Creator. As a result, men and women receive wrath *not* hell. What is wrath?

- **God gave them over** (*Jer. 3:5*) to impurity and **<u>as a result</u>** their bodies were dishonored (*wrath*).
- **God gave them over** (*Psm. 81:12*) to degrading passions and **<u>as a result</u>** the natural sexual interaction among men and women was abandoned (*wrath*). All sin is sin and all sin has a death penalty attached to it. In the biblical text, homosexuality is the lifestyle the Holy Spirit inspired Paul to address in demonstrating the confusion sin generates in the lives of men

and women created in the image of God. And in the context of this passage, it seems a homosexual lifestyle is presented as a willful "exchange" or choice (*as is all sin*).

- **God gave them over** (*Ex. 4:21, 7:3,13,14*) to a depraved mind (*Col. 1:21*) **and the result** is a fallen world "filled with **all** unrighteousness, [*all*] wickedness, [*all*] greed, [*all*] evil; **full of** envy, [*full of*] murder, [*full of*] strife, [*full of*] deceit,[*full of*] malice; they are gossips, slanderers, haters of God, insolent, arrogant, boastful, inventors of evil, disobedient to parents, without understanding, untrustworthy, unloving, unmerciful . . . (*wrath*)"

Be careful what you ask for, you might just get it. And in the case of a defiant sinful world, God gives them what they want. In addition to this treatise on wrath, Paul goes further to instruct his Christian audience in Rome that they're not immune from the consequences (*wrath*) of sin either. Seeing that wrath is *not* hell but the current harmful consequences of willful disobedience, these comments look like a painful reminder to believers of the principle of cause and effect. How we live our lives as born-again believers either brings about compensation or cost.

> But because of **your** [*Christian in the context*] stubbornness and unrepentant heart **you** [*Christian in the context*] are storing up **wrath for yourself** [*Christian in the context*] in the day of wrath and revelation of the righteous judgment of God, who will render to each person [*Christian – 2 Cor. 5:10 / Unbelievers – Mt. 25:32, Rev. 20:11,12*) according to his deeds. (*Rom. 2:5*)

Thus, the presentation of wrath in Romans 1:18-32 and 13:5 and the possibility of wrath in the life of a believer as found in Romans 2:5 precede and provide the context of the passage where eternal life is presented as a reward. With this in mind, eternal life in the context of Romans 2:5-10, can be an earned reward of glory, honor and peace. In contrast, a Christian whose lifestyle is characterized as faithless will be met with extreme disappointment (*wrath, indignation, tribulation, distress*). A believer's good works will result in future compensation – one being the reward of eternal life. Remember, just as "pass" can mean a hand on a knee in a flirtatious manner, "pass" can also mean legislators allowing a law to move forward. Context is as relevant to understanding the term "pass" as much as it is in understanding the phrase "eternal life."

Jesus also expressed eternal life as a reward for conduct. He presented eternal life as a form of earned compensation. In parallel and historical synoptic dialogues with His disciples, He addressed the issue of eternal rewards and how they related to faithfulness in their lives.

> Then Peter said to Him, "Behold, we have left everything and followed You; what then will there be for us?" And Jesus said to them, "Truly I say to you, that you who have followed Me, in the regeneration when the Son of Man will sit on His glorious throne, you also shall sit upon twelve thrones, judging the twelve tribes of Israel. And everyone who has left houses or brothers or sisters or father or mother or children or farms for My name's sake, **will receive many times as much**, and **will inherit eternal life**. But many who are first will be last; and the last, **first."** (*Mt. 19:27-30*)
>
> Peter began to say to Him, "Behold, we have left everything and followed You." Jesus said, "Truly I say to you, there is no one who has left house or brothers or sisters or mother or father or children or farms, for My sake and for the gospel's sake, but that he **will receive a hundred times as much** now in the present age, houses and brothers and sisters and mothers and children and farms, **along with persecutions**; and in the age to come, **eternal life**. But many who are first will be last, and the last, **first.**" (*Mk. 10:28-31*)
>
> Peter said, "Behold, we have left our own homes and followed You." And He said to them, "Truly I say to you, there is no one who has left house or wife or brothers or parents or children, for the sake of the kingdom of God, who **will not receive many times** as much at this time and in the age to come, **eternal life.**" (*Lk 18:28-30*)

Perhaps the initial lessen we're reminded of from these historical accounts is self-concern is not selfishness. Peter was quite blunt with Jesus; "We've left everything for you. What's in it for us!" Christ's response was one of gracious encouragement and commendation. He assured Peter and His men their conduct would result in future compensation – they would rule and reign over Israel with Him from Jerusalem—truly a unique reward. With this as the context, He spoke beyond this immediate group of men to us today in our moment in time. He motivates believers to faithfulness through eternal rewards, one of these rewards being eternal life.

Hebrew Scripture points out the obvious—our homes and families are marvelous treasures.

> Behold, **children** are a **gift** of the Lord, the fruit of the womb is a **reward**. Like arrows in the hand of a warrior, so are the children of one's youth. How **blessed** is the man whose quiver is full of them; They will not be ashamed when they speak with their enemies in the gate. (*Psm. 127:3-5*)
>
> He who finds a **wife** finds a **good thing** and obtains **favor** from the Lord. (*Prov. 18:22*)
>
> An **excellent wife**, who can find? For her **worth is far above jewels.** (*Prov. 31:10*)
>
> Here is what I have seen to be good and fitting: to eat, to drink and **enjoy oneself in all one's labor** in which he toils under the sun during the few years of his life which God has given him; for this is his **reward**. Furthermore, as for every man to whom God has given **riches and wealth**, He has also empowered him to eat from them and to receive his reward and rejoice in his labor; this is the **gift** of God. For he will not often consider the years of his life, because God keeps him occupied with the **gladness of his heart.** (*Eccl 5:18-20*)

Certainly our families are of great value, but the "point" in life is *not* the dot but the line—to live for the eternal. The wonderful fulfillment and joy our loved ones, homes, and occupations bring us appear to be only one percent of the dividend value of the possible return on investment of sacrificial Christian living. Some believers forgo the blessings of a wealth, family and home (*Christ didn't have a home – Mt. 8:20 – so much for the health and wealth gospel*) by choosing to focus their moment in time on spiritual multiplication. Christ assures them their efforts aren't in vain and their life won't be unfulfilling. There are believers whose priorities overlook the temporal comfort of their loved ones and bypass the wealth of the secular world. Christ provides a marvelous return on investment to them.

Mark's account of this event goes beyond nice and lands on honest. He tells us, in addition to rewards, we can expect "persecutions." When we arrange our priorities around the cause of Christ, persecution most likely will be close behind. Seeing it's likely that Peter was Mark's source for the historical events in his gospel, and seeing Peter mentioned suffering no less than 13 times (*1 Pt. 1:11, 2:19, 20, 21, 23, 3:14, 17, 4:13, 15, 16, 19,5:1, 9*) in his epistle, it certainly looks as if faithfulness in our moment in time will result in suffering. When you're over the target expect to take flak.

Thus, in the context of future compensation for the disciples and current payment for faithful Christians, Christ appears to present eternal life as an earned reward also. The defining statement as to what the reward of eternal life is in this passage is "the first will be last, and the last, first." Last place is the place of least honor. I jokingly tell my daughter who competes in track, "Second place is the first to lose." First place is the winner and where the most honor is found. Those Christians who make sacrificial choices in life for Christ will often find themselves with little (*"last place" according to the world*) during this moment in time but with much honor (*"first place"*) in the form of eternal life in the coming kingdom and into eternity.

On another rare occasion, Paul once again presented eternal life as compensation for conduct.

> For the **one** [*believer in the context*] who **sows to his own flesh** will from the flesh **reap corruption**; but the **one** [*believer in the context*] who **sows to the Spirit** will from the Spirit **reap eternal life**. Let **us** [*believers including Paul*] not lose heart in **doing good**, for in due time **we** [*believers including Paul*] will reap if **we** [*believers including Paul*] do not grow weary. (*Gal. 6:8,9*)

In the context, Paul is writing to believers who already possessed eternal life as a gift (*Gal. 3:26*). They were justified. We know this up front from Galatians 1:2 " . . . to the **churches** of Galatia . . ." and throughout Galatians (*4:28,31, 6:1*) when he addresses them as "brethren."

Paul instructs these Christians that if their conduct centered around temporal priorities (*"sow to the flesh"*) the end result would be "corruption"—moral depravity, ruin or frailty (*Dan. 10:8 LXX—Septuagint—Greek translation of the Hebrew Scriptures*). This is a far cry from the abundant life Christ spoke of in John 10:10. In comparison to the conduct of "sowing to the flesh" is a life with a biblically spiritual world-view in mind. The reward for "sow[*ing*] to the Spirit" or "doing good" is eternal life. In this context it appears eternal life, when presented as an earned reward, is a richer and more robust appreciation of the Christian life – the opposite of "corruption."

Paul's letter to Christians in Galatia addressed the issue of justification by faith and not by works.

> ...nevertheless knowing that a man is **not justified by the works** of the Law **but through faith** in Christ Jesus, even **we have believed** in Christ Jesus, so that we may be **justified by faith** in Christ and **not by the works of the Law**; since by the works of the Law no flesh will be justified. (*Gal. 2:16*)

Paul is clear – an acquittal from God is based upon faith alone in Christ alone for eternal life. He disconnects works from justification. But then Paul is just as clear – doing good will result in eternal life. He goes right back and connects eternal life to works. What's going on? As we've seen, when this happens, it's an indicator of the rare occasion which, in the right context, eternal life can be an earned reward. Remember, "pass" can mean a narrow strip of land between mountains or it can mean "hand me the salt." It all depends upon the context.

In looking at the biblical text, eternal life is infrequently presented as a reward for conduct. Context makes all the difference in determining when eternal life is a free gift by faith or an earned reward by conduct. When it's presented as compensation for work, the reward of eternal life seems to be a future honor or a deeper appreciation of the free gift. Who would want to "pass" on that?

CHAPTER 29

Supersizers & Multipliers

All Phoenix Police Officers have to qualify annually with their weapon. In order to maintain State certification, a passing score on a yearly basis needs to be maintained. In my brief moment in time of twenty-five years I've never seen an officer fail to pass. The reason is because the armory staff at the police academy is beyond good, they're outstanding. Their commitment to proper techniques, officer success, and functional trends are just some of the ingredients behind the success rate with officers' shooting qualifications. One way the Department motivates good shooting is by means of an expert shooting badge. Along with this recognized award come career enhancement points. Along with these points come extra wages. All officers carry a gun and are expected to utilize deadly force in a manner consistent with law and policy, but only officers who are expert shooters get special recognition and financial compensation for demonstrated expertise above and beyond the norm (*I call this faithfulness*). Not many obtain this award, but the motivation to pursue it prompts more than a few officers to pay attention to the important skill of squeezing the trigger.

Police officers not only shoot, they drive. The "office" of a patrol officer is his/her police car. Those who drive their "office" well for five years without an at-fault on-duty accident are provided with a safe-driving award (*and more money*). In addition to shooting and driving, another motivator is a sick leave conversion benefit. All officers are provided sick leave, but only those officers who wisely manage 1,714 hours' worth of their paid sick leave benefit get this earned reward. Over the course of a 20+ year career, when officers accumulate at least 1,714 hours of sick leave, they are compensated at a higher payout percentage upon retirement than officers with more leave use and thus a lower bank of hours.

Shooting, driving, and sick leave impact every officer. But only those officers who excel in these employment areas are rewarded – they're "supersized." We see this motivational concept in the New Testament as well when it comes to faithful and exceptional Christian conduct. There won't be a single person who is born-again who will miss out on entering His "eternal kingdom." Similarly, all Christians have eternal life. In addition to this, every believer who dies will be resurrected. But a motivating concept presented in the New Testament to encourage Christians to remain faithful, to excel, and to endure is what I'll call a "multiplier." Exceptional men and women who are born-again will have an "abundant entrance" into the kingdom. Some Christians will be rewarded beyond eternal life with "life indeed." Some believers will experience a "better resurrection." Both Peter and Paul taught the principle of "multipliers" or "supersizers" in conjunction with eternal rewards. Peter wrote:

> Therefore, **brethren**, be all the more diligent to make certain about His calling and choosing you; for as long as you practice these things, you will never **stumble**; for in this way **the entrance** into the eternal kingdom of our Lord and Savior Jesus Christ **will be abundantly supplied** to you. (*2 Pt. 1:10,11*)

Peter is talking to Christians whose eternal destiny is secure. He refers to his audience as "brethren." In his communication with these believers, we see holiness was an important theme in Peter's exhortation to them.

> As obedient **children** [*Christian*], do not be conformed to the former lusts which were yours in your ignorance, but like the Holy One who **called** you, **be holy** yourselves also in all your behavior; because it is written, "You shall **be holy**, for I am holy." (*1 Pt. 1:14-16*)

> For what credit is there if, when you sin and are harshly treated, you endure it with patience? But if when you **do what is right** and **suffer** for it you **patiently endure** it, this finds favor [*grace*] with God. For **you** [*Christian*] have been **called for this purpose**, since Christ also suffered for you, leaving you an example for you to follow in His steps. (*1 Pt. 2:20,21*)

> To sum up, all of you be harmonious, sympathetic, brotherly, kindhearted, and humble in spirit; not returning evil for evil or insult for insult, but giving a blessing instead; for **you were called** for the very purpose [*of giving a blessing*] **that you might inherit a blessing.** (*1 Pt. 3:8,9*)

The standard of the Christian life is to imitate Christ. This is what we're "called" to do. Christ was holy and we should be too. Christ patiently endured and we should too. Christ gave a blessing and we should too. In this context, it's looks as if the subject of being "called" and "chosen" doesn't involve one's eternal destiny but is concerned about one's present lifestyle. Being called and chosen is linked and connected in this context with obedience and holiness. We're called to be holy. In two of His parables, Christ used these terms in conjunction with a believer's obedience.

> Then the king said to the servants, 'Bind him hand and foot, and throw him into the outer darkness; in that place there will be weeping and gnashing of teeth.' For many are **called** [*to the wedding feast for those with righteous lifestyles*] but few are **chosen** [*to be rewarded with this honor*]. (*Mt. 22:13,14*)

> [*Majority Text*] So the last shall be first, and the first last. For many are **called** [*to live faithfully*] but few are **chosen** [*to be honored for doing such*]. (*Mt. 20:16*)

There's no reason to believe Peter was not present when Christ shared these parables (*Mt. 19:27, 20:17, 21:20, 23:1*). In both parables, being "called" and "chosen" are used in tandem with obedience and the resulting honor. Many Christians are invited or called to holiness but few reach the standard and thus few are chosen so as to obtain a reward.

With this context in mind, Peter reminded his audience to make certain about their calling (*a life of holiness*) and their choosing (*their eternal reward*). The admonishment is *not* "make sure you're a Christian and have eternal life." He clearly was already convinced of their eternally secure relationship with the Father by calling them "brethren." In contrast, he admonished these believers to pay attention to their lifestyle so they would "not stumble" and lose the eternal reward that awaited them as compensation. "Stumbling" appears to be a part of a patterned and/or progressive idea used by Peter describing failure in a believer's life: Stumble, entangle, fall.

> For if, after they have escaped the defilements of the world by the knowledge of the Lord and Savior Jesus Christ, they are again **entangled** in them and are overcome, the last state has become worse for them than the first. (*2 Pt. 2:20*)

> You therefore, beloved, knowing this beforehand, be on your guard so that you are not carried away by the error of unprincipled men and **fall** from your own steadfastness. (*2 Pt. 3:17*)

In 2 Peter 1:11 Peter becomes specific as to what reward awaits Christians who are diligent in both pursuing biblical virtues (*2 Pt. 1:1-8*) and holy living. These believers will be rewarded with an abundant entrance into heaven – their entrance will be "multiplied" ("*abundantly supplied*"). All Christians will enter into the presence of the Lord, but only faithful believers will obtain a unique and special entrance to honor and compensate them for their commitment. Peter wasn't the only one who talked about "multipliers." Paul also touched upon the concept of spiritual events in the lives of believers being multiplied or supersized as a reward for faithfulness. Paul wrote:

> More than that, I count all things to be loss in view of the surpassing value of knowing Christ Jesus my Lord, for whom I have suffered the loss of all things, and count them

> but rubbish so that I may gain Christ, and may be found in Him, **not** having a righteousness of my own derived **from the Law**, but that which is **through faith in Christ**, the righteousness which comes from God on **the basis of faith**, that I may know Him and the power of His resurrection and the fellowship of His sufferings, being conformed to His death; **in order that I may attain to the resurrection from the dead.** (*Phil. 3:8-11*)

Paul maintains consistency—faith alone in Christ alone. He restated this tenant to these Philippian Christians that one's positional standing of judicial righteousness (*justification*) before God is obtained not "from the Law" but through "faith in Christ" and "on the basis of faith." But beyond his eternal standing with God, Paul speaks about gaining Christ and knowing not only Him but the "the power of His resurrection and the fellowship of His sufferings." Paul seems to teach that our conduct drives the quality of the friendship (*fellowship*) one has with Jesus and that our suffering and losses on His behalf brings us in line with the pattern of "His death" – sacrificial living fueled by love.

The phrase "in order that" gives us the reason as to why this sacrificial life of faithfulness to Christ was important to Paul. The reason for faithfulness in his life was so that he might "attain to the resurrection from the dead." Scripture is clear that resurrection from the dead, as well as eternal life, is in no way connected to conduct, faithfulness, or obedience but solely on the grace of our "Redeemer."

> As for me, I know that **my Redeemer lives**, and at the last He will take His stand on the earth. Even after my skin is destroyed, yet from **my flesh I shall see God**. (*Job 19:25,26*)

> Now at that time Michael, the great prince who stands guard over the sons of your people, will arise. And there will be a time of distress such as never occurred since there was a nation until that time; and at that time your people, **everyone who is found written in the book, will**

> **be rescued**. Many of **those who sleep in the dust of the ground will awake, these to everlasting life**, but the others to disgrace and everlasting contempt. (*Dan. 12:1,2*)
>
> Jesus said to her, "I am the **resurrection** and the life; he who **believes** in Me **will live even if he dies**, and everyone who lives and believes in Me will never die. Do you believe this?" (*Jn. 11:25,26*)
>
> This is the will of Him who sent Me, that of all that He has given Me I lose nothing, but raise it up on the last day. For this is the will of My Father, that everyone who beholds the Son and **believes in Him** will have eternal life, and I Myself will **raise him up on the last day**. (*Jn. 6:39,40*)
>
> But now Christ has been raised from the dead, the first fruits of those who are asleep. For since by a man came death, by a man also came the resurrection of the dead. For as in Adam all die, so also in Christ all will be **made alive.** (*1 Cor. 15:20-22*)

From the New Testament we see our future resurrection from the dead is the result of a past act of faith alone in Christ alone for eternal life. While Christ was clear that resurrection is the result of faith in Him, Paul goes and links it to conduct. What's going on here? Perhaps Paul is talking about a different kind of resurrection. Remember, "pass" has different meanings depending upon the context.

Paul addressed the issue of resurrection in the phrase "the power of His resurrection." This term uses the normal and typical Greek word for resurrection – "anastasis." It's used 42 times in the New Testament. But there's another word for resurrection Paul used in the same passage. The Greek term Paul used in describing this resurrection, a resurrection linked to conduct, is "ekanastasis." It's a unique term and this is the only place it's found in the New Testament. The only difference between these two words is two letters—the prefix "ek" which means "out of." Paul was *not* trying to obtain "resurrection" by works (*Rom. 4:4,5, Gal. 2:16*). Neither the broad (*Eph. 2:8,9*) or immediate (*Phil.*

3:20) context of Paul's writings lend support to the idea that Paul was working to obtain or maintain his resurrection and justification. Paul was in pursuit of an "out of resurrection," a better or different resurrection by means of his conduct. Paul pressed "on toward the goal for the prize" (*not "gift" / Phil. 3:14*). It's not unreasonable to believe, in the context of this passage and our understanding of resurrection, Paul was teaching faithful Christians will have a better resurrection. Some hold a different yet valid view of this "out of resurrection" as the "present power" to live the Christian life (*Rom. 8:10*).

The writer of Hebrews spoke of better things (*6:9*), a better hope (*7:19*), better promises (*8:6*), better sacrifices (*9:23*), better possessions (*10:34*), a better country (*11:16*), and appears to support Paul's concept of a better resurrection. He tells us in Hebrews 11:35:

> Women received back their dead by resurrection; and others were tortured, not accepting their release, so that they might obtain **a better resurrection.** (*Heb. 11:35*)

The resurrection of all those who die in Christ is guaranteed as a result of faith. But the resurrection of some believers will be "multiplied" or "supersized" as a result of faithfulness. Paul continued with the concept of a multiplying or "supersizing" impact on life – or as Paul put it, "life indeed."

> Instruct those who are rich in this present world not to be conceited or to fix their hope on the uncertainty of riches, but on God, who richly supplies us with all things to enjoy. Instruct them to do good, to be rich in good works, to be generous and ready to share, storing up for themselves the **treasure** of a good foundation for the future, so that they may take hold of that which is **life indeed.** (*1 Tim. 6:17-19*)

The English word "indeed" comes from the Greek term "ontos." It carries the meaning really, certainly, surely, or truly. This term is used in conjunction with freedom, a prophet, innocence, and widows as a method of highlighting or emphasizing a quality.

> So if the Son makes you free, you will be **free indeed.** (*Jn. 8:36*)
>
> "But shall we say, 'From men'?"—they were afraid of the people, for everyone considered John to have been a **real prophet.** (*Mk 11:32*)
>
> Now when the centurion saw what had happened, he began praising God, saying, "**Certainly** this man was **innocent.**" (*Lk. 23:47*)
>
> Honor widows who are **widows indeed.** (*1 Tim. 5:3*)

In his letter to Timothy, Paul pointed out to him Christians who are rich in good works will acquire a deeper appreciation of the free gift of eternal life. Again we see this concept here as we did when eternal life was presented as a reward. All Christians have life, but it seems faithful believers will be compensated with a profound comprehension and awareness of their positional security as a child of God. Perhaps this was a similar concept Jesus was addressing in John 10:10.

> The thief comes only to steal and kill and destroy; I came that they may have **life**, and have it **abundantly** ["*perissos*" – *special, exceptional*]. *(Jn. 10:10)*

Christians whose lifestyles are characterized by faithfulness will not only have their entrance and resurrection multiplied, they'll also have their appreciation of life supersized. What a great and wonderful motivation for us to pursue friendship with Christ and usefulness to the Master in our moment in time.

CHAPTER 30

Miscellany & Reminders

You've given me the privilege to briefly present issues in regards to the biblical concept of eternal rewards. Beyond what you've entertained up to this point, additional rewards Paul and Peter spoke of were the crown of exultation (*1 Ths. 2:19*), the crown of righteousness (*2 Tim. 4:8*), and the crown of glory (*1 Pt. 5:4*). I've heard it said by some we shouldn't hold on to our crowns or our eternal rewards too tightly because we'll just be giving them back – throwing them at God's feet. I struggled with that for two reasons. First, Christ motivates us to work hard in order to win the reward. Do any of us really experience any joy in forfeiting something we worked hard to obtain? I don't. Second, it appears this concept of "casting crowns" comes from Revelation 4:10:

> **the twenty-four elders** will fall down before Him who sits on the throne, and will worship Him who lives forever and ever, and will cast their crowns before the throne, saying, "Worthy are You, our Lord and our God, to receive glory and honor and power; for You created all things, and because of Your will they existed, and were created." (Rev. 4:10,11)

I'm confident I'm not one of the twenty-four elders. Most likely you're not either. This group appears to be a distinct set of beings involved in future end-time events. Because of that, I don't think it will be a conflict with the biblical text if we hang on to what God has graciously allowed us to earn.

I believe the following medley of concepts and reminders will enhance and enrich any further study you might wish to pursue in the area of eternal rewards:

- Live with the end in mind. "Treasure up treasures." *(Mt. 6:19-21)* Our focus determines our conduct (*Mt. 24:48*) and we'll all be evaluated (*Mt. 24:46*).
- The basis of eternal rewards is God's grace. Because of this, God's character (*Mt. 20:13,15*) and a transformed life (*2 Cor. 3:18, Phil. 3:20,21*) will leave no room for envious complaining or comparisons (*1 Cor. 15:39-44*). My reward is an issue between me and HIM.
- Believers will be evaluated on how they used what God gave them; " . . . each one according to his own ability . . ." (*Mt. 25:15*)
- To suffer loss is to miss out on the potential honor and/or opportunity of an eternal reward not the forfeiture of an honor already obtained (*1 Cor. 3:15 "it [reward] shall suffer loss," 1 Jn. 2:28, 2 Jn. 1:8*).
- The "darkness outside" is *not* hell but exclusion from a unique event in the Kingdom (*Mt. 22:13*).
- Sorrow is a possibility as a result of our evaluation by Christ and relief is a certainty (*Rev. 21:4*).
- Showing mercy to others during our moment of time gives us "wiggle room" at the Bema. Being merciful now and disengaging from deserved retribution will generate mercy at our future evaluation (*Mt. 7:2, Heb. 8:12, Jms. 2:12,13*). This is what I call earning "mercy chits."
- <u>Inheriting</u> the kingdom is *not* the same as <u>entering</u> the Kingdom. Possession (*inheritance*) is based upon our faithfulness (*1 Cor. 6:9,10, Gal. 5:19-21, Eph. 5:5*), presence (*entering*) is based upon faith in Christ (*Mt 7:13,21, 18:3, 19:23,24, Jn. 3:3-5,16*). Context remains crucial.
- Wrath is *not* hell – it is the result of God allowing men and women to experience the consequences of sinful choices.
- Some would say individual believers will be privately evaluated by Christ at the Bema Seat (*1 Cor. 4:4*) with no audience in attendance. Others will say since the success and failures of

Adam, Abraham, Job, Noah, David, Solomon, Sampson, Peter, Paul and others were available for all to see, why should we be excluded from public review? You're going to have to determine that one your own.

Conclusion

I received information from a reliable confidential informant (*C.I.*) that an eighty year old man, we'll call him Elmer, was allowing two younger Hispanic males to sell crack cocaine out of his little bungalow. He allowed them to sell in exchange for groceries. The C.I. had just seen drugs sold out of Elmer's place by the two Hispanic males the previous night, so I drew up a search warrant to hit the house the next day.

We served the search warrant without any problems. Inside of the house by the dope, gun, and money were two young Hispanic males. Outside in the backyard on his couch drinking a beer was Elmer. After advising them of their rights, the two Hispanic males told me they were the ones selling the crack cocaine, the money and the drugs belonged to them, and Elmer did not sell drugs but only gave them the use of his home in exchange for the food they would buy him.

I spoke to Elmer next. He admitted the two young males paid him in groceries to sell cocaine out of his house but that was the extent of his involvement. He did not sell drugs. All three males were booked. The two young males were booked for possession of a narcotic drug for sale and Elmer was booked for utilizing a house to sell narcotics.

I attended a preliminary hearing a few days later. This proceeding took place in a justice of the peace court and, for the sake of this account, "Judge Smith" was on the bench. Judge Smith was very supportive of law enforcement and would frequently sign search warrants I brought to him. He was "user friendly." We were in court that day for Elmer to determine if there was probable cause for his arrest. I was notified by the prosecutor they had filed the charge of possession of a narcotic drug (*POND*) for sale against Elmer. I told the attorney that was incorrect. He was arrested and booked for a lesser charge – utilizing a house to sell drugs. The prosecutor seemed indifferent whereas I wasn't. Elmer was eighty years old and had two prior felony convictions for D.U.I. The charge I booked him on could be plead out as a misdemeanor and he could go back home. The charge the prosecutor had filed would mean he would die in prison – this would be his third felony conviction.

I advised the defense attorney of the problems I had with the charges and encouraged him to ask me good questions and I would give him good answers. Defense counsel and I engaged in dialogue under oath similar to the following exchange.

Q. Officer, did you have information my client was selling drugs?
A. No

Q. Did you find my client in possession of narcotic drugs?
A. No

Q. Did you find the two Hispanic males in possession of narcotic drugs?
A. Yes

Q. Did they admit to selling drugs out of my client's house?
A. Yes.

Q. Did they tell you my client sold drugs?
A. No

Q. What did they tell you about my client?
A. They paid him in groceries for the use of his house so they could sell drugs.

Q. Did my client admit he was selling drugs?
A. No

Q. Did my client admit he was paid by the two Hispanic males for the use of his home for them to sell drugs?
A. Yes

Q. Did you arrest my client for selling narcotic drugs?
A. No

Q. Does your police report say you booked my client for selling narcotic drugs?
A. No

Q. What did you book my client for?
A. Utilizing a house to sell drugs.

Q. Does your police report accurately reflect the charges you requested?
A. Yes.

Q. Do you believe the wrong charges of selling narcotic drugs were filed against my client?
A. Yes.

After the testimony, it took less than thirty seconds for Judge Smith to find probable cause Elmer had been in possession of narcotic drugs for sale. It was unbelievable. If you want fair, don't expect to get it in this life. In his zeal to assist the police, Judge Smith completely ignored the clear facts and simple testimony. It's as if he went out of his way to ignore the obvious. I'm sure he believed his motives were pure but in reality, his actions were inappropriate. Later that night, Judge Smith even called me on the phone in an apparent attempt to find approval from me for his ruling. He didn't get it. Thankfully in the end, the charges were amended and Elmer went back home.

Why in the world should I care if an eighty year old male who dabbles in drugs dies in prison? Doesn't that just make our streets all that safer? And besides, you think a guy with two felony convictions would know better. Here's the problem. The ends don't justify the means. They never have and they never will. That's true in a court of law and it's true in our seminaries, churches, and Christian bookstores.

With a great passion to promote godly living, it seems apparent many godly leaders in the evangelical church go out of their way to ignore clear biblical facts and simple scriptural testimony which present eternal life as a free gift which can never be lost. Because of misdirected zeal, being a disciple is equated with being a Christian. Justification and sanctification become merged and mixed into one. Non-biblical terms are created when the concept of faith is needlessly dissected beyond all semblance of common sense. There is an exchange of requirements on the front end of justification for expectations on the back end. Works are moved, shuffled, and relabeled as a "changed life" to keep the banner of "sola fide" still flying (*unfortunately it's at half-mast*). "We are saved by faith alone, but the faith that saves is never alone" is rhetoric which oozes with clear contradiction. Free no longer means free. The end result is the denial of failure in the Christian life. Fruit inspection is married to subjective standards. Works and a changed life have nothing to do with justification, but yet works and a changed life become the only and unchallenged evidence that justification has occurred. When conduct becomes crucial, doubts and paralyzing fear concerning one's eternal destiny are ever present. One never knows how much "fruit" is enough or if they'll persevere in obedience to the end. The motivation of pursuing eternal rewards is infrequently taught, misunderstood or completely ignored. Rewards are seen as an inferior motive. One doesn't have time to pursue eternal rewards if they're always maintaining or proving their possession of eternal life. Worse yet, the gift of eternal life is presented as an earned reward. When context is bypassed, terms like "saved" are forced to focus on heaven and terms like "wrath" and "fire" are pressured to mean hell. A "free gift" becomes costly and "without cost" means a lifelong commitment. A combination of faith, repentance, yielding, willingness, turning, and other good works becomes the norm in obtaining eternal life. And eternal life really isn't eternal because it can be lost or not really received without proper conduct. What is childlike becomes complicated. Grace is described as "cheap."

Theological and political agendas have at least one thing in common – both are quick to dismiss reality. This can cause multiple problems. Agendas make what is clear and simple become difficult and cloudy. Adherents to agendas have a tendency to think too hard. Thus they're masters at ignoring the huge elephant in the middle of the room. This has to happen because agendas don't always line up with reality. Let me share with you one last police story to illustrate my point.

One of the best parts of my job as the PLEA president was the freedom I had to ride with our members in their assignments. This allowed a first-hand view of what was going on, what they needed, and how we could assist them to be successful (*how about this as a management concept for police chiefs to consider*). On one occasion, I received a call from our "day labor squad." This squad's job was to monitor illegal aliens in a certain section of town. That's right, tax-payer dollars were used to pay police officers to watch (*we called it babysitting*) those actively violating federal criminal immigration laws. These officers had a problem and they needed help.

On one day they were told to be visible in the day labor area for police presence. When they stayed in these designated business locations (*where the illegal aliens would solicit work*), the neighbors would call and complain our officers were sitting around in their cars doing nothing. On the next day, police management would then order our officers to circulate in the neighborhoods to keep from bunching up and to keep complaints down. When this happened, the local businesses would call and protest the officers weren't visible and as a result of their absence activity with the illegals was left unchecked. There's a technical police labor mantra for this: damned if you do damned if you don't. Because of this "Catch-22" situation, I received a call from our members and they requested I come out and ride with them to help determine how to apply the Department's new immigration policy as it related to Senate Bill 1070 (*SB1070*). I couldn't put on a police uniform quick enough for the chance to do real police work.

The day I went out on patrol with our two members we were in a marked patrol car and headed out to the designated "day labor" area in question. On the way, a "hot call" (*emergency 911*) came out of a family fight. The location was just a block and a half from the intersection we were at. This was great! Real police work just moments away. I pointed out to the officer who was driving the direction of the fight. His response: "We can't go. We're not allowed to take any calls outside of the day labor activity area." I was shocked. Someone needed help a baseball throw away and politics was preventing common sense intervention by the police. I pulled seniority and demanded we take the call. We were the first unit on the scene and quickly resolved the issue.

We then headed back to the "day labor" area and drove around. It was explained to me every business in the strip mall being patrolled wanted trespassing enforced except for the Wal-Mart. Because of this "no fly zone" with Wal-Mart, it was obvious as to why forty to fifty males in work clothes were congregating in front of that specific merchant and their specific parking lot in the middle of the property. As we continued to drive around, we saw a male in work clothes with a water jug standing under a "no trespassing" sign (*in both English and Spanish*) on the Home Depot property at the far west end of the strip mall. The location, his clothing, and his conduct gave us reasonable suspicion to believe he was not a customer but a day laborer who was trespassing. We stopped and talked to him.

Within five minutes the male admitted to being an illegal alien and ICE verified by phone he had illegally crossed into the country multiple times. ICE asked if we wanted them to come and get him or we could bring our trespasser to their work location. At that point we had two options. We could book the male into the county jail at a cost of $200 to the City of Phoenix or we could take the trespasser directly to ICE for free. Either way, the male was going to be deported – one way cost nothing and the other cost Phoenix taxpayers $200 (*and the cost of two hours for three officers to book him for a total of six man hours at $34 an hour*). I told the ICE agent we were on the way. I contacted a supervisor and he agreed we should take the trespasser to ICE. I documented the contact in a police report requesting trespassing charges be filed against the suspect. This preserved the rights of the Home Depot as a victim of trespassing. We were in and out of ICE in less than fifteen minutes. The next day, an illegal immigrant activist complained I had intentionally abused my police authority by *not* booking the male into jail. A subsequent and public investigation of the "police union president" took seven months to complete. In the end, the allegation of misconduct was unfounded.

This is an example of what happens when the statutory text is ignored, when rhetoric is embraced, and when political agendas are allowed to be injected into police work. This formula is a recipe for disaster. It impedes the singular police function of enforcing the rule of law. Similarly, when the biblical text is ignored, when rhetoric rules the day, and when theological agendas set the standard, a comparable amount of havoc can be created in the Body of Christ. Our fundamental function of fulfilling the Great Commission becomes less than dynamic and far from effective.

Just like my interaction with this foreign illegal national who was breaking the law, my goal in this book was to be fair; to be fair with the biblical text, to be fair with you, and to be fair with reality. My thought process (*my theology*) radically changed in 1991. I was instructed to leave the rhetoric and look at the Word, to let the Bible speak for itself, to use the simple to understand the difficult, to employ the clear to explain the unclear, to never forget – context, context, context, context, and above all, to allow the biblical text to drive my theology not my theology to drive the biblical text.

My hope is you'll entertain the principles I've shared in these pages concerning justification, sanctification, and compensation. My goal was certainly not to offend but to challenge. I've seen life upon life changed and renewed by the beauty and power of God's grace. His Word is reliable and can be trusted beyond the boldest of rhetoric. Sadly, in many churches today, the following seem to be secrets: 1. Eternal life is free. 2. Eternal life is secure. 3. Eternal rewards are real. I'm confident a fair treatment of the biblical text in lieu of embracing theological agendas will highlight these three principles. When we let the biblical text do the driving, we begin to see grace-based principles again and again and again. It's funny how we see more when we let someone else steer. When we're fair with the biblical text, the cohesive consistency of the Bible cracks open and the truth of God's word practically and supernaturally spills out on the needs of a desperate and dying world around us. Grace is very attractive and "without cost" is wonderfully compelling.

Darwinism, like any other religion, requires faith. One must believe you can get something out of nothing. One must believe you can get life from non-life. One must believe chaos produces order. One must believe accidents bring about improvement. One must believe chance is an entity and not a mere descriptor of the outcome of events. This is too hard for me to believe. What's appealing about Christianity is the historical, philosophical, and scientific consistency of the biblical text it relies upon. It's the same biblical text which says, "For by grace you've been saved through faith, and not of yourselves, it is a gift of God, not as a result of works that no one should boast." It's the same biblical text that tells us that even though we are faithless, He remains faithful because He cannot deny Himself. It's the same biblical text which motivates us to "treasure up treasures in heaven." Just because something is simple doesn't mean it isn't true. Just because something is free doesn't mean it's worthless. And just because we fail doesn't mean He's not our Father.

Knowing how to obtain eternal life, knowing we can't lose it, and knowing we'll be rewarded for faithfulness provides the fuel which can make us effective spiritual multipliers. In our brief moment in time, by embracing these three principles, we can become useful to the Master in a way which will dynamically impact eternity.

Closing

God has been nothing but a good Friend to me. He is full of time with a billion things to do. But yet He condescends by spending His timelessness in considering the likes of me (*among sinners I am foremost of all*). The fact He wooed and drew me to Himself has completely captured me in His cause. He is brilliant, good, fair and full of grace and mercy. He is the God of a second chance. Twice in my life I wasn't sure if He existed. All I wanted was the truth. In my detailed and laborious search for reality, I found Him. In all honesty, He let me find Him. Even if you took eternal life off the table, just knowing He is and what He's like is more than enough. Yahweh is the point to this thing called life. And no one is getting out of this thing alive. To get Him is to get the point and that's sufficient for me. Eternal life is gravy poured over the icing of a huge cake. His answers of "No" to my requests have made all the difference in my life. I trust Him. My wealth doesn't consist of millions of dollars and portfolios of assets – my wealth lies in what God has freely given me. I have truth. I have peace. I have eternal life. I have freedom. What else could I ask for? On top of all this, He lets me play – He allows me to engage in the eternal and gives meaning, value, and purpose to my life by showing me the lives He has changed.

In closing, let me share with you my daily prayer which has evolved and developed in my moment of time of more than four decades as a Christian.

I love you Lord and I seek you because I love You.
I live by faith and You don't owe me a thing, but yet you've filled my life with so many good things.
Help me to live for the Cause.
Help me to love people.
Please be with the prisoners.

Please bless Israel and protect Jerusalem.
Please allow the leaders and people of my country to return to biblical standards.
Please give the nations rain for food.
Please allow church leadership to be godly and fair.
Please Spirit, guard and protect my head and my heart. Help me to think right and to feel right.
Help me to stay low, to focus on truth, to have a spiritual mindset, and help me to obey.
Jesus, oh Captain my Captain, please come back.
By faith I ask you to please live Your life through me.

About the Author

Mark Spencer has lived in Phoenix Arizona since 1975, graduated with honors with a finance degree from Northern Arizona University in 1985, met his wife Shannon in 1986 on a Summer Project with Campus Crusade for Christ in Bangkok, Thailand, and was the top overall police recruit from the Phoenix Regional Police Academy in 1987. In 1993 Mark completed his graduate degree in exegetical theology from Western Conservative Baptist Seminary as well as becoming a licensed lay pastor at Scottsdale Bible Church. For fourteen years Mark was an executive board member of the largest police association in Arizona, the Phoenix Law Enforcement Association (*PLEA*). He was the president of PLEA from 2007 until 2011 and, along with the PLEA board of trustees, served over 2,300 rank-and-file Phoenix Police Officers and Detectives. In July 2009, the Arizona Republic reported that Mark, in "his first two years as union president . . . earned . . . a reputation as a harsh critic of police management and a relentless advocate for Phoenix patrol officers." Mark has been interviewed by international (*CNN*) and national (*Fox National News*) cable news outlets, has been quoted in numerous print publications (*The New York Times, The Washington Post, The Nation, The Arizona Republic, Phoenix Magazine*) and has participated on radio talk shows across the country: topics discussed included illegal immigration, police suicide, border violence, and police management pension violations. He has partnered with F.A.I.R. (*Federation for American Immigration Reform*) and Judicial Watch in reference to front-line law enforcement perspectives on illegal immigration and government corruption. His role as the voice of the largest police association in Arizona garnered him the title as being one of "three of the most polarizing figures in Arizona politics" by the left-leaning *Phoenix New Times* in 2011. His retirement from the Phoenix Police Department in January 2012 ended a twenty-five year career in which Mark and the PLEA team cultivated powerful community partnerships and facilitated unprecedented bipartisan support for rights of Arizona law enforcement. Most importantly, during this quarter of a century, Mark saw God change the lives of thousands by means of his professional police platform. By practically applying grace oriented biblical principles with successful real-world strategies, Mark is able to provide a unique but practical perspective which encourages all believers to be "useful to the Master." Mark is an active member of the Free Grace Alliance (*www.freegracealliance.com*) and is the founder and co-director of Bema Investments (*www.bemainvestments.org*), a non-profit corporation which teaches Judeo-Christian leadership principles and facilitates charitable outreach efforts.

Bibliography

Grudem, W. (2000). *Systematic Theology—An Introduction to Biblical Doctrine.* Grand Rapids, MI: Zondervan.

MacArthur, J. (2003). *Hard to Believe.* Nashville, TN: Thomas Nelson.

McVey, S. (1995). *Grace Walk.* Eugene, OR: Harvest House Publishers.

Packer, J. (1991, May). *Tabletalk.*

Packer, J. (1991). *Evangelism and the Sovereignty of God.* Downers Grove,IL: InterVarsity Press.

Piper, J. (1986). *Desiring God.* Sisters, OR: Multnomah Books.

Schreiner, T. & Caneday, A. (2001). *The Race Set Before Us.* Downers Grove, IL: InterVarsity.

Recommended Reading

Absolutely Free, Zane Hodges, Zondervan Publishing House, Grand Rapids, MI, 1989

Calvin and English Calvinism to 1649, R.T. Kendall, Paternoster Press, Carlisle, UK 1997

Confident in Christ: Living by Faith Really Works, Robert N. Wilkin, GES Irving, TX, 1999

The Faith that Saves – The Nature of Faith in the New Testament, Fred Chay and John P. Correia, Schoettle Publishing Co., Haysville, NC, 2008

Free Grace Soteriology, David R. Anderson, Xulon Press, Maitland, FL, 2010

The Reign of the Servant Kings, Joseph C. Dillow, Schoettle Publishing Co., Miami Springs, FL, 1992

Salvation, Earl Radmacher, Word Publishing Nashville, TN, 2000

So Great Salvation – What It Means to Believe In Jesus Christ Charles C. Ryrie Victor Books Wheaton, IL, 1989

Simply Grace, Charles C. Bing, Kregel Publications, Grand Rapids MI, 2009

Understanding Christian Theology, General Editors Charles R. Swindoll and Roy B. Zuck, Thomas Nelson Publishers, Nashville TN, 2003

CPSIA information can be obtained
at www.ICGtesting.com
Printed in the USA
LVOW01s1552010216
473175LV00023B/1507/P

9 781449 748470